The Great American
Housing Bubble

The Great American Housing Bubble

The Road to Collapse

Robert M. Hardaway

 PRAEGER

AN IMPRINT OF ABC-CLIO, LLC
Santa Barbara, California • Denver, Colorado • Oxford, England

Library of Congress Cataloging-in-Publication Data

Hardaway, Robert M., 1946–
   The great American housing bubble : the road to collapse / Robert
M. Hardaway.
      p. cm.
   Includes bibliographical references and index.
   ISBN 978–0–313–38228–4 (hard copy : alk. paper) — ISBN 978–0–313–38229–1
(ebook)
1. Housing—United States—Finance. 2. Housing—Prices—Economic aspects—
United States. 3. Subprime mortgage loans—United States. 4. Financial crises—
United States. I. Title.
HD7293.H238   2011
332.7′20973—dc22   2010046290

ISBN: 978–0–313–38228–4
EISBN: 978–0–313–38229–1

15 14 13 12 11   1 2 3 4 5

This book is also available on the World Wide Web as an eBook.
Visit www.abc-clio.com for details.

Praeger
An Imprint of ABC-CLIO, LLC

ABC-CLIO, LLC
130 Cremona Drive, P.O. Box 1911
Santa Barbara, California 93116-1911

This book is printed on acid-free paper (∞)

Manufactured in the United States of America

Dedicated to
Judy Trejos Swearingen

Contents

List of Tables

Foreword

The Great American Housing Bubble is a title, a current reality and . . . a metaphor. Robert Hardaway is a careful scholar and tells us the sad, perhaps tragic, story of what he designates as "The greatest asset bubble in the economic history of the world." Professor Hardaway's thesis is that this bubble was a self-inflicted wound that caused and is still causing untold suffering and wealth destruction. All economic stakeholders profited from building this bubble as did the politicians who encouraged it. Professor Hardaway shows how public policies like the Community Reinvestment Act forced banks and other lenders to make risky and improvident loans in ways that border on bureaucratic malpractice. The Clinton Administration and the key members of Congress facilitated this bubble and penalized lenders who failed to lower lending standards.

The results were inevitable and, to a few, predictable. There was no conceivable way that many of these borrowers could ever repay their loans, and consequently no way securitized investment vehicle (many of them newly invented) could do anything but collapse.

That explains the title of this book and the reality America finds itself in. But I promised you a "metaphor." The metaphor is mine, not Professor Hardaway's, but it speaks to me from every page of this book: the whole Western World may be a bubble.

The housing bubble may be a microcosm for the whole industrial world. Could our housing and financial services industry be just a bubble within a bubble? A bubble that will make our housing bubble, for all its massive damage, a side show?

The world has been on a borrowing binge. The United States has been adding $100 billion a month to its federal debt and we are not alone. It is unlikely that most European countries can ever repay their debts, and Japan has been struggling for over 20 years to get over its real estate bubble. Worldwide, so much of our economic growth has been debt-driven and this joyride is coming to an end. Belgium, Ireland, Portugal, and Spain face debt loads that are unlikely to be repaid without bailout. But where does the world get the wealth to pay out all the bailouts? What dark dominos, their hour come at last, are creeping to create a worldwide financial crash?

But the national published debt and deficits are not the whole story. Unfunded liabilities hand over most nations like the sword of Damocles. The way national, state, and local governments keep their books would land a private company in jail. Debts do not accrue in governmental accounting, and in the case of the United States, that is estimated to add 50 or 60 trillion dollars in actual debt to the national balance sheet.

The United States has gone from the world's largest creditor nation to the world's largest debtor nation. We have gone from an exporter nation to an importer nation, from a nation of savers to a nation of spenders. We are, as a nation, borrowing to maintain a standard of living we no longer earn.

It is unlikely to end well. In fiscal 2010, the United States paid $441 billion in interest on the federal debt at an average interest rate of 2.3 percent—almost all on short-term obligations which expose us to dramatic increases in interest costs when interest rates rise—as inevitably they must. If we taxed U.S. taxpayers all of their income, we would still have to borrow to meet this year's deficit.

The above gloomy speculation is gratuitous on my part and Professor Hardaway restricts himself wisely to the crisis we are experiencing. It is both a perceptive and an articulate examination of the current housing bubble. But to me it has a universal message: massive credit expansions do not end well.

Richard D. Lamm

Preface

In the aftermath of the great American Housing Bubble Collapse, there has been no shortage of scapegoats upon whom to cast the blame. Unfortunately, the quest for scapegoats has concentrated primarily on those "responsible for the housing bubble collapse." The case is made in this book that this quest is fundamentally misdirected. All bubbles, like all Ponzi schemes, ultimately collapse, the only question being that of timing. While it is true that it took a "perfect storm" of confluent events and influences to administer the final pinprick into the thin skin of the housing balloon, it is submitted herein that all of these "causes" are but trivial considerations compared with the causes of the creation of the bubble itself. Indeed, this perfect storm may actually have been a blessing in disguise for causing the inevitable collapse sooner rather than later—that is, before it got any bigger with even greater potential to cause disastrous economic dislocation.

It is therefore the purpose of this book to focus on what caused the housing bubble itself, with particular emphasis on those government policies and laws that created the incentives for pumping the bubble in the private sector—particularly tax laws and social policies.

In the interests of clarity of presentation, each of the causes of the housing bubble has been isolated and treated in a separate chapter. While this organization has necessitated coverage of individual trees rather than any attempt to present a conceptual forest—a task suitable only for the most powerful super computer not yet created—I have attempted to quantify the impact of the various causes of the housing bubble, as well as setting forth in the conclusion a list of proposed reforms that, if implemented, would prevent future such bubbles from occurring.

No one factor was responsible for creating the housing bubble. In this sense, it required a different kind of "perfect storm" of Jupiter-like duration over a period of 67 years to create the Great American Housing Bubble.

Acknowledgments

Although my name appears as author, in fact this book represents a massive team effort and the contributions of a small army of research assistants—all students at the University of Denver Sturm College of Law—as well as of Professor Michael D. Sousa of the University of Denver Sturm College of Law, who wrote the chapter on bankruptcy laws.

Accordingly, I acknowledge and profusely thank my research assistants and staff at the University of Denver Sturm College of Law, who researched the data, statistics, sources, and authorities that provide the foundation for the conclusions herein. The following student research assistants were invaluable: Allison Blemberg, Andrew Brown, George Curtis, Andrew Frohardt, Danielle Hagen, John Horne, Levi Kendall, Atul Mahajan, Nicholas Mahrt, Amiel Markenson, Joshua Miller, Gabriel Olivares, Krista Poch, John Polk, Claire Rowland, Jay M. Sim, Travis Simpson,Daniel Vedra, Alison Ruggiero, Chad Eimers, and Eileen Carroll.

In addition, I would like to give special thanks to: Lindsey Parlin and Claire Rowland, for their tireless and extensive editing assistance; Jay M. Sim, for his invaluable editing and computer formatting assistance; Daniel Vedra, for his efforts in coordinating and continuously updating the innumerable draft versions of this book; John Horne, for preparing a preliminary draft of the chapter on accounting and the section on the South Sea Bubble in Chapter 6; Levi Kendall, for preparing a draft of Chapter 12 on the Federal Reserve; Andrew Frohardt, for his draft of Chapter 18 on the "Litigation Mess";

Jane Diemer, for her draft on the tulip bubble section in Chapter 6 and her assistance in preparing the appendices; Danielle Hagen for her work on both the appendices and the glossary; John Polk, for assisting in the preparation of the tulip bubble section in Chapter 6; Travis Simpson, for preparing a draft of Chapter 11 on banking practices; and Atul Mahajan, for his draft of Chapter 13 on tax policy.

Most of all, I thank Judy Trejos Swearingen, without whose support this book could not have been written.

Robert M. Hardaway

Introduction

Given the fundamental factors in place that should support the demand for housing, we believe the effect of the troubles in the subprime market will likely be limited . . . Importantly, we see no serious broader spillover to banks or thrift institutions from the problems in the subprime markets.
—Ben Bernanke, chairman of the Federal Reserve (May 17, 2007)[1]

(In order to avoid punishments set forth in the CRA for failure to meet quotas for lending to distressed communities) lenders have had to stretch the rules a bit.
—Chief executive officer of Countrywide Financial[2]

In the aftermath of the Great American Housing Bubble Collapse of 2007–2010, a flurry of books hit the market purporting to explain the collapse. They have blamed it on everything from regulatory failure and clueless regulators, to mark-to-market accounting;[3] from too much regulation,[4] to not enough;[5] from appraiser,[6] auditor,[7] and rating agency[8] conflicts of interest, to the greed of extravagantly compensated and arrogant Wall Street financiers[9] who created exotic financial instruments designed to avoid capital requirements and attain extreme leverage.

From 1940 to 2007, housing prices in the United States rose inexorably to create the greatest asset bubble in the economic history of the world. During that 67-year span, through recession and economic downturns, there was not a single two-year period in which the average price of a house in the United States did not rise. This unrelenting bubble expansion covered up a plethora of sins. Indeed, there was hardly any segment of the economy that was not rewarded for its own sins during the bubble expansion. Homeowners, particularly the richest ones on whom the government showered the most lavish tax subsidies, enjoyed the creation of massive wealth, often overnight. Lenders enjoyed a constant flow of reliable and apparently risk-free mortgage interest income, while Wall Street financial institutions earned multibillion-dollar fees first by buying and then "securitizing" those mortgage loans, rewarding their officers with millions of dollars in bonuses. Hedge funds and money funds made fortunes for their investors by using securitized mortgages as highly leveraged collateral, and they paid millions to their managers for such behavior. Realtors earned high commissions selling homes at bubble prices, risking little liability for steering buyers to predatory lenders. Appraisers, too, risked little liability by bowing to pressure from Realtors to appraise property at what homebuyers—showered with cash from loans requiring low down or no down payments—were willing to pay, since rising prices quickly rendered appraisals obsolete. Last but not least, politicians rode to power on the crest of the bubble and were rewarded for advocating populist policies of expanding homeownership,[10] even among those for whom the burden of homeownership was not sustainable (see Table I.1).

But when the bubble collapsed, as all bubbles in human history have done, all sins were quickly exposed, and everyone affected pointed to everyone but themselves as the cause of the catastrophe that followed.

It has been said that "success has a thousand fathers, and failure is an orphan."[11] With total losses incurred in the aftermath of the housing collapse in the trillions, including "write-downs" resulting from the subprime collapse exceeding a quarter of a trillion in 2008,[12] it is not surprising that virtually every segment of the economy that has had any connection to housing has blamed every segment but its

Table I.1   Median U.S. Housing Prices

1940	$2,938
1950	$7,354
1960	$11,900
1970	$17,000
1980	$47,200
1990	$79,100
2000	$119,600
2008	$260,200

Source: U.S. Census Bureau, http://www.census.gov.

own for the housing collapse. With plenty of blame to go around, it is even less surprising that the collapse has spawned an unprecedented litigation explosion and proved to be a field day for the lawyers representing those who feel victimized by the collapse—which, it seems, is almost everyone.

As home values declined and many homeowners became "upside down" (that is, they owed more money than their house was worth), lending institutions filed foreclosure actions, particularly in the subprime market, which by 2006 exceeded over half a trillion dollars, or more than a quarter of all home mortgages.[13] Foreclosures, most of which were for subprime loans, rose over 75 percent in 2007 alone,[14] exceeding 320,000 in the first two quarters alone.[15] However, what in years past had been straightforward foreclosure actions degenerated into nightmarish litigation tangles in the aftermath of the "securitization" of home mortgage securities,[16] a process whereby the originators of the loan "sold" their mortgages to other financial entities, which in turn "sliced and diced" them into securities sold around the world as investment vehicles.[17] Courts struggled to apply a tangle of ambiguous laws to determine who among the originators, loan purchasers, and investors (if any) had the legal right to foreclose.[18] Complicating this legal morass have been often-vicious disputes over the priority of payments to note holders, a legal issue that has carried over into bankruptcy proceedings (see Table I.2).[19]

Many homeowners who borrowed more money than they could afford to pay back fought back with counterclaims alleging that that their lenders should have known better than to lend to them, but also citing deceptive trade practices, predatory lending, and improper or confusing disclosures. The Securities and Exchange Commission, state attorneys general, and other federal, state, and local entities have

Table I.2 Securitized Subprime Loans

	% of Total Mortgages That Were Subprime	% of Subprime Mortgages That Were Securitized
2001	7.8	54.1
2002	7.4	62.9
2003	8.4	61.1
2004	13.5	75.7
2005	21.3	76.3
2006	20.1	74.8

Source: Mortgage Market Statistical Annual, 2007.

Table I.3   Home Ownership Rates

UK	71%
France	63%
U.S.	69%
Greece	85%

Source: National Association of Home Builders, http://www.nahb.org.

pursued their own lawsuits alleging similar improprieties.[20] Home-owners have also sued subprime lenders for racial discrimination in placing minorities in high-interest subprime loans at a higher rate than white borrowers with similar credit and income.[21] These lawsuits have come in a variety of procedural forms, including class-action lawsuits, Employment Retirement Income Act lawsuits under company-sponsored plans, and shareholder derivative actions (see Table I.3).[22]

Investors in money market funds and hedge funds have sued such funds for failure to diligently manage risk, make prudent investments, and even follow their own internal guidelines for investment.[23] Plaintiffs of such entities as real estate investment trusts have sued investment banks for giving poor advice, and customers have sued banks for engaging in subprime securitization without adequate disclosure.[24] Trust beneficiaries have sued bond trustees for breach of fiduciary duty, and shareholders have sued corporate officers and directors.[25] Rating agencies and appraisers have also been the targets of lawsuits by investors claiming conflict of interest and breach of fiduciary duty. Realtors and developers are also under the threat of suit for recommending mortgage brokers who in turn placed a borrower with a predatory subprime lender.[26]

These are only the tip of the civil litigation iceberg spawned by the housing collapse. On the theory that "somebody has to pay," federal and state prosecutors have initiated thousands of criminal prosecutions related to the housing collapse. Within months of the first signs of collapse in 2007, the FBI alone initiated over 1,200 mortgage-related criminal probes, and established a task force consisting of prosecutors and law enforcement officers from dozens of different federal agencies ranging from the Securities and Exchange Commission and the Federal Reserve, to the Small Business Administration.[27]

It is the theme of this book that many of the more simplistic explanations for the housing bubble collapse have missed the main point, which is not how the housing bubble collapsed, but rather how the bubble was created in the first place; for without the creation of the bubble, there could have been no collapse. While most commentators have agreed on the significant events leading up to the crisis, however, their spin on the significance of those events, and the weight that should be given to each, has led to a polarization of conventional wisdom into two basic camps.

The wisdom of the first camp, led mostly by financial gurus such as George Soros and Paul Krugman, lawyers, and populist politicians, comes down to this simplistic explanation: "deregulation" and "insufficient regulation" of the financial markets were the ultimate culprits in the credit crisis, fed by the "greed" of financial manipulators, corrupt regulators, unscrupulous speculators, and even homeowners themselves. Not surprisingly, solutions proposed by this camp range from "bailing out banks and failing companies" and implementing more layers of regulation, to simply keeping the housing bubble going as long as possible by using taxpayer money to bail out everyone from financial institutions to home buyers who got in over their head.

Implementation of this latter proposal echoes the policies implemented during the Great Depression by a government determined to "keep prices high" by such means as dumping milk into ditches and killing pregnant cows.[28] In a somewhat more civilized version of this policy, government regulators in late 2009 were determined to keep housing prices as high as possible by such means as paying people $4,500 to destroy over half a million functioning automobiles (the so-called "Cash for Clunkers" program) and handing out $7,500 in tax credits to home buyers (regardless of whether the homeowner even owed any tax).[29] When this had little effect, a proposal was submitted in the U.S. Senate in late 2009 to increase the subsidy to $15,000.[30]

The wisdom of the second camp is that the underlying cause of the economic crisis was too much rather than too little regulation,[31] pointing out that regulators are already buried under hundreds of thousands of pages of barely intelligible regulations that they are expected to enforce, and home buyers at closings are confronted with stacks of documents (purportedly required by regulations) which sometimes approach a foot in height. These regulations find their source in a hodge-podge of congressional acts, each enacted in response to some perceived financial crisis in the past, or to promote some perceived social goal, the pursuit of which is likely to attract votes at election time. A litany of these acts can be found in the appendix to this book.

Regulations relating to housing emanating from the tax laws alone amount to hundreds of thousands of pages, requiring the services of a highly paid professional to understand, but regulations enacted under the guise of "social legislation" have proved to be some of the most troublesome, contradictory, and ultimately disastrous. One example of the latter—though a mere tip of the regulatory iceberg—is the Community Reinvestment Act,[32] and in particular the regulations promulgated in the mid-1990s, which set forth bureaucratic sanctions and punishments for banks that did not meet quotas for lending to marginal borrowers who had very little chance of ever paying back the loans.

This second camp also asserts that many of the government regulations enacted in knee-jerk reaction to some perceived economic dislocation of the past have created problems of their own, which in turn have begotten the need for still more regulation to address the new problems created by previous regulation.[33] Acknowledging that the road to hell is often paved with good intentions, many in this second camp concede that well-intentioned regulations may have triggered the creative juices of an elite priesthood of young Wall Street innovators and whiz kids, who in return for multimillion-dollar bonuses created exotic financial instruments to circumvent existing regulations by employing the most extreme levels of leverage imaginable in their pursuit of high returns. With banks and lending institutions now encumbered with literally hundreds of thousands of pages of barely intelligible "regulations," the notion that the solution to the current economic crisis is to promulgate still more thousands of pages of marginally comprehensible legalese is understandably difficult to swallow for those in the second camp. Even less palatable is the suggestion that the best way to deal with the housing bubble is to keep it going as long as possible with government subsidies, thus keeping the price of housing out of reach for the average American.

This ideological split among these two camps on the causes of the housing bubble collapse is perhaps best exemplified by an exchange between Dennis Sewell, writing in the British journal, the *Spectator*, in October 2008, and Roberta Achtenberg, assistant secretary for fair housing and equal opportunity at the Department of Housing and Urban Development (HUD) during the Clinton administration.[34] According to Sewell, it was Achtenberg who pressed the hardest to impose President Clinton's agenda of "increas[ing] home ownership among the poor,"[35] setting up a vast network of regional enforcement offices across the United States to "spearhead an assault on mortgage banks" by accusing them of violating the CRA by practicing discrimination on grounds ranging from race, gender, and sexual to disability. Under Clinton and Achtenberg's regime, banks were graded on how much lending they did to marginal buyers in low-income neighborhoods, and those banks that did not meet quotas received punishments ranging from denials of a bank's petition to merge, expand, or open branch offices, to shutting off access to discount windows. Indeed, so zealous were Achtenberg's minions in pursuing this assault, that Achtenberg herself felt compelled to pull back at one point to issue a clarification that merely because a bank used the word "master bedroom" in a property advertisement was not per se evidence of discrimination, despite "its clear patriarchal and slave-owning resonances."[36] When banks found it difficult to meet the expected quota, Sewell asserts, "Clinton told banks to be more creative."[37] Creative they soon became, "abandoning their formerly rigorous lending criteria." In order to avoid threatened punishment, banks now offered "mortgages with only three percent deposit requirements, and eventually with no deposit requirement at all. The mortgage banks fell over one another to provide loans to low-income households, and especially minority customers."[38]

Asked to respond to Sewell's assertions, Achtenberg called them "laughable," asserting that "with all humility she was only a 'bit player' in her role as assistant Secretary of HUD" and did nothing more than to urge mortgage lenders to "voluntarily improve their best practices and make sure there was no discrimination." Claiming that the deterioration in lending standards had nothing to do with her office, Achtenberg stated that she was "not sure how they came to pass."

If the assistant secretary of HUD during the time when lending standards collapsed does not know "how they came to pass," it is not surprising that virtually no other responsible government official has claimed to know, either.

And so the blame game continues, with a resolution probably left to the historians of the distant future. As reviewed in a later chapter, each side has plenty of ammunition to use against the other. While it is difficult to document such assertions as "Clinton told banks to be more creative," it is certainly true that HUD regulations promulgated under Clinton not only facilitated the securitization of mortgages, but also interpreted the Federal Housing Enterprises Financial Safety and Soundness Act of 1992 as giving HUD the responsibility to ensure not just that government-sponsored entities extend access to mortgage credit to low-income families, but also to *very*-low-income families—a goal that, as a practical matter, could be accomplished only by drastically lowering lending standards. On the other hand, the alacrity with which the large financial institutions such as Bear Stearns took up Clinton's call by leveraging mortgage-backed securities to arguably obscene extremes, lends ample support to those in the first camp who claim that greed and speculative frenzy played an important role in the final collapse (see Table I.4).

But while there may be truth in the blame cast by both camps on each other, it is submitted herein that they are *both* missing the critical point, which is not how the bubble collapsed (inasmuch as *all* bubbles eventually collapse, the only question being one of timing), but rather on how the bubble was created in the first place. Only by answering the latter question can we learn the appropriate lessons that will guide both government and the private sector in insuring that the catastrophe of 2006–2010 is not repeated (see Table I.5).

Many of the books written with the purpose of explaining the housing collapse have attempted to do so by treating all of the purported causes together. While the next chapter offers an overview of all the causes in

Table I.4   U.S. Mortgage Interest Deduction Expenditure (in Billions)

2000	70
2001	71
2002	70
2003	64
2004	66
2005	68
2006	72
2007	76
2008	80

Source: HousingEconomics.com.

Table I.5   Tax Deductions for Home Ownership, by Country

UK	$0
Germany	$0
France	$0
U.S.	$1 million

Notes: The UK abolished the tax credit for housing in a number of steps (1983, 1988, 1991, 2000). Germany abolished mortgage interest tax credit in 1986; France gradually abolished such credit over the period of 1991–2000. In the United States, interest incurred on up to $1 million is deductible.
Source: National Association of Home Builders, http://www.nahb.org.

the form of an allegory to which it is hoped all readers may relate, the primary organization of this book will differ from many others in that it focuses primarily on what caused the bubble, treating each of the purported causes separately in each chapter. Remaining chapters will examine the wider social, economic, environmental, and political ramifications of the housing bubble. Although this organization recognizes that the question of what percentage of the blame should be accorded to each of these causes is probably only resolvable by a super computer with processing power far beyond today's most sophisticated electronic brains, the last chapter proposes what can be learned from examining each of the causes examined and makes recommendations for avoiding similar disasters in the future.

1

Overview: An Allegory

This syndrome is not altogether new. Homes and real estate have always had a peculiar hold on the American psyche. Our founding fathers considered land ownership a prerequisite to voting. A generation later, their pioneer descendents settled the West, drawn largely by an irresistible lure: cheap (or even free) land. We still tell our children the story of the Three Little Pigs (the moral: Build the sturdiest house you can), and spend rainy afternoons marching pieces around Monopoly boards (the lesson: The key to profits is location, location, location). And for decades, many people have had a Sunday-morning ritual that has nothing to do with church: Over coffee they read the real estate listings, even if they've no intention of buying or selling a home.[1]
—Daniel McGinn, *House Lust: America's Obsession with Our Homes*

Once upon a time in the faraway Land of Oz, the people were happy. Or at least they thought they were happy, until one day there arrived from the East a most colorful variety of tulip bulbs. Selling for five cents, the bulbs were so beautiful that people began to covet them for their gardens. People began to realize that they couldn't be really happy unless they could show off these beautiful bulbs in their own gardens.

As the demand for these tulip bulbs increased, however, so did the price. Soon the tulips doubled in price and were selling for 10 cents. However, this rise in price didn't keep people from buying tulips. In fact, just the opposite happened, since people realized that they could have their cake and eat it too. They could buy and enjoy the tulips, and make money at the same time as the price of tulips rose even higher.

Soon, everybody wanted tulips—and not just any old tulips, but the biggest, grandest, and most colorful tulips that could be grown. The bigger and fancier they were, the better. It was not long before the price of the nicest and biggest tulips rose to $100 a bulb—a price that the poorer classes of Oz could not afford.

The politicians of Oz were quick to recognize an opportunity. They began to tout the ownership of beautiful tulips as the "Ozian dream," and something to which all Ozian citizens should aspire. The populist politicians of Oz began to realize that they could get elected on a platform of "A Tulip in Every Garden!" if they could just convince everyone that their worth as human beings was defined by their ownership of tulips; and so they promised that if elected, they would hand out money to all those who voted for them so that they could all buy nice tulips. However, when just handing out money in this fashion reminded some people of the Roman emperors who stayed in power by giving the people bread and circuses, they realized they would have to think of some way to hand out the money in a way in which it wouldn't be so obvious that that's what they were in fact doing.

It so happened that some years before the first tulips arrived from the East, an income tax law had been passed in Oz. This now gave the populists an opportunity to hand out money in the form of tax deductions to all those who bought tulips. It was hoped that some people wouldn't realize that such deductions were just as good as cash, and thus not make the negative connection with bread and circuses. Or maybe they did understand, and didn't mind at all. What made this method of handing out money to the voters even more attractive is that it could be advanced under the populist banner of promoting the "Ozian dream."

At this point, however, the politicians had to deal with an ideological issue. As good populists, they had always supported an agenda of "progressive taxation" in which the richest Ozians paid the highest percentage of their income in taxes. But since the richest Ozians were already buying the most extravagant tulip bulbs, this meant that the richest Ozians would get the biggest tax deductions. In effect, the tax deduction method of handing out money for tulips meant that the government would hand out the most money to the very richest Ozians. Indeed, the more extravagant the tulips the rich bought, the more money the government would give them. Thus, the government might hand out a million dollars or more to a super-rich tulip owner, while giving absolutely nothing to those who were so poor that they couldn't afford to buy any tulips at all.

Fortunately for the populists, this extreme version of regressive taxation didn't seem to bother the voters who elected them to office, especially when it was enacted under the banner of the "Ozian Dream." Indeed, when the wealthiest tulip owners began to complain about having to pay capital gains taxes on the huge profits they made from the tulips they had bought with the money given to them by the populists, the populist politicians responded by passing laws relieving them from even having to pay capital gains taxes on their tulip profits. Capital gains taxes would henceforth be reserved for Ozians foolish enough to have risked their capital on enterprises that might actually produce something—like factories that employed people.

When the rich complained that even this was not enough to shield their windfall gains, they persuaded some state governments to limit the amount of property tax they would have to pay on their most expensive tulips, leaving the state authorities to raise funds for schools and public services by imposing higher sales taxes.

Not surprisingly, the artificial demand for tulips stimulated by government handouts began to push up the price of tulips even higher. Soon tulips were selling for a thousand dollars per bulb. Speculators began to buy tulips not because they were beautiful and graced the finest gardens in the land, but because buying tulips had become a "sure thing" in the investment world. Year after year, the price of tulips rose, until people forgot that there had ever been a time when the price of tulips didn't rise.

While government handouts to tulip purchasers stimulated demand, local government officials soon realized that they too could contribute to the price rise in tulips by restricting the supply. Under the banner of "protecting our neighborhoods," they began to pass zoning restrictions that required tulip owners to have a garden of at least one acre in size on which to properly display their tulips—apparently based on the theory that to display tulips on a smaller plot would downgrade the value of tulips. Since only the richest tulip owners could afford a one-acre garden, those who couldn't afford one-acre gardens were forced to move far away from the neighborhood. This restriction of tulip supply in the original neighborhood greatly benefitted the local government officials themselves, since restricting the supply of tulips in their neighborhood meant that the value of their own tulip gardens rose even more. Although these restrictions had been enacted under the populist banner of "environmentalism," a few of those forced out of the neighborhood began to suspect that the local government officials' idea of environmental policy was "keep the riffraff out." And, of course, "riffraff" was defined as anyone who couldn't afford a one-acre tulip garden. The personal economic windfalls reaped by the local government officials outweighed any concern that their policies were encouraging suburban sprawl by forcing countless Ozians to commute by car to their jobs. Soon most Ozians were totally dependent on their cars, consuming four times the gasoline per capita as in other industrialized nations and pushing up the price of that commodity as well.

At this point, the populist politicians jumped on the environmental bandwagon, advocating such "environmental policies" as making biofuels from corn in order to meet the skyrocketing demand for gasoline by those commuting long distances to their jobs in the neighborhood. Under this environmental policy, it was calculated that the amount of corn used to fill just one tank of an SUV commuting daily to a job from suburbia would be enough to feed a starving Third World child for a year.

Over the course of many years, a national Ozian policy of artificially stimulating demand for tulips, combined with widespread local government policies of restricting supply, caused the price of tulips to rise to the astronomical level of $10,000 for a single tulip bulb. Seeing the price of tulips rise every year for 50 years without respite, speculators began to see and understand the joys of "leverage." If a speculator bought a $10,000 bulb with personal funds, and the price of the bulb rose to $11,000, the speculator would reap a meager 10 percent return. But if the speculator could borrow $9,000, and put up only $1,000 of his own money to buy the bulb, a 10 percent rise in the price of the bulb would mean a *100 percent* return for the speculator.

For virtually every form of investment other than tulip bulbs, such leverage might have created great risk for the speculator. After all, a 10 percent *decline* in the value of an investment instrument would mean that the speculator would lose his entire investment. But that was the beauty of bulbs. They *never* went down in value. Over a period of 50 years, bulb prices had never declined, and if they hadn't declined for that long a period of time, didn't that mean that they probably never *would* decline? Of course, anything was possible (an asteroid might hit the earth, or a super volcano might erupt), but for all intents and purposes, within the human lifespan, tulip bulbs seemed as good as gold. (Maybe even better, since gold sometimes declined.)

Before the time when the price of tulips began their speculator rise, most Ozians had to pay cash for their tulips. Banks had sometimes been willing to finance the purchase of a bulb here and there, but such tulip loans were generally for short periods of time, and a substantial down payment was generally required in order to protect the bank from the risk that the borrower might not be able to repay the loan. Because of the reluctance of banks to lend money for tulips, particularly during a previous economic downturn, the Ozian federal government had begun to set up quasi-governmental entities with funny names like "Tommy Tube" and "Gladys Globe." The idea behind these entities was that in order to foster the Ozian dream of a tulip in every garden, the government would provide "liquidity" in the tulip loan business, provide a "discount window" for banks willing to lend money for tulips, and encourage private lending institutions to lend money for tulips by reducing the risk to those institutions in making such loans.

Not long after the creation of these entities, however, the populist politicians at both the national and the local level began to be hung on their own petard. The national policy of showering taxpayer money on anyone willing to buy a tulip bulb, combined with the local policy of restricting the supply of bulbs, began to cause the price of tulips to rise so high that the average Ozian could no longer afford to buy one—a consequence obviously at odds with the populists' claimed agenda of "A Tulip in Every Garden." A few Ozians even began to refer to the rise in the price of tulips as a "bubble."

A few Ozians familiar with economic history suggested that a possible solution to this problem would have been to slow down the blowing of the bubble by reforming the national policy of handing out money to the richest Ozians to buy tulips, and for local "environmentalists" to stop restricting supply. Not many politicians were willing to listen to such proposals, however, and most of them rejected such a course as politically inexpedient. The politicians were concerned that their richest campaign supporters would never accept the revocation of the extravagant welfare subsidies they had long enjoyed, and that even their middle-class supporters would oppose the revocation of a benefit that had long given them an economic advantage over those too poor to buy any tulips at all. Staying in power and being reelected was far more important than slowing down a bubble, even if economic history taught that it would inevitably burst—hopefully after they were all retired and enjoying the wealth created by their own tulip gardens. Likewise, local environmentalists were not eager to compromise the value of their own tulip gardens by reducing restrictions on the size of tulip gardens in their neighborhoods.

Rather, both the populists and environmentalists took the course of least political resistance. If people couldn't afford to buy houses anymore, the government would simply print more "funny money" and hand it out to their constituents so that they could keep buying, and thus keep the bubble going as long as possible—maybe even forever! That way, wouldn't everyone be happy? Affluent voters who already owned tulips would be more than pleased by the vast increases in their personal wealth in the form of tulips. After all, they could still afford to buy even more expensive tulips by selling the tulips they already had, which had raised so much in value. Best of all, the populists could continue being elected on a platform of the Ozian Dream.

Not surprisingly, the tax deductions for tulips passed by the Ozian congress showered 75 percent of its benefits on those in the top one-fifth of income distribution.[2]

Yet there remained some loose ends. Some populists represented districts that were not affluent, and in which there lived people so poor that they had never even owned a tulip. Many of these poorer people were beginning to understand and resent the government policy of showering the very richest Ozians with the most extravagant welfare subsidies, while they got left with nothing—or worse, herded into government housing "projects" rife with crime and vermin.

How would populists get the votes of these poorer citizens? Here, the solution was but a variant of the policy of showering the rich with subsidies, and best of all, it would also help keep the bubble going as long as possible. Although the populists couldn't really stomach handing out money outright to the poor in the same fashion that it handed out subsidies to the rich, it could accomplish very nearly the same result by *lending it to them*, though preferably without regard to whether they could actually pay it back. The trick was to get *someone else* to do the actual lending, thus letting the government off the hook (in theory, at least). This was done by promulgating "regulations" that punished banks that did not lend money to those who would never have qualified for tulip loans under traditional loan standards.[3] Typical of these new government regulations was the soon-to-become-infamous "Tulip Reinvestment Act" (TRA),[4] which had been passed on the wildly popular political agenda of promoting tulip ownership by those who theretofore couldn't afford to buy tulips. Later, a popular Ozian president promoted a policy of increasing tulip ownership by two and a half million people by "grading" banks according to how many loans they gave to marginal borrowers; those banks that got low grades were duly punished by a variety of means.

Apologists for the TRA reacted furiously to any suggestion that the TRA had done anything more than restrict "discriminatory" tulip loan practices, and took great pains to point out that only a small percentage of the total number of banks were formally governed by the TRA. But some Ozians saw that these apologists had missed the main point, which was not how many banks were formally governed by the TRA, but rather that the Ozian government was now sending a clear message to *all* aspiring tulip owners and lenders: *tulip prices will keep going up, so tulip purchasers and tulip lenders can invest in tulips with minimal risk.*

These regulations presaged the final stages of the tulip bubble blowoff. Implicit too was the subtext: neither banks formally covered by the regulations nor investment banks not covered had to worry about whether an unqualified buyer would be able to repay a tulip loan, since tulips were rising so fast and so high that any hard-pressed tulip owner could later "refinance" his tulip loan, take out the equity, and use the proceeds to make payments on the new loan. In fact, so great would be the withdrawn equity, that there would be enough left over for a new car, a round-the-world luxury cruise, or an elite private school education for their kids.

But even these latter-day government "regulations" were not enough in themselves to precipitate the final climactic blowoff of the bubble. It remained for the full import of the government's message of an eternal bubble to be absorbed and acted upon by banks, lending institutions, investors, tulip owners, and aspiring tulip owners. Based upon belief in the validity of that underlying message sent to them by the government, each of these groups responded in a totally rational way.

Ozians who in years past would never even have considered buying stocks "on margin," even with modest leverage of 1 to 1 (i.e., borrowing one dollar for every dollar invested), now rushed with wild abandon to leverage their investment in tulips on a margin of as high as *100 to 1* (i.e., borrowing 99 cents for every dollar invested in a tulip).

People began to ask, was this behavior of buying tulips "on margin" irrational, risky, or greedy? To the contrary, given the government's message, it made perfect economic sense for a tulip investor to put a penny down on each dollar borrowed, and then sit back and enjoy not only the rise in the price of the tulip purchased, but the generous check the government sent her (in the form of a tax refund) for having the good sense to buy a tulip on 99 percent margin. After all, even if the price of tulips went up only 5 percent a year, and the investor was paying only 5 percent interest on the loan, she was nevertheless effectively receiving the exquisite joy of owning the tulip for *free* (after taking into account the check from the government). If the price of tulips went up by more than 5 percent, the tulip investor would be on her way to making a windfall profit and building massive wealth. (In some regions of Oz, tulips were actually rising by 25% *per month*).[5]

But were tulip buyers who took this course of action really irrational? Were they any "greedier" than the millions of wealthy Ozians who gladly accepted government welfare checks in the form of tax rebates on their tulip loans, or the thousands of politicians who rode to lucrative office on a wave of tulip mania?

Banks too were quick to realize the financial implications of the government's strongly worded message of an eternal bubble. In the days before the government began "regulating" banks, banks were circumspect in giving loans, particularly on tulips. After all, if even one borrower defaulted, that one loss might eat up the bank's profits for the entire year. Accordingly, banks often required at least a 50 percent down payment, or in later years, at least a 20 percent down payment. But now that "Tommy Tube" and "Gladys Globe" were offering to buy up many of the banks' tulip loans, banks began to sense that their real opportunity for profit lay not in the anemic interest rates they charged on tulip loans, but rather on the fees they charged for originating the loans. The faster they could originate loans, pocket the lucrative fees, and unload them on Tommy and Gladys, the more money they could make. Although banks still had to be concerned about "runs" (when panicked depositors all tried to withdraw their money at the same time), even this concern had been all but eliminated by the federal deposit insurance of Oz, which insured deposits up to as much as $250,000.

In this frenzy of profit-seeking in the tulip loan business, it was not surprising that a "shadow" banking system arose. Since older regulations prohibiting commercial banks from conducting investment banking business had recently been abrogated, both commercial and investment banks soon began looking for ways to allocate their cash to higher-yielding investments without (technically) violating the capital ratio regulations. Small groups of bright, professional "whiz kids" at the lending institutions soon came up with the idea of "structured investment vehicles" (SIVs).[6] These were paper entities set up by banks and investment houses, which were theoretically independent of its parent, but which were in practice closely tied to it financially. Unloading their liabilities onto these SIVs theoretically enabled banks and investment houses to avoid the capital regulations by keeping substantial liabilities off of the bank's books.

The net result of this development was that while most commercial banks were themselves protected from the threat of a run, the entire "shadow" banking system, acting as it did under the regulatory radar, was left entirely unprotected from runs. Although the Ozian government promulgated thousands of pages of regulations, they were so complicated that not even the regulator themselves fully understood them, and left the way open for Palisade investment bankers to stay one step ahead of the regulators by inventing instruments of leverage and calling them by funny names.

Concurrent with the creation of a shadow banking system was the attempt by lending institutions to "jack up" the returns on their investments. This involved a two-step process.

First, banks had to find a way to "sell" all those tulip loans that they had not been able to unload on Tommy Tube and Gladys Globe. The largest category of such loans was so-called "subprime" tulip loans, which did not meet all of Tommy's and Gladys' loan requirements. These were loans made to marginal tulip buyers, many of whom could not verify income, and who had no money at all for a down payment. While such loans paid an attractive interest rate, this high rate of return was outweighed by the risk of default. Accordingly, it became most important to banks that they find a way to unload as many of these types of loans as they could as quickly as possible—preferably on Tommy or Gladys (implicitly back by the Ozian government and taxpayers), but if not on them, at least on private investors who had faith in the government message that tulip prices would always go up, and never down.

At this point, banks recognized a problem in finding such investors. Mortgages came in relatively large units of hundreds of thousands of dollars per mortgage, beyond the financial ability of many investors to purchase such large units. Was there some way these mortgages could by sliced up into smaller units more amenable to purchase by smaller investors?

Another problem was that before investing in such mortgages, most investors (and their advisors) would inevitably seek the comfort of being able to ascertain in advance the "risk level" of each unit of investment so as to better soundly judge the proper price to bid for each unit.

Here, the small priesthoods of young Turks at Palisade investment banks came up with a solution.[7] After purchasing the tulip loans, the

Palisade brokers would quickly slice and dice them, cut them up into little pieces called "securities," and then resell them to investors around the world. Best of all, all of these investment units could be sold on the basis that they were backed by the most secure collateral known to humankind: *tulips!* Though clear legal mechanisms for securitizing tulip loans had not yet been fully developed, populist politicians eager for any means to promote its "Tulip in Every Garden" agenda again quickly came to the rescue, passing a series of "regulations" permitting, and even encouraging, this slicing-and-dicing process.

To make these securities even more attractive to investors desperate for secure, high-yielding securities, they could be bundled according to "tranches" (categories of securities with their own investment grades).[8] Securities derived from tulip loans to the most creditworthy borrowers could be lumped into senior tranches. The bankers could then go to rating agencies to whom the bankers paid fees, and pressure them into awarding a "Triple-A" rating for the senior tranches, with lower ratings for securities derived from tulip loans made to less creditworthy borrowers, including "subprime" borrowers.

Rating agencies eager to please those investment banks that paid those fees rationalized the Triple-A rating they gave these securities, which were derived from loans made to creditworthy borrowers, on two grounds. First, the original borrowers had good credit ratings, and second, the securities were "diversified"—that is, a small slice of thousands of different tulip loans went into the creation of a single investment unit.

These securitized investment units were given the name "collateralized debt obligations" (CDOs), reflecting that each of the securitized tulip bulb investment units was backed by the collateral of real tulips.

Because these rating agencies were beholden to paymasters for fees, few were willing to recognize that these rationales rested squarely on the validity of the Ozian government's underlying message that there was minimal risk that the collateral of all these securities would ever actually decline in value. Fewer still were willing to recognize that the requirement of "diversification" was hardly satisfied by the simple expedient of buying loans secured by a variety of different tulips. That was because, regardless of the wide variety of tulips that served as collateral, the *collateral for all the tranches consisted entirely of tulips, and nothing but tulips.*

With the securitization process well underway, investment banks could now make money by using senior CDOs as collateral to borrow money at low rates from money market entities and hedge funds, and lend it out at higher rates to finance corporate mergers and buyouts. Their profit was the difference between the rates at which they borrowed and lent money.

Although the "securitization" of tulip loans permitted lending institutions to make considerable profits from their slicing-and-dicing fees, competitive pressures for still higher returns led the great Palisade investment banks to think of ways to "juice up" their investment returns. Though no banker liked to use the term "leverage," they sought ways to employ leverage without actually using that term in creating exotic financial instruments.

If banks had to use their own capital to buy the CDOs that served as collateral for the money they borrowed, their potential profits were limited. But if they could use only five cents of their own capital for each dollar's worth of a CDO, and borrow the other 95 cents at low Triple-A rates, they could increase their profits exponentially in a way similar to the way a purchaser of stock can reap huge profits by borrowing 95 cents to purchase a share of stock selling for one dollar. Even if the stock only rises modestly from a price of $1.00 a share to $1.05 a share, the investor still makes a huge 100 percent return on his five-cent investment. (Of course, if the value of the collateral for his loan declines by only five cents, the investor is totally wiped out).

However, two potential obstacles could block any attempt by the bankers to engage in the extreme leverage they needed to use in order to juice up their profits.

The first was the possible application of Ozian government capital requirements. Because such capital regulations varied in amount according to the institution and investment vehicle, it was not always clear how a particular capital requirement might restrict the use of leverage by a particular investment bank. Fairly clear were the capital requirements for federally chartered commercial banks, which enjoyed federal deposit insurance; but the applicability of capital requirements to institutions in the "shadow banking system," and in particular to institutions that had created SIVs on which to dump their obligations, was far from clear. Were SIVs really financially independent from the parent institutions which had created them, or were they simply paper entities with interlocking financial obligations created for the sole purpose of avoiding whatever capital requirements might otherwise be applicable?

Further complicating the quest for leverage was the fact that several years previously, bankers from around the world had set forth an international standard under which investment banks could leverage their loans at no greater than 12 to 1 (i.e., banks must keep in their vaults at least $8 for every $100 it lent out).

Assuming that these capital regulations restricting leverage could somehow be circumvented, there remained the problem of employing extreme leverage without it becoming apparent to potential investors that such risky leverage was in fact being employed. Solving this problem was how the small priesthoods of young Palisade whiz kids at the major investment banks and brokerage houses on the Palisades earned their multimillion-dollar bonuses.

Meeting at a five-star beach resort on Florida's Gold Coast, a group of these whiz kids from the investment bank of P. R. Gordon met for a week of sun and fun. But they also did some real "work," devising new kinds of very imaginative, "exotic" investment instruments using complex mathematical formulas. Under the guise of "risk management," they devised instruments that later morphed into vehicles that came to be known as "credit derivatives," "inverse floaters," "LIBOR squared," "BISTROs," "synthetic collateralized debt obligations," and "credit default swaps." Sometimes all of these instruments were lumped together and called simply called a form of "derivative"; but all served the primary purpose of circumventing capital regulations. This left the way open to engage in leverage that would otherwise have been prohibited by those same capital requirements.

Some of these exotic new financial instruments were nothing more than variations on tried-and-true instruments for hedging. For example, investors had long been able to buy "puts," or to "sell short," as a means of earning returns when the value of a stock or other collateral declined in value. Using similar financial instruments, an airline might "hedge" its exposure to rising fuel prices by buying a financial instrument that entitled it to buy fuel in the future at a particular price. But that same instrument could also be used by speculators betting on a rise in fuel prices, and the returns on such an instrument could be spectacular if purchased using extreme leverage of as much as 100 to 1. Such leverage was intensified by the proliferation of small, undercapitalized companies that offered to "insure" the holders of CDOs against default. Banks could then tout not only that their loans were Triple A, but also that they were "insured" against loss. These insurance policies were themselves "securitized" and sold as "credit default swaps."

But while leverage in the stock or pork belly markets might be risky, few doubted the safety of leverage in the tulip loan markets since, according to the Ozian government message, *tulip prices, unlike stocks and pork bellies, never went down.*

Though such "derivatives" were denounced by financier Felix Rohatyn as "financial hydrogen bombs, built on personal computers by twenty-six-year-olds with MBAs," the risk of employing such instruments was considered minimal by those who believed in the Ozian government's implicit message that all such leverage was essentially safe as long as the collateral upon which it was based was in the form of tulips.

That's the story of how the tulip bubble in the Land of Oz was created, in much the same way as the Tulip Bubble in Holland in 1593 was created. In that bubble, tulip bulbs originally selling for five cents eventually sold for as much as today's equivalent of $100,000 *per bulb.*

How the Oz bubble actually burst amounts to little more than a predictable postscript, inasmuch as the real story is not in how the bubble burst (all bubbles inevitably burst), but rather in how the bubble was created. For without a bubble, there can be no bursting of the bubble.

But for those curious about how the Oz bubble burst, here's a short summary of how it happened:

Like a large fire that starts with a tiny match, bubbles are pricked by something as small and seemingly inconsequential as a tiny needle. In the case of Oz, it was nothing more than a very slight leveling off of tulip prices caused by a saturation of the tulip market. Banks seeking to avoid punishment under the TRA regulations eventually scraped the bottom of the barrel in trying to find enough marginal buyers willing to mortgage their entire future by taking on tulip loans they couldn't ever afford to pay back. But this very slight leveling off of tulip prices had a disproportionate effect on those subprime borrowers who had assumed loans they couldn't afford based on the implicit promise of their government that tulip prices would never decline. These borrowers had also accepted at face value the more explicit representations of their realtors and bankers who had assured them that if their loan payments ever got too burdensome, they could simply "refinance" their tulip loans, and take out the equity in their tulips, which surely would have increased in value. They could then use the excess equity to buy a new car and take a grand vacation.

Because many of these subprime borrowers had either put no money down, or "borrowed" their down payment, even this slight leveling of tulip prices put them "under water"—that is, after paying realtor fees and closing costs (often themselves borrowed), they owed more than the value of their tulips. Slowly, but inexorably, they began to default. Many had nothing to lose by walking away from their tulips, since they hadn't put so much as a dime into the tulips they had purchased.

At first, this caused little concern among the Ozian "regulators." After all, the subprime tulip loans constituted a relatively small percentage of the total number of tulip loans outstanding, and myopic "regulators" couldn't see how a few defaults in the subprime market could possibly affect the vast market of prime tulip loans in which the vast majority of borrowers were diligently making their payments.

What the regulators and whiz kids had failed to learn in their economics classes at prestigious universities, and which could not be quantified in the complicated risk management and mathematical formulas concocted on their super computers, was the critical psychological element of investor *confidence*.

Rather than sitting at their computers and concocting mathematical formulas and exotic financial instruments, both bewildered regulators and greedy whiz kids might have done far better to watch the Frank Capra film *It's a Wonderful Life*, starring Jimmy Stewart and Donna Reed. In that film, Stewart took over his family's small-town bank serving the needs of the community in which it lived by taking deposits from customers and lending it out to townspeople to buy their homes. The bank's practices were sound, and the amount of capital it kept in reserve was more than sufficient by prevailing banking standards. Although the film was not explicit on this point, we can assume that the bank kept a prudent 20 percent of its assets in the form of cash in order to meet the demands of depositors who wished to withdraw money from their accounts on any given day. On an ordinary day, it was probably rare that as much as even 1 percent of the money in customer's accounts were withdrawn, so the capital reserve of 20 percent proved more than ample to meet daily cash requirements.

But on one particular day, one of the bank's employees lost an envelope of cash containing the day's deposits. This relatively small loss was observed by one of the bank's customers, who became so alarmed that it might undermine the financial integrity of the bank that he told his friends. The rumor of the bank's imminent failure spread like wildfire around the town. By evening, virtually every depositor in the entire town was lined up to withdraw all their money, and they wanted it immediately.

The problem was that depositors had been implicitly promised by the bank when they deposited their money that they could withdraw their money any time they wished. The home loans, however, were long-term extensions of credit, and the bank could not demand repayment of those loans on short notice. Thus the indomitable Jimmy Stewart was faced with the classic "run" on the bank in which he could not hope to pay off all the depositors who demanded the return of their money *immediately*.

The seemingly inconsequential loss on some subprime tulip loans in the Land of Oz may be compared to the relatively small loss of the day's deposits by the employee of Jimmy Stewart's bank in *It's a Wonderful Life*. This was because the loss, albeit relatively small, undermined that critical element of confidence on the part of investors.

True, many of the banks in the Land of Oz were protected from runs by virtue of the fact that depositors of those banks never feared losing their money because the Ozian Deposit Insurance Corporation, backed by the Ozian federal government, guaranteed those deposits. But the problem in the Land of Oz was not so much with the banks covered by deposit insurance. Rather, it was with those giant investment banks, the SIVs, and those institutions in the "shadow" banking world that were *not* insured by the Ozian Deposit Insurance Corporation.

Just as in *It's a Wonderful Life*, investors who lent money to the big investment banks, in what was known as the "repo" market, panicked overnight. Up to that time, these investors had been confident that their overnight loans to the investment banks were fully collateralized by CDOs, which were in turn backed by tulips, which they had always assumed would never fall in value. Now these investors were scared. The source of their biggest fear was the fact that they couldn't verify the actual value of all the CDOs that had served as collateral for their loans in the past because they had been so sliced and diced as to be incomprehensible. If subprime loans were defaulting, who could say what a fall in tulips might do to higher-rated CDOs? Who now really knew the true underlying value of the tulips that served as the collateral for the CDOs, now that the mortgages by which they were backed had been so thoroughly sliced, diced, and mixed together in a toxic stew?

Not only did the traditional overnight repo lenders (such as money market funds, hedge funds, etc.) decline to lend Hound Bearns any more money, but they demanded that all current loans either be paid off immediately, or that Hound Bearns come up with billions of additional collateral.

In the same way that the fear of the depositors in Jimmy Stewart's bank was irrational, so the fear of the repo investors in Ozian investment banks may have been irrational. But this was beside the point, because for whatever reason, rational or not, confidence had been lost. The run on the shadow banking system was on.

Aghast that their primary investment sources were no longer willing to lend to them in the overnight repo market, the major investment banks desperately tried to sell their CDOs on the open market to raise cash. But by now, virtually no one was willing to buy them—at *any* price. With no one willing to buy them, the critical question arose as to what they were actually worth.

To the consternation of the big investment banks, another government "regulation," enacted in response to a previous economic crisis, forbade financial institutions from valuing their assets based on their intrinsic value; rather, these regulations required that banks instead value their assets based on their *current market* price. That meant that the current market price of CDOs, which had a face value of many hundreds of billions of dollars but could not be immediately sold in the market at any price, now had to be valued at effectively *zero*. Within a day, the value of what had once been value as billions of dollars of CDOs now sunk to effectively zero, and their books now showed negligible assets and overwhelming liabilities. They were failing for the same reason that Jimmy Stewart's bank faced failure.

When the major Palisades investment firm of Hound Bearns, which did business around the world, couldn't borrow money on its mound of CDOs, it faced total and instant ruin. Regulators recognized that if Hound Bearns failed, investor confidence around the entire world would erode overnight, and there would be a run not only on the entire financial system of Oz, *but the financial system of the entire world*. With confidence totally eroded, investors were now afraid to invest in anything except Ozian government bonds, which were now so oversold that they effectively provided negative returns. Stock prices crashed, companies unable to get loans to finance their operations shut down, workers were fired, and unemployment skyrocketed.

Panicked regulators now rushed about like chickens with their heads cut off, desperately trying to find another major investment bank willing to "buy" Hound Bearns, which had been selling for $62 a share just days before. But not even the venerable P. R. Gordon investment bank was willing to buy if it meant taking on Hound's mountain of CDOs, now effectively valued at zero. Finally, P. R. Gordon agreed to pay $2 a share for Hound Bearns if the Ozian government would assume the lion's share of Hound Bearns' liabilities at taxpayer expense.

A major shareholder of Hound found his $60 billion stake in Hound reduced to $12 million *overnight*.

And so it went, as a panicked Ozian government, throwing concerns about future inflation to the wind, desperately tried to keep the financial system afloat by printing paper money by the trillions and handing it out to hard-pressed financial institutions and businesses without regard to whether those businesses had any chance of succeeding. They even printed $20 billion to give to a failing car company, and then, when that was consumed in a matter of weeks, printed $30 billion more so that they could hang on a little longer while paying above-market wages and honoring bloated pension funds that had never been actually funded.

In the meantime, tulip prices across the land plunged, plagued in part by margin calls on tulip loans, but most of all by disillusionment, demoralization, and the erosion of confidence in a government that had created the tulip bulb bubble by deceptive messages, populist demagoguery, and misguided regulation.

There we shall leave the story of Oz, and turn to how was created the Great American Housing Bubble.

2

Blind Faith

What kind of monster has been created here? It's like you know a cute kid who then grew up and created a horrible crime. All this just totally blows your mind.[1]
—E-mail from a former member of J. P. Morgan group to another after major investment banks worldwide suffered multibillion-dollar losses in the aftermath of the subprime mortgage market crash (December 2007).

When my parents moved to Denver, Colorado, shortly after World War II, they bought a spacious two-bedroom house near Fitzsimmons Army hospital for $2,995. Their house payments were about $25 a month. Although the house was comfortable, my mother often said that her dream was to "some day live in a $10,000 house."

About five years before my parents bought that house, one of the most enduring and long-lasting bubbles in economic history had begun. Ever since the Great Depression and up until 2006, there had not been a single two-year period in which the average price of housing did not rise on a nationwide basis.[2] Nor did housing prices during that time simply rise in an amount commensurate with the inflation rate, but rather rose at a rate significantly above the official government-reported Consumer Price Index.[3]

History reveals that most economic crises are precipitated by the collapse of a "bubble"—a frenzied rise in prices driven by speculation—in some major component of an economy. In 1929, a bubble in the stock market and its subsequent collapse precipitated the Great Depression. Exacerbating that collapse was the Smoot-Hawley Act, which set forth high tariffs on imported goods under the misguided belief that by making the cost of imported goods more expensive, they were "protecting domestic jobs." Predictably, countries around the world retaliated with their own punitive tariffs. The predictable economic result was that international trade declined precipitously along with world output, thus triggering the stock market collapse.

After the stock market crash in 1929, Herbert Hoover tried to save the economy by "bailing out the big banks and corporations."[4] If this failed strategy sounds familiar, it is because that same policy is being implemented by U.S. policy makers and regulators trying to deal with the real estate crash in 2007–2009—witness the $50 billion bailout of General Motors in 2009,[5] and the billions for investment banks. Worse, policy makers are also adopting many of the failed strategies of the Roosevelt administration, which came to power in 1933.

In 1932, and again in 1936, Roosevelt ran on a platform of "balancing the budget" by declining to reduce taxes at a time when consumer demand had dropped precipitously due to a lack of purchasing power,[6] and asked for authority to cut the federal budget. Disastrous government policies such as paying the richest farmers not to grow food at a time when people were starving, killing pigs and pregnant cows[7] in order to raise prices, and paying subsistence wages of a dime an hour for manual labor on such make-work projects such as the Forest Conservation Corps, led to the Great Roosevelt Depression of 1937, which made the Hoover Depression of 1929 look like a picnic.

Indeed, so disastrous were Roosevelt's economic policies that in 1937, an exasperated John Maynard Keynes, the Noble Prize–winning British economist, felt compelled to write an urgent letter to Roosevelt, desperately urging him to abandon his bankrupt platform of "balancing the budget," and instead use fiscal policy to expand purchasing power and create jobs. Not only did Roosevelt ignore this desperate plea, but he inexplicably compounded the economic crisis by choosing that very year as the time to extract even more purchasing power from the taxpayers by implementing an additional payroll tax. In the end, only the purchasing power unleashed by the government for war goods in World War II brought the U.S. out of depression.

Desperate to mitigate the housing bubble collapse, U.S. policy makers in 2009 are implementing such strategies as handing out $8,000 checks to homebuyers to stimulate demand and push up house prices. These same policy makers continue to give the wealthiest homeowners hundreds of thousands of dollars in the form of tax benefits, while giving nothing to the one-third of the population who rent or are too poor to buy a house.

The agenda of the populist camp is illustrated by the all-too-familiar talk show financial expert who opines that "it would be the greatest tragedy if housing prices were permitted to the fall to the level where people could afford to buy them." Support for this characterization can be found in the policy recommendations of George Soros, who has argued that the best solution to the subprime mortgage crisis is to "contain the collapse of home prices."[8]

In other words, stripped to its essence, the policy agenda of the populist camp is to keep the bubble going as long as possible[9]—the very same policy proposal that governments have been espousing since the Tulip Bulb collapse of 1642,[10] and always with predictable results.

Whether this is a viable policy can best be determined after examining how the housing bubble was created in the first place.

In 1983, the Bureau of Labor Statistics (BLS) was faced with an awkward dilemma. If it continued to include the skyrocketing prices of housing in the official Consumer Price Index, the CPI might reflect an overall inflation rate of 15 percent or higher, thereby making the U.S. economy look like some kind of dysfunctional banana republic. Worse, such an official inflation rate would alert bond traders, who traditionally seek a 2 percent rate of return above inflation, to the real inflation rate, thus causing them to demand bond yields of as high as 17 percent or more.[11]

The BLS solution, implemented without fanfare or publicity, was as simple as it was bold: exclude the cost of housing as a component of the CPI, and substitute a so-called "Owner Equivalency Rent" that would reflect only the lower rents offered by many speculators eager to mitigate their holding costs.

The result of this statistical sleight of hand was immediate and gratifying, as the "official" inflation rate dropped dramatically virtually overnight, thus allowing government policymakers to "have their cake and eat it too"; i.e., to keep the housing bubble going even longer before catastrophic collapse, even to astronomical levels, while not alarming the bond traders who were only too happy to pretend to their customers that inflation was so tame that investors should be satisfied with lower rates of return on their bonds.

With the true inflation rate so camouflaged, even the most unsophisticated speculator could be dazzled by the prospect of earning windfall capital gains by purchasing and selling homes while enjoying low payments and interest rates made possible by the long-term bond traders.

Between 1997 and 2005, the average price of a home in the United States increased by 80 percent, and in some areas such as California and Florida, the average price increased by up to 25 percent a month.[12] When the Internet and dot-com bubble collapsed in 2000, frustrated investors and speculators alike quickly jumped into what they believed was a different kind of bubble—an everlasting bubble that would never collapse, but would just keep expanding forever.

"They're not making any more land," realtors would chant, egged on by everyone from financial planners and advisors to the highest government policy makers and politicians—particularly the populist politicians who saw "homeownership" as more important than virtually anything else in American society and were glad to be elected on what they perceived as a platform on which no one could oppose them.

Indeed, in a variation of the populist creed of the speculative frenzy of the 1920s ("two chickens in every pot"), so confident did these populist politicians become, and so confident were they that the housing bubble would go on forever, that they convinced even themselves that homeownership should be extended even to those who could not afford it (affordability being thought to be irrelevant if any home buyer could count on virtually guaranteed capital gains and declining interest rates). As early as 1977, Congress had begun passing such acts as the Community Reinvestment Act, which provided for severe punishments for banks that did not lend to such marginal borrowers.[13]

By 2005, even the most respected economists and government regulators such as Federal Reserve Board chairman Alan Greenspan had jumped on the bandwagon. Conveniently professing a belief that regulators should only take action after a bubble collapse rather than trying to prevent it, Greenspan turbocharged the housing bubble by reducing interest rates to such a low level that even the most unsophisticated home buyers realized instinctively what the BLS had tried so hard to hide—namely, that the government was actually *paying* home buyers to purchase houses by charging interest rates far below the real inflation rate. As a result, home buyers began to expect it as their due that they could borrow money when it was at one value, and repay the debt with devalued money over 30 years as the value of their home rose inexorably.

Despite those who saw danger in such an explosive expansion of the housing bubble, Greenspan further professed his opinion that the housing bubble, if there even was one, was "different" from other bubbles. Oblivious to the burgeoning role of the Internet in reducing transaction costs, Greenspan insisted that speculation could not possibly take root in housing since high transaction costs would deter speculators. He further insisted that any bubble collapse would be confined to local markets, and could not possibly collapse on a national level.

In many ways, Greenspan was justified in thinking that housing bubble might go on forever. After all, for the past 70 years, there had not been *a single year* in which housing prices had declined on a national level, although as Greenspan had conceded, it had sometimes declined in local areas. The closest the housing market had come to a decline was in the late 1980s, though even then, housing did not decline on a nationwide basis.

Nor was Greenspan alone in his confidence that the housing bubble was "different"—the classic famous last words of all those who rationalize attempts to ride a bubble. In 2005, Ben Bernanke, then chairman of the President's Council of Economic Advisors, declared that "Although speculative activity (in housing) has increased in some areas, at a national level, these price increases reflect strong economic fundamentals."[14] The same year, David Lereah, chief economist of the National Association of Realtors, declared that onlookers "should (not) be concerned that home prices are rising faster than family income . . . home prices are likely to continue to rise above historical norms."[15]

EARLY WARNINGS

The first hints of trouble in the American housing market came to light in the spring of 2006, when the rise in home prices began to moderate and even slightly decline in some areas of the country. At that time, as much as 40 percent of all homes were being purchased not as permanent residences, but rather for speculation or for second homes.[16] Although few homeowners took much notice of these early warning signs, even moderate declines during that period began to spook the most aggressive speculators, who had been buying houses with the expectation of "flipping" them for double-digit gains within months of purchase. When these speculators began to cash out and head for the exits, the first stages of what later became a panic had begun.[17]

WARNINGS UNHEEDED

Few people in a bubble realize they are in one until it collapses around them. Only in retrospect can the outlines and perimeters of the bubble be discerned. Like an Agatha Christie novel in which seemingly trivial clues leading to the identify of the murderer only become apparent upon a rereading of the text, so the warning signs of a bubble alert only the most perspicacious observer in advance of its collapse.

In 1929, on the eve of the Great Depression, Joseph P. Kennedy is said to have seen the warning sign of imminent stock market collapse when the boy shining his shoes began giving him advice on the latest hot stocks to buy. Kennedy cashed out just in time, preserving his fortune which was one of the few to survive the Depression.

In 2006, a similar warning might have been found in the effusion of television reality shows, with titles like *Flip This House*, purportedly showing how huge profits could be made by buying houses and then quickly selling them.

But, just as the reader of an Agatha Christie novel is surprised by the final denouement, so most Americans were bewildered by the collapse of the housing bubble around them, followed by a domino effect of dizzying rapidity causing collateral economic damage, first in the United States and then around the world. On August 6, 2007, American Home Mortgage filed for bankruptcy, followed two days later by the suspension of investment funds by the large French bank, BNP Paribus.[18] On September 8, a depression-style bank run on British bank Northern Rock led to a government takeover of that bank, followed by the collapse of Countrywide Financial on January 11, 2008, the distress sale of Bear Stearns for $2 a share on March 16, the effective government takeover of Fannie Mae and Freddie Mac on September 15, and perhaps most disconcerting of all to the average investor, the staggering loss of $8 billion by Merrill Lynch, obliging that former investor powerhouse to seek emergency capital infusions from such dubious sources as the Kuwaiti Investment Authority in order to stay afloat.[19]

By late 2008, such catastrophic events induced a panic-stricken U.S. government to run the presses at full blast to print off trillions of dollar bills in a desperate attempt to restore "liquidity" to the markets. What began as a relatively trivial loss of a mere quarter-trillion in subprime loan losses in the United States had resulted in a cumulative loss in world gross national product of $4.7 trillion, and a loss of over *$26 trillion* in stock market capitalization[20]—thus revealing for the first time that the American housing bubble was the critical bottom card in a world-wide house of cards. How the American housing bubble collapse brought down the world's economy is one of the matters discussed in this book.

IGNORING THE LESSONS OF ECONOMIC HISTORY

Looking back, the great "blowoff" (the final stages of a bubble) in the American housing market occurred during the years 2004–2007. In fact, however, the Great American Housing Bubble was not a new phenomenon in the economic history of the world. A review of that history shows that economic bubbles have occurred with unnerving frequency an average of every 10 to 20 years since the days of the Roman Empire. Indeed, within the memory of many home buyers today, there have occurred the Internet and dot.com bubble of 1997–2000, the savings-and-loan collapse of 1988–1990, and the stock market collapse of 1973–1974. For those few who actually study economic history, one can also read about the stock market bubble of the 1920s, the Panic of 1907, and, skipping back over a century or so in which bubbles occurred with regularity, the South Sea bubble in England, and the Tulip Bulb bubble in Holland.

What is most alarming about such bubbles is not so much that they have occurred, but that so few lessons were learned from them, with the result that the mistakes that led to them continued to be repeated. Indeed, the salient limiting factor in learning lessons from prior bubbles appears to be the living memory of those who mindlessly blunder into the bubble of the current day.

What makes this failure to learn from prior bubbles all the more stark is that each and every bubble in history shares common features and characteristics—from the Tulip Bulb mania of 1642, to the American housing bubble of the twentieth century.

The old adage that "only the burnt fool's finger goes wandering back to the fire" is most appropriate when applied to humankind's experience with bubbles. It is submitted herein, however, that as applied to economic bubbles, the "foolishness" cited in the adage refers not to any basic defect in intrinsic human intelligence, but rather to a combination of human factors including allowing emotion and greed to overcome reason; a lack of education in economics, economic theory, and economic history (which can be laid directly at the doors of our educational system); and to the often-pathological refusal or inability to apply what economic history so clearly teaches. As the remaining chapters of this book will document, foolishness in the form of failure to learn the lessons of economic history has not been limited to unsophisticated investors, but extends to those at the highest level of banking and finance, as well as to the highest levels of government policy makers.

THE NEGLECT OF ECONOMICS IN THE PUBLIC SCHOOL CURRICULUM

While courses in social studies and rainforest math proliferate in our public schools, scant attention and focus is placed on economic theory, let alone economic history. While it is true that there have been latter-day efforts to address "financial illiteracy" in the form of courses and programs teaching "personal finance" to the masses, such programs have traditionally focused on such basic personal financial skills as balancing a checkbook or handling a credit card. While such courses are undoubtedly helpful—indeed, recommended to all—they fall far short of instilling that kind of basic understanding of macroeconomic principles that will enable voters to make sound decisions in electing officials who will apply sound economic principles in formulating economic policy.

This is not to suggest that teaching personal financial skills is not important. A sample of high school pupils aged 17 to 18 failed to answer even half of the basic questions posed in 2006 by researchers at the State University of New York, Buffalo. The researchers reported that "[l]ess than one quarter knew that income tax could be levied on interest earned in a savings account; three fifths did not know the difference between a company pension, Social Security, and a 401(k) personal savings account."[21]

Currently, only three states require that students take a course on personal finance.[22] Laura Levine, the head of Jump$tart, a loose coalition of 180 organizations in America that purport to promote financial literacy, has noted that "school principals will usually agree that financial literacy is worth teaching, but they are reluctant to give it time and resources."[23]

While some progress is being made in some high school curricula that teach balancing a checkbook and managing a credit card along the lines of a "home economics" course, the most serious deficiency in the current public school curriculum is in the teaching of basic economic theory. This deficiency in turn has led to adults often deferring to so-called financial "experts" or voting for politicians with little or no knowledge of fundamental economic principles and laws. As will be seen in the chapters that follow, this deficiency has contributed to the housing bubble collapse and the economic devastation suffered it its wake.

The chapters that follow will highlight in turn each of the economic fallacies flowing from such deficiencies, and the belief in those fallacies by voters, financial experts, and politicians that led to the current economic disaster. A few pointed illustrations make the point here for purposes of this introduction.

BLIND FAITH IN THE PRIESTHOOD OF FINANCIAL "EXPERTS"

In 2007, Gillian Tett was awarded the Wincott Prize, the premier British award for financial journalism, for her capital markets coverage. In 2008, she was honored as British Business Journalist of the year. Her 2009 book, *Fool's Gold: How the Bold Dream of A Small Tribe at J. P. Morgan was Corrupted by Wall Street Greed and Unleashed a Catastrophe*,[24] tells the story of Terri Duhon, who in 1998 was hired by J. P. Morgan to help develop "exotic" financial instruments that later became known by such colorful names as "BISTROs" (later called "synthetic collateralized debt obligations"), LIBORS squared, "inverse floaters," "credit default swaps," and "credit derivatives."

Ten years before, according to Tett, Duhon had been a high school student in Louisiana. When she told her family she was going to work in a bank, they assumed she was going to be a teller. Little did they know that she would soon be handling at J. P. Morgan *billions* of dollars of financial instruments so exotic and complex that even her superiors and chief executive officers didn't fully understand them.[25]

Indeed, the evidence now suggests that even government regulators did not understand the gush of new financial "exotics" that emanated from financial institutions in the aftermath of the Internet and dot-com bubble collapse in 2000. Without understanding these instruments, regulators were at a loss as to how to regulate them.

With stocks no longer offering the windfall returns to which many investors had become accustomed in the 1990s, many investors demanded equally high returns in alternative investment vehicles. To meet this demand, financial institutions had to figure out a way to get around the capital requirements that limited how much of their capital could be retained in liquid assets in proportion to what was invested. This was because liquid assets offered little if any returns.

Banks have traditionally made their money by accepting low-interest-bearing deposits and then lending it out to borrowers at higher rates of interest. In order to make an acceptable profit, it is necessary to lend out as much as possible at the higher rates of interest, and to retain as little as possible in cash. However, if depositors ever lose confidence in the soundness of the bank, they may engage in a "run" on the bank, in which depositors ask for all their money back at the same time. Since the bank retains only a percentage of its deposits on hand, a run may cause a bank to fail, because depositors may demand the right to receive their money immediately, whereas many of the bank loans may be long-term loans that need not be repaid for many years.

Generally, the more money that a bank retains in cash, the lower the risk of a run, which is why government regulations require that a certain percentage of deposits be retained by the bank in cash and not lent out. After the Great Depression of the 1930s, the government also established the Federal Deposit Insurance Corporation (FDIC). In return for insurance premiums paid by the banks, the FDIC "insures" the accounts of depositors up to a certain maximum amount. With accounts insured, the threat of a run caused by a lack of confidence was thought to be minimized.

In trying to meet the demands for high returns in the aftermath of the Internet and dot-com bubble collapse, financial institutions began looking for ways to get around the capital requirements. They finally settled on two methods. First, they created the "exotic" financial instruments, which for all their complexity came down to one dynamic: leverage. Second, they sought to remove loans from their books by transferring them to separate entities (known as SIVs, or "structured investment vehicles"), thus avoiding the capital requirements that would be triggered by keeping those loans on the books of the financial institution itself.

By such methods, the small elites of young turks at the great investment banks, hedge funds, and what is now termed the "shadow banking system" (entities created by financial institutions but in theory separate from the banking system itself, such a SIVs), established themselves as a kind of priesthood to whom investors would have to prostrate themselves in order to receive investment guidance.

Like the priests of ancient Egypt who had their own hieroglyphic language that outsiders could not understand, so their modern counterparts in the exotics departments of the biggest financial institutions developed their own arcane language and created instruments so complex that not even the management of their own institutions could understand them. Investors desperate for guidance in seeking high returns were ultimately at their mercy.

A massive study undertaken by Jenson in 1968 found that "active mutual fund managers were unable to add value and, in fact, tended to underperform the market by approximately the amount of their added expenses."[26] A follow up study by Burton Malkiel, professor of economics at Princeton University, showed that over the previous decade, about three-quarters of actively managed funds failed to beat the stock index, and that "the median large-capitalization professionally managed equity fund has underperformed the S&P 500 index by almost 2 percentage points over the past 10-, 15- and 20-year periods ... [The data] shows similar results in different market and against different bench marks."[27] Even so, Malkiel pointed out that the "survivorship bias" in the data is substantial in that "poorly performing funds tend to be merged into other funds in the mutual fund's family complex, thus burying the records of many of the underperformers."[28] Malkiel first made this point more colorfully in his book, *A Random Walk down Wall Street*, in which he noted that "a blindfolded chimpanzee throwing darts at the Wall Street Journal could select a portfolio that would do as well as the experts."[29]

Unfortunately, few investors are aware of such studies and thus are easy prey for anyone who comes forward claiming to be an expert with superior prescient skills in determining in advance how a particular stock or investment will perform. Indeed, so desperate is this average investor to defer to such "experts" that they are willing to pay extravagant fees for the privilege of being advised by them.

In an up market, of course, such fees are easily disguised in the returns; in a down market, they are equally disguised by the fact that everyone, everywhere also seems to be losing money. Managers of funds that have in fact managed to outperform the market are always keen to tout their success as justification for their high fees, usually cherry-picking the time periods in which their funds managed to outperform.

Of course, an astute investor will recognize that even some of the blindfolded chimpanzees will occasionally outperform the market by pure chance, in the same way that a gambler who walks into a casino and plays roulette will sometimes come out a winner. And of course, the 20 percent of gamblers who do win at roulette can then tout their great skill and prescience in having picked out the winning numbers by highlighting the cherry-picked periods in which they came out ahead and advertising them as "proof" of the kind of skill and genius worthy of reward in the form of million-dollar bonuses.

In normal economic times, the only harm done by the financial experts is the extraction of billions of dollars of potential returns from the pockets of their investors. But sometimes the blind faith investors put in experts can lead to much more dire consequences. The housing bubble collapse serves as an illustration. By now, some of the events leading to the housing bubble "blowoff" and subsequent collapse have become familiar to anyone who reads newspapers or even tunes in to the talking heads of television talk shows, and are explained in detail in the chapters to follow.

3

Greed

"Greed" has become the favorite whipping boy of the populist politicians seeking to avoid responsibility for the consequences of their own policies and political agenda. This factor should therefore be examined closely before moving on.

Greed as an explanation of economic collapse can only have meaning if it is determined to whom the attribute is directed, how it is manifested, and, most critical of all, how it is defined. Each of these touchstones will be examined in turn.

Most anthropologists concede that at least some forms of greed can be found in every member of the human race. Indeed, greed has been recognized as an important factor in the rise of civilization, and a common characteristic of humans who during the course of evolution have sought to improve their condition in life.

Perhaps a good place to start is to create a spectrum of greed, and then examine where on that spectrum one might find the kind of greed referred to by those who attribute the collapse of the housing bubble to greed.

Several years ago, I had an occasion to take a taxi from the Moscow airport in Russia. The driver spoke admissible English, and in the midst of a traffic jam, I had a chance to inquire about the state of taxi regulation in Russia. It turns out that there was none. Whereas under the prior communist regime, taxis were heavily regulated, now anyone could be a taxi driver. Indeed, he informed me that probably half of all drivers on the street picked up people who waved them down on the street, and bargained for a fare that would offset the cost of gas. He informed me that he now worked 16 hours a day as a driver, earning money to support his family. Under the former communist regime, he was only permitted to work seven hours a day, five days a week.

When he asked his bosses for permission to work extra hours in order to make extra money, he was told that working extra hours was strictly forbidden. In fact, he was derided for even requesting permission to work extra hours on grounds that doing so exhibited the sinister capitalist characteristic of "greed"—the desire to make more money than his comrades so that he could have more material things than they did and lord his wealth over them.

Desiring to make more money in order to raise one's standard of living is certainly one definition of greed. But the notion that any human societal system could eliminate that kind of greed has, of course, proved ephemeral. Even under communism, party bosses sought to gain economic privileges for themselves in the form of summer dachas (all in the name of the "people," of course) and other special privileges.

Consider this example closer to home: one of the most overwhelmingly popular subsidy programs ever implemented by the U.S. government has been the home mortgage deduction—a disguised subsidy to the richest Americans. Indeed, more than 70 percent of Americans received no benefit at all from the home interest deduction, either because they don't own a home or don't have income high enough to justify itemizing deductions and foregoing the standard deduction.[1] Fifty-five percent of these subsidies go to the top 12 percent of American homeowners, and 63 percent of federal largess goes directly into the pockets of the top 20 percent of income earners,[2] many of whom use the money to purchase the biggest and most luxurious homes.

Are the richest 30 percent of Americans who hog the housing subsidy at the expense of the poor "greedy"? Or are they simply graciously accepting the largess that their representatives in Congress have decided to heap upon them? Were all the people who bought houses on the expectation of ever-rising home prices "greedy," or should that epithet be applied only to the great majority of home buyers who actually did make money? Or to the wealthier homebuyers who made small fortunes and created great wealth for themselves?

Consider now the Wall Street "whiz kids" who in the mid-to-late 1990s began winning multimillion-dollar bonuses for inventing the exotic financial instruments employing extreme leverage to juice up returns. To the extent that some of them may have crossed the line, the more precise term to describe them would be criminal perpetrators of fraud. But, given that the government message to them for 60 years had been "houses never go down," was it any greedier for the whiz kids to create instruments leveraging a "sure thing" than it was for the average American to put their money into a money market fund paying high interest in order to enjoy the fruits of the whiz kids' inventions?

Finally, consider the politicians who rode their way to power by promulgating policies that created the housing bubble. Can they fairly escape the "greed" label if they can reasonably rationalize their behavior by protesting that they only had the "public interest" in mind? Or should the fact that most politicians who implemented such programs ended up personally enjoying the lion's share of wealth created by such programs give the lie to such protests?

In short, attempts to blame the housing bubble collapse on "greed" must fail. Greed as an explanation is too broad in that it applies to virtually every human, with the possible exception of Mother Teresa.

4

Regulation

[We must place] greater reliance on the forces of competition and less
reliance on the restraints of regulation.
    —President John F. Kennedy in his 1962 Transportation Message[1]

Before considering the role of regulation, or the lack thereof in the
housing bubble collapse, it is first necessary to examine the extent of
regulation in the American economy as a whole.

According to a 2009 study by the Competitive Enterprise Institute
("Ten Thousand Commandments: an Annual Snapshot of the Federal
Regulatory System"),[2] in 2008, federal regulatory agencies issued
3,830 "final rules," each of which consisted of hundreds, often
thousands of pages of barely intelligible rules. The study found that
"the total regulatory compliance costs of all these regulations hit
$1.172 *trillion* [emphasis added] in 2008 alone"—or almost as much as
the entire amount the government raised in individual tax revenues
for the same year. More regulations are in the pipeline: "Sixty-one
federal departments, agencies, and commissions have 4004 regulations
in play in various stages of implementation—180 are 'economically
significant rules, packing at least $100 million in economic impact.' "
Many of the agencies implementing these regulations have overlapping
responsibilities, and very often, agencies with such overlapping
responsibilities have no idea what the other agencies are doing.

Although there are various cost-benefit analyses applied to these
thousands of regulations, the report points out that "it largely amounts
to agency self-policing; agencies that perform 'audits' of their own rules
rarely admit that the rule's benefits do not justify the costs involved."

It has been over a thousand years since the first attempts by a
civilized society to regulate economic activity by fiat. As early as

310 AD, the Roman emperor Diocletian attempted to regulate prices by issuing an edict that imposed the death penalty for violations of a law setting a "just price" for consumer goods.[3]

The history of economic regulation reveals a now-familiar pattern: a failure to learn from pervious mistakes and a misguided hope that basic economic laws can be made to disappear if they are commanded to do so. Because of the failure to teach basic economic theory in the public schools, there are those who continue to believe that economic wealth can be increased by simply printing more money, that real prices can be lowered or raised by waving a regulatory wand, and that an efficient industry can be mandated by government fiat.[4]

For example, strict rent controls in France from 1914 to 1948 resulted in an almost complete cessation of building during that period;[5] and New York City, which failed to learn from that experience, later instituted rent controls that resulted in the tragic abandonment of thousands of apartments at a time when shelter was desperately needed. So called "wage-price" controls during the Nixon administration in 1974 resulted in black markets and renewed inflation.[6]

Like Diocletian, populist governments often have a difficult time deciding whether to order prices down in order to protect the consumer, or order them up in order to protect an industry (and their workers). This ambivalence has often led to conflicting, inconsistent, and ultimately self-defeating regulatory practices. Accordingly, George Stigler in his landmark article, "The Theory of Regulation," set forth the following law of regulation: "Every industry or occupation that has enough political power to utilize the state will seek to control entry."[7] Controlling entry limits the number of competitors in an industry and, by inhibiting competition, keeps prices high.

In accordance with this law of regulation, the government in 1938 passed the so-called Civil Aeronautics Act,[8] which strictly regulated entry into the airline industry. So rigid was this regulation that between 1950 and 1974, not a single firm was permitted to enter the industry, despite 79 applications to do so. This fact is even more startling when one considers that the airline industry expanded by some 23,800 percentage points during this period.[9]

Not content with the suppression of competition that might have helped consumers, the Civil Aeronautics Board (CAB) during this period actually fixed prices on behalf of the incumbent carriers (behavior that would have been criminal had the industry itself engaged in it), and instead, like Diocletian, made it a crime to charge lower fares than that mandated by government.

Unfortunately for the consumer, industry and labor groups in the past 100 years in the United States have generally been better organized than consumer groups, and thus better able to exert political pressure to institute a regulatory agenda of keeping prices high in order to protect industry rather than the consumer. In particular, the populist agenda of the 1930s was directed primarily to keeping prices high by such policies as dumping milk into ditches and killing pregnant cows at a time when people were starving.

In 1981, Levine acknowledged that "the scholarly view of the regulatory process (has) changed from one of controlling private behavior for the public benefit to one of use of government power for private or sectional gain,"[10] and in 1977, Jean Luc Migue postulated that "it seems fair to say that among economists the most widely accepted theory of government regulation is that, as a rule, regulation is acquired by the industry regulated and is designed and operated primarily for its benefit."

Perhaps most illustrative of Stigler's Law that "every industry or occupation that has enough political power to utilize the state will seek to control entry" is the history of the railroad industry in America. In 1880, before the implementation of Diocletian-style regulation, passengers and businesses had 12 competitive railroads and routes between Atlanta and St. Louis to choose from. By 1900, there were 1,224 operating railroads. However, competition between these carriers resulted in such low prices to consumers that the railroad tycoons, thirsty for higher profits, soon began demanding "regulation" of fares. Prohibited by the Sherman Antitrust Act from legally colluding to fix higher prices by agreement among themselves, the rail kings began lobbying in Congress for a bill by which the government would set prices for them. Thus, in 1884, rail magnate John P. Green testified before the House Committee on Commerce, that "a large majority of the railroads in the U.S. would be delighted if a railroad commission or any other power could set rates (which) would insure them six per cent dividends."[11]

So great was the political and financial power of the railroads that, in accordance with Stigler's Law, Congress responded by passing the Interstate Commerce Act in 1887,[12] which fixed higher rates and limited entry. The *New York Press* tried to warn the American public about the consequences of such anticonsumer legislation, declaring that the railroad magnates had written the entire bill, and "this explains why the railroad lobbies did not raise a note of public or private protest against the Hepburn bill in the House." These warnings did not go unheeded, but in 1906, Congress tightened the price fixing and regulatory controls by passing the Hepburn Act. As a result, by 1980, the number of competitors had been reduced to but seven inefficient, lumbering oligopolists carrying over 85 percent of rail traffic.[13]

The first shot in the popular revolt against this kind of heavy-handed anticonsumer regulation was fired by John F. Kennedy in his Transportation Message of 1962, in which he called for greater reliance on the forces of competition and less reliance on the restraints of regulation.[14] Thirteen years later, the U.S. Senate Subcommittee of the CAB, under Senator Ted Kennedy, in oversight hearings revealed and exposed to the American public the fact that airline fares were 40 to 100 percent higher than they would be under deregulation, and that consumers had been bilked out of $3.5 billion by government "regulation."[15] As documentation of this conclusion, the hearings documented that fares in intrastate areas not regulated by the CAB were 50–70 percent of those fares regulated by the CAB over the same distance.[16] Finally, in 1978, the Carter administration pushed through the Airline Deregulation Act of 1978, which eased entry restrictions and opened the way for airlines to compete with each other. Deregulation in trucking soon followed, and in 1980, the Staggers Railroad Act of 1980, relaxed, though did not eliminate, government regulatory controls over the railroads.

The results of deregulation were as dramatic as they were sweeping. In the airline industry, fares declined despite steep increases in fuel costs. Whereas during regulation air travel was considered a luxury available only to a rich elite, middle-class passengers accustomed to "taking the bus" across the country on Greyhound or Trailways during the 1950s and 1960s now found air travel affordable, causing passenger traffic to more than triple in the aftermath of deregulation. By 1983, there were more city-pair markets receiving nonstop service than in 1978, the market share of new entrants more than tripled, and fatal crashes per 100,000 takeoffs declined dramatically, from 0.10 in 1978 to 0.08 in 1982

In an example of "creeping re-regulation," in recent years, regulators and airline executives have found ways via the back door to limit entry to competitors. Airlines that had financed long-term leases with airports took advantage of the "majority in interest" clauses in their leases to limit access to gates of competitors at major airports, and regulation continued in the granting of airport slots at high-traffic airports. Rather than condemning such slots and making them available to new entrants in a fair auction process, the major trunks were permitted to keep them as a means of limiting entry by their competitors. As a result, many of the new competitors who entered the industry in the aftermath of deregulation found themselves being pushed out by such policies, which have come in a form of disguised regulation. The unfortunate result has been a trend back toward an industry dominated by a handful of major trunk carriers that are able to fix fares in a de facto manner by posting (offering) fares on airline reservation systems and then seeing if they are "accepted" by their very few competitors. In such a manner, few airlines now ever get caught for antitrust violations of price-fixing laws in an increasingly concentrated industry.

Whatever the merits of deregulation in the transportation, service, and manufacturing industries, the case continues to be made that the benefits of deregulation cannot be carried over to the financial sector. The financial sector, it is claimed, is fundamentally different than other sectors in that the financial structure is the primary infrastructure for the entire economy, and must therefore be subject to a wide variety of government regulations.

Before addressing this claim, it is first necessary to define some terms. Although the term "regulation" is often used loosely to refer to both economic and health-and-safety regulations, such use blurs very different aspects of economic activity.

Examples of economic regulation are those which were promulgated by the CAB during the height of airline regulation. Airlines seeking entry into the airline industry were arbitrarily forbidden to do so by draconian economic regulations designed to protect incumbent carriers from any competition whatsoever. This kind of regulatory regime founds its roots in the policies of the Great Depression, which were to "keep prices high." By effectively forbidding the entry of competitors who might be able to provide air travel at a lower cost, this agenda was promoted.

Likewise, CAB regulations also fixed ticket prices on behalf of the airlines. Had the airlines themselves attempted to fix prices, they would have been subject to severe criminal sanctions, including imprisonment. By having the government fix prices for them, the airlines immunized themselves from criminal sanctions. The government itself was immune from criminal prosecution, under laws that provided them with immunity. With ticket prices fixed, incumbents were not only protected from competition from new entrants, but were now even protected from competition between *them*. Despite the fact that consumers cared more about price than other amenities, airlines were now reduced to competing with each other by offering to provide the most free cigarettes or offering Polynesian pubs.

Not content with regulating entry and prices, the CAB even promulgated regulations directing airlines to where they could fly. Whenever a congressman needed to satisfy the demands of a campaign contributor, pressure could be administratively directed toward the CAB to order one airline or another to provide service regardless of whether such service was economically viable.

Entry control, price fixing, and route regulations were the prime example of "economic" regulations, designed to protect large companies from competition with little or no consideration given to the needs of consumers. Health-and-safety regulation, on the other hand, is an entirely different sort of regulation. Examples of this type of regulation in the airline industry would be airworthiness regulations, and regulations providing for safety inspections of all airlines. Such regulations would be applicable to all competitors in an industry. Such health-and-safety regulation serves an entirely different purposed than economic regulation—namely the health and safety of the flying public. It was not surprising, then, that in the aftermath of airline deregulation in 1979, safety improved dramatically as much of the regulatory energy and resources previously dedicated to economic regulation were directed toward health-and-safety regulation.

The failure to recognize the important differences between economic and safety regulation has caused confusion among the voting public not exposed to the subject of economics in the public schools—a confusion that politicians have been quick to exploit.

In the aftermath of airline deregulation, there was a dramatic rise in the demand for air travel.[17] When air traffic congestion arose at airports not equipped to deal with such increases in demand, those who had opposed deregulation blamed deregulation for the problem. In the "good old days" before deregulation, air travel was considered a luxury available only to the elite, and most people took either Trailways or Greyhound buses for cross-country travel, or if willing to pay a bit more, the train. Consequently there was little congestion on the airlines, and wealthy travelers enjoyed the "civility" of half-filled airlines, were pampered by attentive and attractive air "hostesses," and showered with free cigarettes and liquor. No wonder that those who could afford to travel in those days bemoaned the loss of civility that came with deregulation. Especially galling was having to rub shoulders with the "Great Unwashed" who now filled all the seats on the airliners. Of course, deregulation was the cause of all this lack of "civility."

Nevertheless, economic deregulation did bring reduced fares, a dramatic rise in air travel, more efficient allocation of resources, greater service to small communities, a reduction in taxpayer-supported subsidies, safer travel, and deconcentration of power in the industry.

This experience with economic deregulation highlights the critical importance of distinguishing between economic and safety regulation. In many ways, it would be better if a different word than "regulation" could be used to describe both. In the meantime, policy makers must be content with using either the adjectives "economic" or "health and safety" in the describing the kind of regulation to which they refer.

The difference between the two might be noted in the meatpacking industry. Economic regulation in that industry would take the form of keeping competitors out of the industry, price fixing, or dictating to meatpackers what kind of animals to raise. Health-and-safety regulation would take the form of requiring frequent inspections of meatpacking facilities to protect the public from contaminated meat.

Making the distinction between economic and safety regulation in the financial industry is even more important. An example of safety regulation in the financial sphere would be capital requirements. Such regulations might require that a bank or financial institution set aside a certain percentage of its assets in cash or high-grade and short-term securities, such as government bonds, or that it require a certain percentage of down payment in lending money to home buyers. Other safety regulations would be those requiring banks to pay annual premiums to a federal deposit insurance entity, such as the Federal Deposit Insurance Corporation (FDIC).

In addition, responsible safety regulation of the financial sector should consist not only of requirements for frequent audits and inspections, but also the establishment of a federal rating agency that would assign ratings to the financial instruments created and issued by financial institutions. Currently, ratings of such instruments are issued by private companies, such as Moody's, who are often, in one way or another, on the payroll of the very institutions issuing the financial instruments to be rated. This would be akin to airline inspectors being hired by the airlines, or meat inspectors hired by the meatpacking companies.

Unfortunately, however, the government has failed to implement such safety regulations as might create an independent, government-sponsored rating agency. Rather, politicians have allocated the bulk of their energies toward economic regulation of the financial system in the form of regulations purporting to tell banks to whom to lend. Perhaps the most notorious example of this latter type of economic regulation was the Community Reinvestment Act, which actually threatened to impose severe penalties on banks that did not lend to constituencies favored by the politicians who promulgated the act. An additional flood of economic regulation was promulgated in the mid-1990s by the administration then in power, designed not only to put more enforcement teeth into the CRA, but also to induce the private sector to expand the "securitization" of mortgages by camouflaging the risk or subprime mortgages through a complicated process of slicing and dicing (see Appendix A for an explanation of this process).

The most pernicious of all the economic regulations have taken the form of handing out subsidies to high-income Americans to buy houses in the form of "tax deductions." Seemingly more benign, but in the end even more disastrous when combined with other government regulations designed to hype up a housing bubble, was the policy adopted by the government as early as the Great Depression to initiate the entire securitization process through the creation of quasi-government entities such as Fannie Mae, and later Freddie Mac. Indeed, the primary purpose of these entities was to provide "liquidity" in the mortgage industry by creating an agency that would buy mortgages from various lenders around the country, and then securitize them in the form of bonds issued to investors in the entities.

Had housing regulation been limited to this type of regulation and implemented on a responsible basis, the intrusion of government into the mortgage business might have created a more orderly bubble that could have been absorbed by a growing economy over a long period of time before collapse. Combined with the massive housing subsidies to the rich, however, naked economic regulation in the form of the CRA and its progeny, the securitization regulations of the mid-1990s,[18] and the subsequent collapse of responsible lending standards in the aftermath of securitization, the creation of a system in which government played the major role in a financial business inevitably led to abuses that no economy on earth could have sustained.

Calls for "more regulation" as a means to prevent future financial crises rarely distinguish between the types of regulation called for, thus creating a danger that the wrong kind of regulation will ultimately be implemented.

Safety regulation of financial institutions need be neither complicated nor byzantine, and should include two primary requirements for all financial institutions subject to federal jurisdiction: (1) a capital requirement of 20 percent, (2) home loan standards requiring at least 20 percent down and payments no greater than one-third of the verified income of the borrower over the term of the loan. In addition, a separate government department should be established that rates all financial instruments issued by financial institutions.

Enhancement, promulgation, and strict enforcement of safety regulations should be accompanied by the abrogation of economic regulations. (Currently, more than 90 percent of all government financial regulations fall into this category.) Home buyers and consumers have been burned badly by regulations issued by government entities purporting to tell financial institutions to whom to lend. Any discrimination in lending should be dealt with forcefully and vigorously by enforcement of the civil rights laws.

Perhaps most urgent is the need for reform of the antiquated 1913 tax code, in which extravagant subsidies for housing were granted to the very richest Americans at the expense of the very poorest. Second to CRA and the securitization regulations promulgated during the 1990s, no other single factor contributed more to the housing bubble, which raised housing prices to levels unaffordable to the average American.

5

Local Exclusionary Practices

It is an axiomatic economic principle that prices are determined by the intersection of demand and supply. Thus far, regulations contributing to the housing bubble by means of juicing up demand by means of handouts, subsidies, and easy money have been considered in previous chapters. It remains to examine how local regulations restricting supply have also contributed to the housing bubble.

Ever since the 1926 Supreme Court decision in *Village of Euclid v. Ambler Realty Co.*[1] gave constitutional sanction to the power of local governments, urban planning and land development has remained largely a matter of local control. Accordingly, local governments and zoning boards have been free to promulgate exclusionary zoning restrictions designed to promote the interests of their own communities, often at the expense of others.

Zoning by its very nature is exclusionary. Accordingly, developments excluded by zoning restrictions have no choice but to find alternatives. In many cases, these alternatives result in sprawl located further and further out from an urban core.

By way of example, one recent study of land development in the outer areas of the Washington, D.C., metropolitan area has revealed that more than half the land is subject to local zoning restrictions requiring lot sizes of between 3 and 25 acres of land.[2] While protecting the land and home values of current homeowners by insuring that low-income and multiunit dwellings are kept far away from the wealthy estates, such restrictions limit the supply of housing in those areas. California is another area where such local restrictions place enormous pressures on supply, and thus ultimately on price (see Tables 5.1 and 5.2).

Table 5.1   Average Size (Sq. Ft) of an American Home

1900	950
1950	1000
2000	2265
2005	2436

Source: National Association of Home Builders, http://www.nahb.org.

Table 5.2   Ratio of Home Prices to Household Income

2001	3.1
2002	3.3
2003	3.6
2004	4
2005	4.3
2006	4.3

Source: http://www.businessweek.com/investor/content/oct2008/pi20081017_950382_page_2.htm

Many of the current homeowners in control of local zoning boards make no attempt to conceal their personal financial interests in policies of exclusion, and even appeal to their fellow homeowners' personal financial interest in support of exclusionary policies. Others, however, have felt the need to find a more socially acceptable rationale than personal self-interest, if for no reason other than to appease their own consciences. Accordingly, many of these exclusionary policies have rested on the premise that low-density use actually helps to promote the preservation of open space, farmland, and forests.

In fact, however, studies have shown that such exclusionary practices have the exact opposite effect. In particular, Peter Whoriskey's article, entitled "Density Limits Only Add to Sprawl: Large Lots Eat Up Areas Countryside," revealed quite clearly that such exclusionary practices have "accelerated the consumption of woods and fields and pushed developers outward in their search for home sites."[3]

Edward Ziegler has concluded in his treatise *Land Use Regulation* that "exclusionary zoning and slow-growth regulations ... have the effect of raising housing costs and prices within the community and within the region."[4] He further concludes that:

Since local zoning and growth management programs can significantly limit the supply of housing available for sale within a community and, cumulatively, within a region, it's not difficult, particularly in a strong housing market, to see the potential connection between such limits on housing supply and inflated housing prices. According to one recent report on the housing industry, demand for new housing in this country may be exceeding building permits issued for new housing units; by over half a million units each year. This problem is particularly acute in California.[5]

Making matters even worse, these kind of exclusionary practices have been upheld by the courts. In *Construction Industry Association of Sonoma County v. the City of Petaluma*,[6] the Ninth Circuit Court of Appeals upheld the city of Petaluma's "freeze" on development on grounds that its exclusionary practices were implemented as a means to "preserve its small town character, its open spaces and low density of population, and grow at an orderly and deliberate pace." In that case, the city of Petaluma was successful in convincing the court that the basis for its exclusionary practices were for "environmental reasons." Since that case, however, considerable cynicism has been expressed regarding the true motives of those local governments engaging in such practices (see Tables 5.3 and 5.4). James Clingermayer, in an article in *Urban Affairs*, has noted that, despite claims of acting in the interests of the "environment," in fact, such practices are associated with "high home values, high income levels, and (preservation) of the white population."[7]

Mark Baldassare, in his "Trouble in Paradise: The Suburban Transformation in America," recognized that rich homeowners have now learned to give "environmental concerns" as the rationale for the exclusionary practices they support in order to increase their chances of having such practices upheld by the courts.[8]

On at least some occasions, the courts have seen through the environmental camouflage and recognized exclusionary practices for what they truly are. In *Windwood Estate v. Gretkowski*, the court recognized that the

Table 5.3   Rooms per House, by Country

Austria	3.2
Finland	3.6
France	3.8
Germany	4.5
U.S.	5.6

Source: National Association of Home Builders, http://www.nahb.org.

Table 5.4   Savings Rates Compared

	U.S.	France	Germany
1993	5.5	12.2	12.2
1994	5.1	11.8	11.8
1995	5.0	12.4	11.2
1996	4.1	11.9	10.8
1997	3.3	12.6	10.2
1998	4.2	12.2	10.2
1999	2.6	12.0	9.6
2000	2.2	11.9	9.4
2001	1.9	12.1	9.4
2002	2.2	13.8	10.0
2003	2.2	12.4	10.2
2004	2.0	12.4	10.6
2005	0.3	11.9	10.8
2006	0.8	12.0	10.8

Source: OECD Economic Outlook 82, no. 2 (December 2007).

true basis for the local government restrictions were "concerns about socioeconomic background and income level potential residents."[9] A journalist reporting on this case observed that:

> While trying to develop affordable homes and bring the American dream of home ownership to an expanded class of citizens, Woodwind Estates ran smack into the NIMBY (not-in-my-backyard) syndrome. Neighbors of the proposed project didn't like the idea, at least, not in their neighborhood. Banding together (as such groups always do) . . . the Concerned Neighbors of Windwood Estates . . . sought to stop the project by peppering the Strott Township Planning Commission with euphemisms. They were concerned about the income level of potential residents, as well as their socioeconomic background. Fretting about the effects of such people on local property values, they urged projects denial simply because they were opposed to low income residents moving into their community.[10]

In other words, many local governments' idea of "environmentalism" is simply to "keep the riffraff out"—or at least as far away as possible. Little or no consideration is given to where the "riffraff" will go once they are excluded. Dan Silver, head of the Los Angeles–based Endangered Habitats League, has considered this question, however, and concluded that "rather than preventing growth, the traditional anti-sprawl lawsuit simply diverts development into another neighborhood or the suburb."[11]

As affluent homeowners' true motives for excluding people based on their socioeconomic status, race, or culture becomes more transparent, the grounds for legally challenging their exclusionary practices have become somewhat broader. As a practical matter, however, this has not always led to any real diminution in such practices. Housing developers, especially those seeking to build affordable housing, have neither the time nor the resources to engage in costly litigation initiated by greedy homeowners eager to enhance the windfalls they stand to gain if the riffraff is excluded from their areas. Such cases can drag on for years, during which housing developers most often throw in the towel and give up their plans to build affordable housing.

The net result, of course, is that as a practical matter, the supply of housing is squeezed by local governments and affluent homeowners eager to relegate the riffraff to outlying areas from which they are doomed to long commutes to get to work. Such long commutes in the hinterland of sprawl have contributed significantly to the number of fatal automobile accidents—2.5 million deaths since 1950, or the equivalent of a 9/11 terrorist attack every month for 60 years.

Yet, it turns out that contributing to the housing bubble may have been the least of the disastrous social consequences of local exclusionary practices. Edward Ziegler's massive study of urban sprawl has concluded that such sprawl "increases air and water pollution [and] increases the consumption of oil and the emission of green house gases from automobiles," and concludes that "[c]ities that tout their Green Development initiatives . . . should be honest enough to count their 'zoning policy' responsibility for their 'exclusion-driven GHG emissions' from the automobile drivers of workers in the city who must find housing elsewhere and from their own city residents who need to drive elsewhere to find jobs."[12]

6

Bubbles of the Past

Our descendants doubtless will laugh at the human insanity of our age.[1]

Holland boasts of its yearly tulip festivals, and hundred of thousands of tourists each year flock there to enjoy the beauty of their tulips. However, these same tulips are perhaps better known for their involvement in the most iconic speculation bubble in history, the Dutch Tulip Mania. It has achieved this iconic status as a speculation bubble in part because the idea of paying such incredible prices for a simple flower is fantastic in itself, and combined with the steep rise and dramatic fall of tulip bulb prices, it is an example that leaps to mind whenever speculation bubbles, irrational exuberance, or herding is discussed.

In the late sixteenth century, Holland was becoming a booming economic landscape, its people luxuriously living off the popular trade industry in Amsterdam. The canals of Amsterdam provided the perfect port for foreign exotic goods, and the city used this to the advantage its own citizens. This trade in exotic foreign goods brought the tulip to Holland.

The tulip originated in the Ottoman Empire and was traded across Europe and through Amsterdam beginning in the 1600s. The vibrant flower became a must-have for the Dutch population because of their desire to show off their economic success through large estates surrounded by immaculate flower gardens.[2]

Tulips are an unpredictable species because they have to be planted and grown in order to see the beauty or rarity of the bloom. Therefore, the tulip bloom was an investment for gardeners, who wanted the most beautiful, varied, and rare species at the centers of their gardens. To remedy the possibility of an expensive bulb that may produce only an average bloom, there was a modified transaction process, and contracts were made strictly "in good faith."[3] Dutchmen would deposit money, plant the bulbs, and make further agreed-upon payments based on the results of the blooms.

The standard tulip was sought after, but only the more unique varieties commanded staggeringly high prices. A variation in tulip bulbs, caused by the Tulip Burst Virus, created vivid secondary color marks on the petals of the tulip flower, referred to as burst tulips.[4] As these coloring patterns were not genetic traits, the patterns could not be reproduced through breeding. The only method of culturing more "burst tulips" was through culturing the buds of tulips that were already infected with the virus.[5] Additionally, the virus also had the effect of reducing the effectiveness of the methods used to culture more bulbs, resulting in a small, relatively static supply of a desirable good.

While the actual value of the tulip bulb was hard to quantify, high-society merchants and traders, called *bloemists* (or, in English, simply florists), assessed the bulbs based on their color, their variance, their shape, and, most importantly, their rarity.[6] At the height of their value, broken tulips were valued at prices similar to that of houses. There is one recorded incident in which a speculator offered 12 acres of building land for a single bulb.[7] Tulips were sold in exchange for art, and valued as highly as gold and silver. With its increasing popularity amid the elite, lower-society members began giving up their occupations for an opportunity in the tulip trade business. The demand for tulips was so great that tulips were traded on the stock exchanges of many towns across Europe. Futures contracts for the purchase of tulip bulbs, where speculators agreed to purchase bulbs in the future at a set price, were signed.[8] Individuals began showing the first symptoms of gambling as they attempted to make profits from the rise and fall of the cost.[9]

Many speculative reasons for the tulip market crash in Holland exist. According to Robert Van Order, "To have a bubble, you need two things ... One is inelastic supply and the other is bad information."[10] As the burst tulips could not be reproduced through breeding, their supply was relatively static. A static price with an increasing demand will naturally drive prices higher. As prices increased, bulbs became a viable investment option, with purchases being made with the intent of reselling them on a later date at a profit.[11] The information available regarding investment in tulips was not insufficient for proper decision making. Commonly available knowledge was that tulip investment was a sure thing. Tulip investment was a reasonably good investment vehicle; investors rarely suffered a loss before the crash of 1637.[12] Without the ability to forecast an eventual crash, tulip investors were operating under the assumption that tulip prices would never fall. More and more people flocked to the growing tulip speculation industry, and any suggestions that the prices could not be sustained were dismissed by the populace.

While the economic conditions of Holland at the time were ripe for a boom, with increasing currency, colonial opportunities, and a strong state, the tulip bubble could not be sustained.

> The crisis came unexpectedly. On February 4th, 1637, the possibility of the tulips becoming definitely unsalable was mentioned for the first time. From then to the end of May 1637, all attempts of coordination between florists, bulb growers as well as by the States of Holland were met with failure. Bulbs worth tens of thousands of U.S. dollars (in present value) in early 1637 became valueless a few months later.[13]

Yet how could something once sought after so eagerly and priced to impress fall so drastically in value?

One of the reasons for this large devaluation was that the price of tulips no longer reflected their intrinsic value; rather, everyone just valued the profits not the bulbs.[14] The value of the tulip bulbs was relative—at first for its beauty and rarity, then for its investment value. Dutch traders had valued tulips for their social worth, in order to gain the highest profits, and not for their actual worth. Similar to the current American economic and housing market collapse, the Dutchmen did not realize the fallout of overestimating the market value of tulip bulbs until after the fact. Dutch Tulip Mania is a fascinating period of history that has become the iconic example of a speculation bubble.

SOUTH SEA BUBBLE

> As Fishes on each other prey,
> The Great Ones swallowing up the Small;
> So fares it in the Southern Sea:
> But Whale Directors eat up all.
>
> When Stock is high, they come between,
> Making by second-hand their Offers;
> Then cunningly retire unseen,
> With each a Million in his Coffers.[15]
>
> —From Jonathan Swift, "The South Sea Project"

The South Sea Company is another famous example of a 18th century bubble.[16] In response to the English Parliament's rising debt, South Sea conjured a method of converting Parliament's debt into stock. South Sea successfully outbid Bank of England for the right to acquire this debt by offering £7.6M (British pounds). The agreement between Parliament and South Sea was in exchange for Parliament's £31.5M debt, South Sea received £31.5M worth of its own stock, held by Parliament.[17]

How does South Sea raise money to cover this debt as well as profit at the same time? In addition to being paid interest (4-5%), South Sea was also allowed to issue stock. It did not, however, set its initial stock price at the nominal value of £100.[18] South Sea was also able to increase the number of buyers by using leveraging. Using leveraging, buyers may enter the market with only a fraction of the total cash needed to pay for the total number of shares and borrow the rest.[19] This fraction is known as "margin."[20] South Sea, in issuing shares of stock in four intervals, allowed buyers to put up only one-fifth of the total stock value they wanted to purchase of the first and fourth intervals, and only one-tenth of the total value of the second and third intervals.[21]

When a company issues stock, it is then charged with increasing its value thereby increasing the value of the company. South Sea was no different. However, it needed "help" from Parliament in passing law in South Sea's favor; the methods it employed were suspect.[22] For example, during the first two intervals of stock issuance South Sea issued "call options"[23] (options to buy stock at a price at a predetermined value). If this predetermined value is below the market value, then a person exercises his or her call option, buys at this lower value, and sells at the market value. South Sea gave members of Parliament these call options in order to give Parliament incentive to see the stock's value increase.[24]

The first issuance of stock took place on April, 14, 1720 with an offering of £300.[25] The second offering was issued on April 29th at £400.[26] Between the second and third issuance (June 16th), South Sea's stock value sharply rose from somewhere between £300 and £400, to £800.[27] The stock saw its peak value of £1,050 on June 25th. Just prior to June 25th, South Sea closed its books in order to determine dividends payable to shareholders.[28] Unfortunately for South Sea, its better days were behind it.

When the books were reopened in mid-August, South Sea's stock value began to fall dramatically. Over a one-month span between mid-September and mid-October, the value fell from £520 to £170.[29] The South Sea Bubble had certainly burst.

During South Sea's dramatic upswing, several other start-up companies entered the market hoping to see similar gains.[30] However, several of these companies were fake.[31] Garber identified two companies that were legitimate, and therefore competed for available purchaser of stock. Parliament, having been paid in options by South Sea, passed the Bubble Act mid-June which forbid companies from seeking new ventures without being authorized.[32] Once Parliament began enforcing the Act, companies lost their value because they could no longer proceed with their ventures.[33] Consequently, shareholders began dumping their shares to avoid further losses.

One theory holds that the South Sea Bubble is a prime example of irrational behavior: Investors either didn't fully understand the risks involved or they based their judgment based on the successively lucrative subscriptions without paying respect to how unsound their initial valuations of the risk might have been.[34]

While the theory holding that irrational behavior by investors suggests several possible causes for the irrational behavior, the main thrust of the argument is that given the South Sea Company was predicated on practically no assets (merely a fixed interest payment from the government and one cargo ship a year to South America), that no rational investor would've participated in the incredibly risky debt conversion scheme. Among the reasons for why irrational behavior could have taken over is that gambling was very pervasive in the early 1700's and the similarity between successive lottery draws of the 1711 National Lottery and the successively more lucrative seeming subscriptions.[35]

THE EVENTS LEADING TO THE GREAT DEPRESSION

Few other eras in the history of the United States inspire as much fancy and nostalgia as the 1920s. Most high school history classes regard it as the "Roaring Twenties": an epoch of uninterrupted social and economic expansion. Indeed, the decade preceding the Great Depression witnessed the passage of the Nineteenth Amendment, the Harlem renaissance, art deco, the growth of cinema, and one of the longest periods of economic expansion in U.S. history. Mass production brought what were once luxury goods into the homes of millions of Americans. However, most historians fail to account for the Federal Reserve's role in both creating and ending this era.

The 1920s can be fairly characterized as the era that changed consumption patterns in America. During the interwar years, Americans spent increasingly more of their income on durable goods. A durable good is one that has an expected service life of three years or longer and tends to be more expensive than a perishable or nondurable good.[36] These often include books, china, jewelry, sewing machines, lamps, automobiles, yachts, and eyeglasses, to name but a few.[37] In the first three decades of the twentieth century, Americans tripled their consumption of large-ticket items. Between 1899 and 1908, households spent $79 on average annually on durable goods.[38] Between 1919 and 1928, that number grew to $267. The change in the type of goods purchased is equally as significant. Prior to World War I, 43 percent of durable purchases went to major durables, primarily furniture; while after the war, 64 percent went to major durables, now primarily automobiles.[39]

Two trends explain this change in consumption: rising household income, and increased purchases of automobiles, televisions, and radios. Between 1899 and 1929, gross domestic product per capita increased from $5,515 to $8,016 in 2005 dollar terms.[40] When real incomes rise faster than the cost of consumer staples, consumption tends to shift away from perishable items to durables. Over this time period, total expenditures on perishables decreased from 44.6 percent to 38.4 percent of total consumption.[41] During the Great Depression, expenditures on perishables returned to their historical averages and did not decrease until the postwar economic boom.[42] During this time, however, consumers changed the items that they purchased. In the first decade of the twentieth century, consumers spent less than 4 percent of their annual expenditures on cars, televisions, and radios.[43] By 1929, they spent 31.7 percent on automobiles and 6.7 percent on televisions and radios.[44]

Despite the rapid and continued economic expansion during the 1920s, consumers astonishingly paid for their expenditures by decreasing their savings and borrowing. During prosperous years, we ordinarily expect personal savings to rise, reflecting the overall health of the economy. Not so in the 1920s, where household savings decreased by nearly a third. Between 1922 and 1929, personal saving averaged 3.9 percent, which is rather shocking considering the prewar average was 5.5 percent.[45] Perhaps we should not be surprised to find that just as the housing bubble began to reach its limits in 2005 and 2006, personal savings remained below 2.5 percent and even turned negative in the third quarter of 2005.[46]

Decreases in savings alone did not account for the rapid rise in consumer durables. The 1920s saw the first-ever rapid expansion of consumer credit. While installment selling dates back to as early as the Romans and Mesopotamia, its wide-scale use did not rise to a critical mass until the Industrial Revolution.[47] Installment contracts were the primary source of finance for durable goods purchases prior to World War II. Unlike a loan, the buyer in an installment sale does not receive any monetary proceeds. Instead, the buyer owes the balance of the purchase price plus a predetermined finance charge. The contract is a promise to pay the remaining payments, not the promise to repay a specific sum. While auto purchases were the primary source of installment contracts, finance companies offered installment financing on everything from "mechanical refrigerators, radios, air conditioners, oil burners, automatic stokers, household facilities, pumps, dairy equipment, and other chattels."[48]

The increased demand for durables and the need for purchase financing led to the creation and expansion of finance companies. Finance companies had a dual role in the rapid expansion of consumption. As has already been noted, they provided financing directly to consumers for purchases. Equally important, they provided inventory financing for dealers.[49] With the expansion of assembly line production techniques, car manufacturers required dealers to maintain a larger inventory during slow selling seasons.[50] Unable to secure financing from banks or manufacturers, dealers turned to finance companies to fund their inventory.[51] As a result, the number of finance companies doubled during the decade, from 100 in 1920 to well over 1,000 in 1928.[52] By the end of the decade, consumer nonmortgage debt had risen from 4.7 percent of household income in 1920 to 9.3 percent in 1929.[53]

The expansion of credit and increased purchases meant that corporations, particularly manufacturers, experienced vast increases in profitability. In 1922, the net profit for all U.S. corporations stood at $4.38 billion. By 1929 it had nearly doubled to $8.083 billion. Corporate dividends grew correspondingly, and companies paid a majority of profits to stockowners. This, combined with the apparent success of the Federal Reserve (Fed) in taming the economy, led many to believe that stock prices would only go up. As such, stocks made a reasonable investment. While many have pointed to the stock market and collapse as the cause of the Great Depression, the monetary policies probably caused the collapse that led to the Depression.

While the Federal Reserve had been particularly lax about the volume and expansion of credit during the 1920s, many at the Fed believed in the real bills doctrine. The real bills doctrine held that "loans should only be made for productive purposes to accommodate the needs of the business community and should be self liquidating."[54] Any loans not backed by real bills were speculative per se and would necessarily lead to inflation.[55] In early 1929, the Board of Governors of the Federal Reserve made its intentions clear with respect to broker loans in a letter sent to member banks:

> The board has no disposition to assume authority to interfere with the loan practices of member banks so long as they do not involve the Federal Reserve banks. It has, however, a grave responsibility whenever there is evidence that member banks are maintaining speculative security loans with the aid of Federal Reserve credit. When such is the case the Federal Reserve Bank becomes either a contributing or a sustaining factor in the current volume of speculative security credit. This is not in harmony with the intent of the Federal Reserve Act, nor is it conducive to the wholesome operation of the banking and credit system of the country.

As a result of this perception within the Fed, the board launched a highly contractionary policy at the end of 1927. During this time, the Fed significantly decreased the amount of credit available, raising the rates on bankers' acceptances from 3 percent to 4.5 percent and the discount rate from 3.5 percent to 5 percent.[56] While the Fed may have intended only to prick the stock bubble, the policy had disastrous consequences for the remainder of the economy. The crash along with the increase of debt on household balance sheets led consumers to defer consumption, thereby choking output.

Most contemporary observers feel that the Depression could have been mitigated or possibly avoided had the Federal Reserve pursued a policy of expanding the money supply.[57] As the money supply contracted and interest rates increased, consumers needed less output. This put additional pressure on prices and in turn discouraged consumption.[58] This approach would be essentially what policy makers are trying to accomplish today. Rather than acknowledge that there was an excessive and speculative bubble that should have been extinguished, the policy makers attempt to perpetuate the bubble through increased consumption. Perhaps it is easier to subsidize consumption when it is of a home, but not when it is of a Singer sewing machine or Victrola.

Economic Education

The failure of American public education has been well documented.[1] In one international comparative study of educational progress in math and science conducted by the International Assessment of Educational Progress, it was reported that "13 year olds in the United States ranked among the lowest of all those taking the tests."[2] In math, for example, American students ranked 19th out of 20th, managing to nudge out Jordan.

Measuring the performance of American public school students in such subjects as economics, however, would be difficult, given that few public schools offer rigorous courses in macroeconomics. The schools which do offer a class in economics often offer nothing little more than a course on balancing a checkbook.

In 2006, the National Center for Education Statistics tested a representative sample of public school students.[3] Results of these tests showed that about half of the students tested understood what banks did with the money customers deposited into their checking account.[4] Only 36 percent could identify the government's primary source of revenue. Less than one third could explain how interest rates might affect a decision to borrow money. Perhaps most disheartening, only half understood the impact of removing trade barriers between countries, and only 40 percent understood why industries and labor unions seek protectionist measures such as high tariffs. In the end, only 3 percent performed at an "advanced" level.[5]

The failure to understand such basic economic concepts as the law of supply and demand and the law of comparative advantage serves as a significant factor in the housing bubble collapse. Perhaps most alarming is the failure of schools to teach economic history. Those versed in even basic economic history would be familiar with such economic catastrophes of the past, such as the South Sea Bubble, the Tulip Bubble, and the kind of economic policies that led to the stock market bubble of the 1920's and the Great Depression. They would understand how Ponzi schemes work, and what economic warning signs which signal the rise of an economic bubble.

Homebuyers with even a rudimentary understanding of economics would understand the implications of negative amortization, adjustable rate mortgages pursuant to which their monthly payments could double or triple, the effect of interest rates on monthly payments, and the budgetary consequences if their home declined in value.

Perhaps even more alarming than the lack of economic knowledge among homebuyers is the exhibited lack of economic understanding by elected politicians. Though the very notion that home prices could continue to spiral up forever would be anathema to any person with a rudimentary knowledge of economic history, politicians won votes and elections win votes by perpetuating the myth that home ownership was so risk free that even those with marginal credit and no payment could get in on the government's gravy train if only banks could be coerced into lending vast sums of money to them by threatening them with sanctions and punitive measures if they did not (as was provided for in the Community Reinvestment Act[6] and the housing regulations promulgated by Congress in the mid-1990's.

Government regulators have also revealed a fundamental misunderstanding of economics. Apparently under the impression that confronting homebuyers with foot high stack of documents and fine print warnings at closings were a reasonable (though perfunctory) way to implement a myriad of government regulations, these regulators failed to undertake even the most basic of warnings to homebuyers with marginal credit and who were making no down payment—something along the lines of the following in 16 point bold print:

> I understand that my monthly payment may double in six months, and that my interest rate may double by next year. I further understand that, statistically, given my low down payment and unsatisfactory credit history, my chances of losing my home to foreclosure in within three years exceeds 90%

But perhaps the greatest concern for the lack of education in economic laws should be reserved for the very highest echelons of the economic regulation establishment. By way of example, consider this economic analysis by none other than the Chairman of Federal

Reserve Ben Barnanke on May 17, 2007, on the very verge of the financial collapse of the housing bubble:

> Given the fundamental factors in place that should support the demand for housing, we believe the effect of the trouble in the subprime market ... will likely be limited ... Importantly, we see no serious broader spillover to banks or thrift institutions from the problems in the subprime market.

8

Speculation

You know it is time to sell when your shoe shine boy starts giving you
stock tips.
—Attributed to Joseph P. Kennedy, who secured his fortune by selling
his investments just prior to the stock market collapse.

Another favorite scapegoat of the housing bubble collapse has been
"speculation," a term that turns out to be as elusive as "greed."

Consider who may have been the earliest speculators in history:
those who bought grain during the good harvest years in ancient
Egypt and stored it in the hope that in case of a famine, they could sell
their grain for a huge profit.

If the Nile flooded and the crops were good, the speculators were
wiped out, and understandably, no tears were shed for them. But
when famine did come, the speculators made a handsome profit
selling for high prices. Rarely appreciated—then, or since, for
that matter—was that had the speculators not taken their risk, there
would have been *no food at all* available at any price when the crops
failed, and there would have been famine. Whatever public service the
speculators might have served, however, society has never seen fit to
pin a medal on them inasmuch as they acted purely with motives of
greed and self-interest.

Indeed, the main ideological difference between capitalism and
socialism has been that the former accepts that humans inevitably act
most vigorously in their own self-interest, and seeks to harness that
self-interest for the public good; socialism, on the other hand, is based
on the premise that humans can be forced to act for the public good
rather than in their self-interest. A capitalist society learns to resist
envying those who speculate and become rich as a consequence,

instead concentrating on a social safety net for those who fail; social-ism rejects in theory that those acting purely in their self-interest should ever be rewarded and is willing to accept poverty for all its citizens other than the privileged members of the political elite who run the show.

Nevertheless, the social and economic case for speculators rests on the assumption that economic system in which they act is both transparent and fair in the use of that government power that regulates and provides the infrastructure of that system. When a gambler enters a casino and puts her money down on red at the roulette wheel, she has every right to assume that the roulette wheel has not been rigged. She has a right to know what the odds are, and, in the case of a casino, that the odds are against her. If she wins, the government will take its cut in the form of taxes; if she loses, few tears are shed for her since she acted in her own self-interest, and it is only fair that she must accept the consequences of losing her bet.

But what of the speculator who cheats by rigging the roulette wheel? And what of a government that secretly rigs or manipulates the wheel in a way that will maximize its own cut of the winnings? The difference is that between speculation and fraudulent behavior. A capitalist system can tolerate, even encourage the former; but it should recognize and punish the latter.

Consider now the role of "speculation" in both the creation of the housing bubble, and in its inevitable collapse. As early as 1913, the government pursued a policy of pushing up housing prices, although it is not at all clear that it realized that was what it was doing. At first, the means for doing so were modest, limited to granting a tax deduction to anyone who paid interest on a mortgage. Because so few people paid income taxes in 1913, however, the effect on the housing bubble was minimal. By the mid-1930s, the government took a more proactive role in promoting homeownership by establishing the Federal Housing Administration. Later came the creation of Fannie Mae and Freddie Mac (see chapter 11, *infra*, for a detailed discussion). In 1977, Congress passed the Community Reinvestment Act, which first set forth the goal of expanding home ownership in depressed areas. Finally, in 1992–1993, the Department of Housing and Urban Development set forth rigid quotas for Fannie Mae to meet in purchasing mortgages: "30 percent should be to located in central cities; 30 percent should be to (low) income ... families."[1] In 1995, the quotas were increased, requiring that 42 percent of Fannie Mae purchases be for mortgages on housing located in "central cities ... and other underserved areas."[2] In order to meet these goals, banks began to reduce or eliminate down payments, to relax income qualification requirements, and to devise "creative" financing instruments such as adjustable rate and negatively amortizing loans. No one would ever suspect the government of encouraging marginal buyers to buy houses with no down payment unless it was prepared to keep home prices surging to ensure that few such buyers would find themselves "upside down" (in which a position in which they owed more than their house was worth).

Not surprisingly, "speculators" were the first to grasp the government's implicit promise to stimulate the housing bubble to new and dizzying heights, and soon began buying houses in frenzy in order to "flip" them for quick profits.

In light of these undisputed activities, it is tempting to blame the speculators. After all, by buying houses "on spec," they were indeed contributing to the escalation in home prices. However, it should be considered that the government itself laid the groundwork for this speculative frenzy in the first place. It was as if the government had deposited a slot machine in the living room of a potential speculator, along with a promise that if they pulled the handle, the could not lose. Based on government policy, the buying of houses for quick profit could no longer be described as speculation at all, but rather as a rational and prudent investment—far safer than buying stocks or even long-term U.S. government bonds, which could fall dramatically in value if interest rates ever rose (as they did in 1974).

In the aftermath of the 1995 HUD regulations, it was not surprising that many mortgage companies began to dramatically increase the employment of predatory lending practices. While such practices should always be punished in accordance with applicable law, it cannot be ignored that such predatory lenders were emboldened to engage in such practices by government policies. The chances of such practices being discovered were minimal as long as the housing bubble continued to expand. A home buyer who obtained a home loan he could not afford was hardly likely to complain if his home doubled in value, thus enabling even the most marginal borrower to take cash out of his equity and refinance. Only when the bubble inevitably burst did buyers who were unable to refinance begin to justify their defaults on grounds of predatory lending grounds.

If it is a stretch to analogize the Clinton HUD regulations of 1995 to a rigging of the roulette wheel, it is not a long stretch by any means. Politicians were being elected and gaining political power based on a promise to their constituencies to get them into houses they could not afford. These same politicians were rigging the wheel by pursuing policies designed to keep the bubble going as long as possible (or at least until they were safely retired on their generous government pensions).

The irony, of course, is that in pursuing policies that resulted in pushing home prices far above the capacity of the average American to afford them, the politicians did so under the banner of "expanding homeownership. Like all Ponzi schemes, the government was initially successful, increasing the number of homeowners by almost two million. Not transparent to the constituencies they served, however, was the fact that a fair proportion of these new "homeowners" were not owners at all—at least in any meaningful sense of the word. Many had put no money down, with even their closing costs being lent to them by "predatory" lenders. In many cases, they got into homes for less cash outlay than would have been required had they wanted to rent an apartment. When foreclosures loomed, the same politicians who had risen to power by creating the housing bubble now claimed that the only solution to the housing bubble collapse they had created was to pursue policies that would prevent homeowners from being "pushed from their homes."

An example of policies now being proposed was that lenders be forced to reduce the interest, and even the principal of the loans they had extended. If enacted by federal legislation, such proposals would be in direct violation of the due process clause of the U.S. Constitution, which forbids the taking of property without due process. If enacted by the states, such legislation would be in violation of Art. 1, Section 10, of the U.S. Constitution, which forbids states to "impair the obligation of contracts."

To deprive a lender of his property in this way would be similar to passing a law that said if a customer went to a bank and deposited $1,000, the government would be free to ordain that the bank only has to return half of that to the customer. (Of course, any person may petition for bankruptcy, and homeowners are always free to discharge their debts upon compliance with current bankruptcy laws).

Still another "solution" proposed by the politicians who created the bubble is to keep the bubble going as long as possible. An example of this agenda is the 2009 bill that hands out $8,000 to people who want to buy a house.[3] Although this subsidy is to be handed out in the form of tax credit, there is no requirement in the bill that the recipient of such largess actually owe any taxes at all as a prerequisite to qualifying for the cash credit. Since most people who qualify for the credit do not pay any federal income taxes, the tax credit is effectively a cash subsidy paid for by all taxpayers.

Not considered by government officials at all is a policy that would allow house prices to fall to levels affordable by the average American family. As long as government policies are directed toward bubble expansion rather than on preventing bubbles in the future, there appears to be little prospect of preventing bubble collapses in the future.

Speculation played an important role in the recent housing bubble. When housing prices were soaring, people began scooping up houses as investments, hoping to make a quick profit. However, when the housing bubble burst, those investments turned into losing bets. This is not the first time speculation has ended in burst bubbles and lost investments. So, why do people continue to speculate? The media plays an integral role in hyping the idea of speculation. There is also the "everyone-else-is-doing-it" theory. Furthermore, psychological theories, such as observational learning, conditioning, and social identity, may explain speculation's allure. When speculation acts as a trend, the results can be devastating. However, speculation is not without merits. Speculation can stimulate economic growth and benefit society, but only if done responsibly.

"Flipping houses is the most tried-and-true way to make a fortune in real estate."[4] This proclamation from the hit A&E television show *Flip This House* illuminates the role speculation plays in housing bubbles. Flipping houses is the practice of buying a house, making renovations that increase the value of the property, and then selling the property for a profit. Houses can also be flipped in the same manner that stocks are traded. Houses that are expected to increase in value are purchased and, once the value increases, the buyer flips the house for a profit. "Flippers often look for distressed properties, foreclosed properties, or residences in poor condition that they can repair and put back on the market at a higher price. Flippers take advantage of any excited or hyped market psychology that exists," states Christopher Cagan, director of research at First American Real Estate Solutions of Anaheim.[5]

The misconception bred by *Flip This House* is that it is always possible to make a fortune flipping houses, that housing prices will perpetually increase. While Christopher Cagan found that flippers who resold during the "sweet spot," three to six months after the purchase, usually received an annualized rate of return 20 to 40 percent or more above the market appreciation rate, he focused his study on three of the hottest zip codes in the country.[6] Furthermore, if the value of the house goes down in three to six months, the "sweet spot" turns into the "rotten spot." Cagan admits that, "At some time the market must slow down, level off or even decline."[7] Housing markets are constantly fluctuating, and flipping houses is a tried-and-true way to lose a fortune when the market goes sour.

GAMBLING ON HOUSES

> The safest way to double your money is to fold it over once and put it in your pocket.
>
> —Kin Hubbard

Gambling is to bet on an uncertain outcome.[8] Gambling also refers to when monetary gain is pursued without the use of skill.[9] In this light, speculation is not the same as gambling. Speculation occurs when "one backs" one's own opinion against the established one or against "the market's."[10] There are risks associated with both gambling and speculation, but speculation is more of an educated guess, while gambling is left merely to chance. However, what happens when the established opinion is incorrect?

"Plasma TV screens? Check. Over-the-top bathrooms? Check. Huge hot tubs? Check. This season of *Cribs* has it all, so you can spend your time daydreaming about how the other half lives."[11] As the plug for the popular television show *Cribs* describes, the established opinion in America is that status is dependent on huge mansions with lavish accessories. The plug also implies that half of America is living in a luxury house. In 2007, the median sales price of existing single-family homes for metropolitan areas in the United States was $217,800.[12] Clearly, the implication gleaned from *Cribs* is inaccurate. When people base their opinion on this inaccurate representation the housing market, speculation acts as an uneducated guess. Using this misinformation as the basis for buying an investment home is particularly dangerous.

When the public believes that lavish houses will continue to be symbols of status, the demand for these houses increases, and their prices jump. As long as lavish houses continue as status symbols, the demand will continue to boost prices. This is analogous to the demand for tulip bulbs in Holland in the mid-seventeenth century. As long as tulips continued to act as status symbols, the demand for tulips intensified, and their prices kept climbing. Then, people realized that a tulip was just a flower. A similar realization struck the American housing markets. Demand for houses had pushed prices through the roof. When the reality of the houses' actual worth reared its head, demand and prices shrunk, causing the housing bubble to burst.

Buying a house has always been part of the American dream. It represents an individual's or family's independence. A homeowner is like a king, free to do as he pleases within the confines of the kingdom. However, history has not given us many castle-flipping kings. The twentieth century has, on the other hand, given us a rampant increase in house-flipping home buyers. The twentieth century has also given us the Las Vegas' "Strip" of casinos, legalized gambling through the Indian Gaming Regulatory Act, and the widely televised World Series of Poker. It appears that gambling is the zeitgeist of the times.

Taking out risky loans to finance investment mansions is not that different from playing the lottery or shooting craps; both are losing propositions. Gamblers know that the odds are against them. However, the extremely slight chance that they may win keeps them scratching tickets and rolling dice. Similarly, hapless home buyers know, or should know, that they cannot afford houses beyond their means, even if they plan on flipping the house for a profit. There is always a risk that the house will not increase in value or that it will not sell. Still, the National Association of Realtors reported that, in 2005, 27.7 percent of all homes purchased were investment properties.[13]

Since the 1970s, casino "gambling" has been referred to as "gaming."[14] Poker is now a "sport" on ESPN. Flipping houses is viewed as a viable means to make a living. In the eighteenth and nineteenth centuries, gambling and lotteries were condemned.[15] In the twentieth and twenty-first centuries, "gaming" is not only an accepted activity, but is encouraged.

People gamble for money. Many betting games are referred to as "entertainment," but the entertaining aspect of gambling is winning money. When people are down on their luck, the tendency to gamble increases because people are in greater need of money. Gambling, especially in churches and bingo halls, was rampant during the Great Depression.[16] During this time, lotteries were legalized, and gambling on horses and car races was prolific.[17] The worse the economic situation, the greater the tendency will be for people to gamble. It is quite the opposite scenario for house speculation. As house prices increase and the future looks brighter, more people are inclined to invest in houses. This makes sense because, if house values did not increase, no money could be made by flipping them. This is the very nature of housing speculation. However, the very nature of speculation breeds something that ruins gamblers and bankrupts home investors: optimism.

"A pessimist sees the difficulty in every opportunity; an optimist sees the opportunity in every difficulty," said Winston Churchill.[18] This statement summarizes the fatal pitfall awaiting every housing speculator. The tendency to see property values as ever-increasing blinds the investor to the reality that values always level out or decline. This is the nature of any speculative market. In this sense, property values are like waves. Investors want to buy properties when the wave is first forming, when prices are low. They want to sell when the wave has grown larger, when prices have increased. The ideal time to sell would be when the wave peaks or just before it breaks, just before prices decrease. Therein lies the gamble: guessing when the wave will peak.

It would defy the laws of physics to have a wave that infinitely increased in size. So, too, would it be unreasonable to expect house values to infinitely increase. However, this is the fantasy that causes home investors to cling to their properties, waiting for the prices to increase, as the crashing wave of property value dashes them on the rocks of foreclosures and bankruptcies. The lethal potential of the market dynamics is driven by the market values themselves. The Tulip Bulb Bubble exemplifies this.

When the price of a single tulip increases by several dollars and then decreases by several dollars, the likelihood of adverse effects are minimal. This is likened to a swelling wave that does not crash. It merely undulates. However, when the price of a single tulip increases by hundreds or even thousands of dollars, the value is more volatile, and the inevitable decrease in value is more likely to be violent. This is likened to a tidal wave that crashes when it can no longer support itself. Optimism for infinitely increasing property values is like hoping for a tidal wave.

Optimists are also less likely to heed the warnings of past losses. In a study comparing the gambling expectations and behaviors of optimists and pessimists, researchers found that optimists had higher expectations for winning casino games that had only a slight chance for success.[19] Also, the researchers found that optimists were more likely than pessimists to maintain high expectations of winning, even after suffering losses.[20] Finally, they found that optimists were more

prone to continue gambling after losing when compared to pessimists.[21] Casinos want their patrons to continue to gamble. So, it is in
the casinos' best interests to encourage gamblers to be optimistic about
their chances of winning. Casinos do this through advertising.

Advertising for housing speculation is notably more subtle than
casino advertising, but the same marketing principles are used. There
are three purposes that housing investment advertising attempts to
attain: the recruitment of people who may want to invest in houses,
but have not yet; the retention of current housing investors; and the
normalization of housing speculation in the eyes of the investors.

"Get 'em while they're young." Television shows like *Cribs* and *Flip
This House* are marketed to young adults. There is a very good reason
for this. A high proportion of males between the ages of 18 and 24
are frequent gamblers.[22] Gambling advertising, like these television
shows that encourage housing speculation, is aimed at people
between the ages of 14 and 17.[23] This population may have limited
means to gamble.[24] However, the purpose of the advertising is to
groom and nurture gambling tendencies so that when the target
audience reaches the age at which they can legally gamble, they are more
likely to gamble frequently.[25] It is the same with housing investment
advertising. If young people are groomed to think that housing
speculation is the "most tried-and-true way to make a fortune in real
estate," they will be more inclined to flip houses when they are given
the financial means to do so.

Housing investment advertising aims to encourage current housing
speculators to keep investing in the market, even if the market is in
decline. As noted earlier, the best way to do this is to keep current
investors optimistic about property values. This is accomplished
through a slew of resources. One of the most effective advertising
outlets for this information is news reports. News reports that paint
future property values as bright and sunny bolster speculators' belief
that prices are going to increase and that there is money to be made
in the market. News reports, especially from reputable sources, can
be particularly dangerous when their housing value forecasts do not
pan out. Optimism in news reports during the Great Depression
exacerbated the economic crisis. Right after the stock market plunged
in October 1929, the *New York Times* spoke of the market "regain[ing]
its poise and stability," while the *Washington Post* heralded the
"passing of the crisis."[26] In reality, the Great Depression was just
beginning. Today, newspapers and television news programs are
flooded with reports of foreclosures, declining property values, and

panic in the housing market. This is not 1929. "I think as business journalists have been burned many times for not sounding the alarm before previous drops in the market or big corporate failures, which many of them now bend over backwards to avoid being wronged," states Chris Roush, a business journalism professor at the University of North Carolina, on the trend toward more negative news reporting.[27] While news reports are becoming more wary of depicting markets in a blindingly optimistic light, other advertising outlets continue to suggest that property values will raise again soon, thus attempting to retain current investors who might otherwise jump the housing speculation ship.

Housing speculation advertising, as well as gambling advertising, attempts to normalize the activity. They theory behind normalization is that, if people believe that housing speculation is a widely acceptable means of making money, they will be more willing to engage in housing speculation. In gambling advertising, normalization serves to decrease the negative stigma attached to frequent gambling.[28] Likewise, housing speculation advertising attempts to downplay the risks of speculative investment by showing that housing speculation is a widely accepted and economically beneficial activity. The normalization of housing speculation is especially dangerous because humans are social animals and prone to conformity. When people participate in an activity such as housing speculation, ignoring or at least downplaying the risks associated with the activity because it is held to be acceptable by the majority of people, the outcome can be disastrous.

"No down payment!" "No closing costs!" "No finance charges!" When consumers hear these phrases, they should also be hearing the adage "If it sounds too good to be true, it probably is." So, why did so many home buyers blindly fall victim to unscrupulous lenders touting questionable loans in order to buy investment homes they could not afford? One explanation is that everyone was flipping houses. As previously stated, humans are social animals. Social influences factor greatly in our daily activities, especially risky ones. Risky activities are inherently susceptible to social influence because people are more likely to engage in risky behavior if they have a social support network that condones the behavior. There are many psychological theories that attempt to explain how social influence affects our decisions. Some of the most applicable to the psychology of housing speculation are observational learning, classical conditioning, and social identity.[29]

9

Psychology

Markets are mirrors of the human psyche...they can become depressed...even suffer complete breakdowns.

Harvard Financial Historian Niall Ferguson[1]

In 1961, Albert Bandura conducted a research study that analyzed the way children learn from observing.[2] Bandura took two groups of children, the control group and the experimental group, and let them draw pictures in a room in which an adult was playing with Tinkertoys.[3] The experimental group watched the adult stop playing and beat up a bobo doll for 10 minutes while yelling violent phrases.[4] The control group did not witness the violent outburst. Bandura hypothesized that the "subjects exposed to aggressive models would reproduce aggressive acts resembling those of their models and would differ in this respect both from subjects who served nonaggressive models and from those who had no prior exposure to any models."[5] Next, Bandura took the children to another room and let them play with toys.[6] After a couple of minutes, the experimenter stated that "these were her very best toys, that she did not let just anyone play with them."[7] Bandura then took the toys away from the children, telling them that the toys were "for the other children."[8] He then took each frustrated child, individually, to another room in which there were different toys, one of which was a Bobo doll.[9] Bandura found that the children in the experimental group were much more likely to lash out at the Bobo doll than the children in the control group who had not witnessed the adult's prior aggression toward the Bobo doll.[10]

From a young age, children are taught to respect adults. When they see someone they respect and look up to behaving in a certain manner, they are more likely to imitate that behavior. This characteristic follows people throughout their lives. Teenagers see their favorite rock stars with tattoos and, all of the sudden, tattoo parlors are flooded with teens getting similar tattoos. Young professionals see Tiger Woods driving a sporty new SUV and then they want to have one. When people we admire and respect behave in a certain way, we imitate that behavior. So, when young adults see their favorite rappers and rock stars showing off their extravagant mansions on *Cribs*, they want to imitate the behavior and have extravagant mansions as well. When people see ordinary people, like themselves, getting rich on *Flip This House*, they want to imitate that behavior to produce the desired reward, money.

CLASSICAL CONDITIONING

In 1927, Ivan Pavlov conducted one of the most important and influential studies on learning and behavior. Pavlov, in his studies of salivary secretions in dogs, realized that dogs invariably salivate when food is placed in their mouths.[11] He also realized that dogs salivate when presented with a stimulus associated with food such as a food bowl or the person who normally provides the food.[12] Pavlov experimented by making a sound, such as a ringing bell, every time the dog received food, and he measured the amount of saliva the dogs produced.[13] Pavlov hypothesized that the dog would associate the sound of the bell with the receipt of food. He named this phenomenon "signalization."[14] After a period of training, Pavlov made the same sound but did not provide any food, and then measured the amount of saliva produced.[15] Pavlov found that, where dogs did not need to be conditioned to salivate when presented with food, they needed to be conditioned to salivate at the sound of a bell.[16] This "conditioned response" to a "conditioned stimulus" is applicable to humans as well as to dogs.

House investment advertising conditions people to think about the luxuries and wealth waiting to be acquired by speculations every time they here the word "flip." Prior to the housing speculation frenzy, people associated the word "flip" with trampolines or hamburgers. "Flip" is now a buzzword for speculatively investing in a house in order to make a profit selling the house once the value increases. "Speculatively investing in a house in order to make a profit selling the house once the value increases" is too much information for a person to be conditioned to. Thus, a word that sounds good, is simple, and expresses the behavior in a novel way is employed. People do not think about the risks involved in housing speculation. They just think that "it's hip to flip."[17]

SOCIAL IDENTITY

High school is the fertile crescent of cliques. There are the preps, jocks, freaks, geeks, and myriad other social stratifications. There are the "cool" kids and the "losers." No one wants to be a "loser." Everyone wants to fit in. Once people click with a certain clique, they shun other cliques with opposite ideals. That is the conclusion that Muzafer Sherif came to in his 1966 experiment.[18]

Sherif took 22 boys to a Boy Scout camp and separated them into two teams.[19] One team was named "The Rattlers," and the other was named "The Eagles."[20] The teams competed against each other in various activities, and the more they competed, the more hostile they became toward the other team, and the more they exhibited fanatic pride in their own group.[21] Much like the way fans of rival sports teams harass each other, the boys taunted and threatened the other team members and even instigated fistfights.[22] Sherif's experiment depicts the way groups affect individual psyches. This effect is found in every type of group because it is the individuals' pride in the group that holds the group together.

Housing investment advertisements utilize "in-groups" and "out-groups" to encourage people to invest in speculative housing markets. The quote from *Cribs* is particularly appropriate here. "You can spend your time daydreaming about how the other half lives."[23] This quote separates the "haves" from the "have-nots," the "in-group" from the "out-group." This quote says, "Don't be a loser without a million-dollar mansion. Be cool like 'the other half' and get one!" To be seen as a loser is to be viewed as having an "undesirable group membership."[24] The essence of *Flip This House* is that people can become exceedingly wealthy by flipping houses. Just like the kids in the Sherif experiment taunted the other team when they won, the rich house flippers on *Flip This House* taunt their audience by dangling their newly acquired wealth in their faces.

FLIPPING AS A FAD

Joel Best has observed that in the 1980s, Reebok Pumps were the shoes that you "had to have." When they first came out, masses of people swarmed shoe stores, hoping to get a pair of the sneaker that you could "inflate." Pumps maintained its dominance in the shoe market for a time, but then, it seemed out of nowhere, no one was wearing them anymore. The shoes you "had to have" became Air Jordans. Similarly, speculative markets, such as investment properties, are like fads. Investors are always on the lookout for up-and-coming markets. When tulips were an emerging market in Holland, investors flooded the market, and then the market died, much like the rise and fall of Reebok Pumps. Similarly, the recent housing bubble followed the same rise and fall. There are three stages of a fad: emerging, surging, and purging.[25]

Why did housing speculation emerge as a hot investment market as opposed to any other market? Sociologist Herbert Blumer described the selection process by which speculative markets are chosen as "collective selection."[26] According to Blumer, there are two elements to collective selection: news about an emerging market, and people's decision to invest in it.[27] A speculative market invariably starts small, with only a limited number of people investing. Housing speculation is not a new idea. People have been flipping houses since there were houses to flip. Word got around, through news reports, word of mouth, and other avenues that there was a lot of money to be made through housing speculation. Thus, housing speculation emerged as the hot new investment market.

Then, housing speculation surged. Surging is "the period when a fad's popularity grows most rapidly, when lots of people adopt the novelty."[28] People are passionate about money. When the word spread that there was untapped money waiting in the housing market, people became very excited. As more and more people got caught up in the house-flipping frenzy, the housing market atmosphere turned electric. More and more people began investing in houses with the intention to resell them for profit. Just like the optimistic gamblers with diamonds glittering in their eyes, the house flippers could only see the soaring cost of houses, not the inevitable crashing of their property-value wave. Similarly, "in gambling, optimists do not benefit from their upbeat disposition."[29]

Then, there was a "collapse trigger,"[30] or "growing disenchantment with an already adopted innovation."[31] Property values began to drop. This instilled fear in housing investors. Their fear translated into further drops in property values. Housing speculation was beginning to become the undesirable investment market. Not wanting to be associated with the "losers," more investors jumped ship. Prices plummeted, and the Great American Housing Bubble had burst.

RESPONSIBLE SPECULATION

> Those who cannot remember the past are condemned to repeat it.
> —George Santayana

In retrospect, it is easy to see how people were swept up in the sea of enthusiasm for house flipping. In our culture of gambling, flipping seemed like a pretty safe bet, and it could have been, if people had been more careful. After all, speculation is not inherently bad. When Christopher Columbus discovered America, he was speculating that he could find a quicker route to the East Indies. Speculation fuels progressive ideas such as new forms of energy and new technological advances. When speculators optimistically dive into untested markets without using due care, then they are more likely to be burned by bursting bubbles. In his book *Flavor of the Day: Why Smart People Fall for Fads*, Joel Best gives four rules outlining how to protect yourself from the adverse effects of fading fads. Speculative market bubbles follow practically the same path as fads. So, the rules Best gives should be considered when speculating, in any market:

1. *"Don't forget what happened last time."*[32] The second part that should be included in this statement is, "and apply that knowledge to the current situation." It is all very well to remember the Tulip Bulb Bubble or the South Sea Bubble, but in order to learn from past bubbles, one must look for the "emerging" and the "surging" so that they do not get caught in the "purging." Like waves, all bubbles act the same. Bubbles are just formed from different speculative markets. Bubbles are "nothing more mysterious than the law of supply and demand."[33]
2. *"Be skeptical about astonishing claims."*[34] The "other half" does not live like the celebrities on *MTV Cribs*. Only a very small fraction of the population lives that extravagantly. Being skeptical means asking critical questions. "Why don't I see any of these mega-mansions in my town?" "Do I know anyone who has gotten rich flipping houses like the people on *Flip This House*?" These questions can help potential investors think rationally about a speculative market before pouring money into a potential pitfall.
3. *"Continue to insist on persuasive evidence."*[35] Just because the current market research suggests that prices will continue to climb does not mean they will. It is imperative to always ask why. If *Flip This House* tells you that "flipping houses is the most tried-and-true way to make a fortune in real estate," just ask why.[36] Why will property values go up? If the reason is only because an exorbitant amount of people are

investing in the market, you can be sure a bubble is brewing and the best course is to stay away.

4. *"Don't focus on the fear of being left behind."*[37] Just because everyone else is doing it does not mean it is a good idea. Speculation can be profitable and encourage economic growth, but it should not be engaged in as merely a way of keeping up with the Joneses. History repeats itself, and while the next speculative market bubble is unlikely to be a housing market, these bubbles will continue to occur until investors learn to speculate with care and not be blinded by the diamonds in their eyes.

THE "MONEY ILLUSION"

All the aforementioned psychological and mental phenomena (plus a few forthcoming additional ones) contradict classic economical arguments.In other words, that actors in the market do not behave rationally and in turn that prices do not accurately reflect market value.[38] Money illusion—what some economists are now arguing contributed mightily to the real estate bubble—"occurs when people ignore obvious information about the distorting effects of inflation on a purchase and, in an irrational leap, decide that the thing is worth much more than it really is."[39] Scientific research has shown that this illusion evinces itself as a sensory perception in the ventromedial prefrontal cortex (VMPFC) of the human brain, a trigger that helped lead American society to wildly view houses as "always a great investment because of the misbegotten perception that prices inexorably rise."[40]

The thrust of money illusion is as follows: humans recognize a large sum of money, and their brain becomes excited; the brains ignore other information suggesting that nominal monetary value (and its equivalent—a house, for instance) is not worth what it sounds like due to the ever-changing buying power of money; this leads to irrational decision making in the real estate market. Says Yale University economics professor Robert J. Shiller

> Since people are likely to remember the price they paid for their house from many years ago but remember few other prices from then, they have the mistaken impression that home prices have gone up more than other prices, giving a mistakenly exaggerated impression of the investment potential of houses.[41]

How does this occur? A scientific brain study showed the brain illuminates, or responds, when shown an increasing amount of money with no regard for offsetting effects such as inflation.[42] This type of irrational behavior belies the classical theory of economics and operates in tandem with the Reebok Pumps fad, high school–era social strata, conditional responses, and Pavlovian impulses.

Several theorists now contend that market prices and human-investing decisions, rather than being based on complete and accurate information working in a metaphysical manner towards perfect market equilibrium, are based on such irrationality.[43] The classical view would hold that "the risks of a bubble bursting would be reflected in existing market prices"—the so-called efficient-market hypothesis.[44] The emerging view is that the real estate market and its corresponding bubble prices (and subsequent burst) became subject to money illusion and other irrational behaviors. Among those irrational behaviors include "animal spirits,"— which "drive people to overconfidence and rash decision making during a boom"—and heuristics, which leads to biases such as confirmation bias, availability bias, and hindsight bias.[45] These biases, in turn, led to certain irrational market-actor behaviors that contributed to the bubble.[46] "Emotion-driven decision making complements cognitive biases— money illusion's failure to account for inflation, for instance—that lead to poor investment logic."[47]

This "poor investment logic" can be left at the door, and responsible speculation and other types of real estate investment can flourish. Ultimately, several ideas are taking root, such as MIT professor Andrew Lo's adaptive-market model, based on a Darwin-like evolution approach (market actors, such as hedge funds and banks, are considered "species" that sometimes react based on heuristics leading to irrational investing).[48] This theory acknowledges that the classical theory of economics operates *most* of the time, but adds that sometimes the actors in the market operate based on biases or money illusion, or some other behavioral, emotion-driven technique, because it is competing with other "species."[49] By calculating the "why" of market prices, and having policy regulations designed to sense when bubbles are forming and adapt to them, economic catastrophes can be averted.

10

Bankruptcy Laws

Michael D. Sousa

For better or for worse, we live in an age of consumer credit. To that end, it is beyond contention that the use of consumer credit has become a part of American culture.[1] Indeed, borrowing and lending by American consumers have been prevalent practices since the late nineteenth century.[2] But it is in the past few decades that the average American has become indebted and overextended like never before.

Given the vibrancy in the housing market prior to the recession, commingled with readily available credit and the boom of the subprime mortgage industry, many Americans are finding themselves buried by inescapable mortgage debt. The epidemic of mortgage defaults and consequent foreclosures are jeopardizing any economic recovery. As it now stands, nearly three million homes are in serious default (nonpayment for 90 days or more) or foreclosure,[3] and current estimates suggest that more than six million mortgages will end in foreclosure by 2012.[4] Whether the failure to maintain regular mortgage payments stem from an ill-advised underwriting process, a homeowner's inability to continue paying after initial teaser rates reset, or a sudden life-altering event such as a death, job loss, or divorce, which saps more of a homeowner's earnings, it is clear that for three to six million Americans, a respite is needed for their mounting financial obligations.

Over a decade ago, Professor Elizabeth Warren commented on the necessity of consumers having a break from their indebtedness as follows: "Americans need a safety valve to deal with the financial consequences of misfortunes they may encounter. They need a way to declare a halt to creditor collection actions when they have no reasonable possibility of repaying. They need the chance to remain productive members of society, not driven underground or into joblessness by unpayable debt."[5] The safety valve to which Professor Warren alluded, and to which many Americans have turned and will continue to turn, is filing for bankruptcy relief. In the past two years, the subject of bankruptcy and the economic plight of the American consumer have become part of the national consciousness.

Individual consumers contemplating filing for bankruptcy protection generally choose between Chapter 7 and Chapter 13. In a Chapter 7 bankruptcy, or liquidation, the debtor, in exchange for giving up most of his or her existing property for immediate distribution to creditors, is in most cases relieved of any ongoing personal liability for the pre-petition indebtedness, and can keep his or her future income from the claims of the pre-bankruptcy creditors.[6] This dynamic is called the "fresh-start" for the individual debtor.[7] In contrast, if a consumer wishes to retain his or her pre-petition assets, and has sufficient ongoing income to repay some portion of pre-petition indebtedness, then the debtor may well opt to file for relief under Chapter 13 of the Bankruptcy Code. In short, Chapter 13 is intended to serve as the financial rehabilitation chapter for individual consumer debtors. In a Chapter 13 case, the debtor retains his or her property and pays creditors some portion of their claims over a three- to five-year time frame in accordance with a court-approved plan.[8]

Because Chapter 13 enables debtors to retain their existing assets, most consumers who choose to file for Chapter 13 are homeowners trying to save their homes from impending foreclosure.[9] However, the current bankruptcy laws serve little utility in enabling many homeowners to retain their homes because the Bankruptcy Code forbids debtors from modifying most residential mortgages by reducing the debt owed to the current market value of the property, otherwise known as a "cram-down."[10]

Upon the filing of a bankruptcy petition, the efforts of the mortgage lender to collect any defaults or institute or continue foreclosure proceedings must cease.[11] Thus, a consumer debtor can prevent in the first instance the foreclosure of his or her house by resorting to the bankruptcy process. Moreover, the Bankruptcy Code provides that a Chapter 13 debtor can "cure" any pre-petition defaults, and provide for the curing of the defaults over the life of the Chapter 13 plan (i.e., three to five years).[12] This right to cure any outstanding defaults exists even if the mortgage lender has accelerated the mortgage debt, and even if state law or the loan contract between the parties does not provide such a right.[13] Consequently, this right to repay mortgage arrears over time provides families with the opportunity under bankruptcy law to save their homes from foreclosure.[14]

In order to retain a home in Chapter 13, the Bankruptcy Code requires that the debtor continues to make his or her regularly scheduled mortgage payments to the lender, while at the same time repaying any arrearages on the mortgage loan through the life of the plan. As a recent scholarly article on this issue correctly noted, "Chapter 13 bankruptcy is well-suited to aid families who have defaulted on their mortgage loans due to a temporary loss of income (e.g., unemployment, illness, divorce)."[15] However, for the tens of thousands, if not millions, of homeowners that cannot afford their regular mortgage payments because (1) their monthly payments have escalated due to the resetting of initial teaser rates or initial interest-only payments, (2) the homeowners now find themselves "underwater" on their homes (i.e., they owe more on the mortgage loans than the current value of their homes), or (3) they have suffered a permanent loss of income, the bankruptcy process does not provide a remedy.

In its current incarnation, the Bankruptcy Code provides that a debtor cannot modify the terms of a mortgage in real property that is the debtor's "principal residence."[16] Stated affirmatively, a debtor cannot use the bankruptcy process to change the payment schedule, reduce the contractual interest rate, or cram-down the amount of the indebtedness to the market value of the property. "This restriction on loan modification can make it nearly impossible for debtors with unaffordable mortgage payments to save their homes from foreclosure through the bankruptcy process."[17] Because of the inflexibility of the existing Bankruptcy Code with respect to the modification of home mortgages, thousands of debtors with unaffordable mortgages will be unable to save their homes from the foreclosure process. But the rigidity of the Bankruptcy Code has another deleterious effect on the current economic crisis. That is, because thousands of homeowners are underwater (namely, owing more on the loan than the property's fair value), and because the Bankruptcy Code does not permit these debtors to cram-down the outstanding indebtedness to the current value of the property, the bankruptcy law incentivizes homeowners to abandon their properties. Such a result only serves to perpetuate the current home mortgage crisis through declining property values and an increased inventory of homes to be sold "on the cheap."

11

Banking Practices and Redlining

We are determined to make every American citizen the subject of his country's interest and concern . . . the test of our progress is not whether we add more to the abundance of those who have much; it is whether we provide enough for those who have too little.
                                                    —Franklin Delano Roosevelt

Since the early 1900s, homeownership has been an inherent part of the American dream. After World War II, the United States experienced an economic boom, and postwar legislation along with aggressive home building enabled housing affordability. With the affordability of loans accompanying the postwar housing development market, a family without a home became increasingly rare, a mark of poverty. Homeownership as the American dream shifted into the idea of home-ownership as an American right. In a 1944 State of the Union address, Franklin Delano Roosevelt referred to the "Economic Bill of Rights," a second bill of rights focused on the essential material and financial interests of Americans, "regardless of station, race, or creed," which includes "the right of every family to a decent home."[1] During his tenure as president, Roosevelt enacted a housing policy to fulfill his intention of establishing homeownership as an inherent American right, creating the Home Owner Loan Corporation (HOLC) and passing the National Housing Act and G.I. Bill of Rights. Despite the objective of homeownership for all, these policies gave rise to the practice of redlining, discriminatory lending based on geographic location, essentially drawing a "red line" around areas of high minority concentration.

In 1934, Roosevelt and his progressive, pro-government administration created the HOLC, a temporary agency that addressed the restrictive mortgage system of the Depression era.

Homeowners were unable to pay their mortgage based on high rates, and potential home buyers were unable to make the high down payment required for homes; banks, on shaky ground during the harsh economic times of the Great Depression, were unwilling or unable to renegotiate loan terms to accommodate individual circumstances. The HOLC stepped in and offered credit at an increased interest rate to home buyers, and used this interest to refinance old mortgages. While the HOLC showed an incredible loan success rate of 80 percent and returned a profit to the U.S. Treasury, it also established the practice of red-lining, often discriminating against minority groups in "risky neighborhoods."

As a government agency, the HOLC was a public service organization; however, it was also designed as a profit-making business venture. As a result, the HOLC loaned only to low-risk investors. In order to determine a low-risk investor, the HOLC developed Residential Security Maps based on four categories: Most Desirable Lending Neighborhoods, Desirable Lending Neighborhoods, Declining Neighborhoods, and Risky Neighborhoods. The criterion for the guidelines was based on preferential order of race and prevalence in the neighborhoods. For example, a "Most Desirable Lending Neighborhood" was a "new, homogenous, and in demand in good times and bad" community, while a "Declining Neighborhood" stood on the edge of "undesirable elements." Risky neighborhoods consisted almost entirely of black ghettos, and residents of these neighborhoods were not desirable homeownership loan candidates.

The Federal Housing Administration (FHA), developed shortly after the HOLC, employed these racially restrictive policies in its own mortgage-lending practice. The FHA originally dealt with the GI Bill of Rights, which offered loans to returning war veterans for both education and housing. While African American veterans benefited from the bill's educational provisions, the FHA denied them access to the veteran homeownership loan programs, resulting in less than 1 percent of all African Americans obtaining a mortgage at this time. This type of "structural racism" reflected societal views of the times.

BANKING PRACTICES

> Beautiful credit! The foundation of modern society. Who shall say this is not the age of mutual trust, of unlimited reliance on human promises? That is a peculiar condition of modern society which enables a whole country to instantly recognize point and meaning to the familiar newspaper anecdote,

which puts into the speculator in lands and mines this remark: "I wasn't worth a cent two years ago, and now I owe two million dollars."

—Mark Twain[2]

The reality of the subprime crisis is that banks lent money to many people in terms and amounts they could not ever hope to repay, on collateral that was highly overvalued. Regions such as Southern California and the greater Boston metroplex have experienced housing bubbles in the past not unlike the one we deal with today. The shift away from localized lending in the late 1990s contributed to the malaise and turned what tended to be a localized problem into a national, then global epidemic.

At the end of the previous century, lending occurred directly between banks and customers. If someone wanted to purchase or refinance a house, that person went to his or her local bank to ask for a loan. Innovations and deregulation in technology, communication, and banking started to increase the distance between the consumer and the lender, which eventually led to an overall decrease in underwriting standards. As telecommunications costs decreased and the Internet as a business model grew, mortgage brokers were able to target an ever-growing audience. Similarly, as large national and regional banks bought smaller rivals and expanded into wider markets, lending decisions could be more efficiently made at a centralized location. Large banks and finance companies could then rely on brokers and smaller banks that served those areas to originate loans, rather than establish an expensive, local workforce.

As loan originators became larger, the secondary market for mortgage-related securities played an increasingly important and dispositive role. By transforming the way that banks and originators made profits, the secondary market removed incentives to originate high-quality loans. Instead, banks derived profits from selling the loans rather than from holding them. As these organizations grew larger, so did their lending apparatus. As a result, lenders needed to maintain a high volume of originations to cover the high fixed costs of a national lending platform. After the Federal Reserve began raising interest rates in 2004, lenders increasingly turned to marginal borrowers to maintain lending levels.

In 2007, the market began to break down. Housing prices leveled off and the tide went out, revealing that many borrowers could not actually afford their houses. Banks that retained interests in the mortgage-related securities that they sold began to suffer. As defaults grew, the value of outstanding securities decreased or vanished, revealing that many participants were undercapitalized. Low regulatory oversight had allowed banks to become highly leveraged, borrowing upwards of $30 in capital for each dollar of equity. Consequently, even small changes in the value of securities led to banks needing massive amounts of capital.

After several large failures, the government intervened. Finding that banks could not raise capital in private markets, the Treasury and Federal Reserve, along with some help from Congress, then began recapitalizing banks, insurance companies, and even Fannie Mae and Freddie Mac. The price tag has approached several trillion dollars and housing prices have not yet found a bottom, indicating the cost may still rise.

THE ORIGINATE-TO-DISTRIBUTE MODEL

The fallout from the subprime crises often conjures feelings of nostalgia and a desire to return to the banking of George Bailey evinced in the Frank Capra classic *It's a Wonderful Life*. While the Bailey Building and Loan Association lent money more safely and simply, modern finance has devised ways to do it more abundantly. Lenders write mortgages using their own capital and then distribute them as debt securities to the secondary debt market, creating liquidity and enabling them to write new loans. The secondary market for mortgages currently exceeds $10 trillion.[3] The market disperses risk among myriad participants, increases liquidity of lenders, and lowers costs through competition.[4] As a result, homeownership spiked to a record of 69 percent in 2004, and ownership by minorities increased by 3.1 million between 2002 and 2008.[5]

The originate-to-distribute model created the economic turmoil by failing to manage the incentives of the parties involved. Because each player passes the risk along to the next party, he relieves himself of default liability. Prior to distribution in the secondary market, loans pass through several layers whereby each actor profits by loan approval rather than performance. A description of the actors along with their incentives follows.

LOAN ORIGINATION

Beginning with home purchase, real estate agents reap the greatest financial benefit of any loan transaction. A typical commission ranges from 5 to 6 percent of the sales price, and can be larger depending on the location of the property.[6] Low barriers to entry and high benefits have attracted many people to become real estate agents, all of whom rely heavily on financing to earn their commissions. Agents are the only party involved in a transaction from beginning to end; they usually have the best knowledge of a buyer's financial situation, and they often refer the buyer to a lender or act as mortgage broker themselves. Consequently, the agent has perhaps the largest single incentive to make sure that a home purchase goes through.

As banks steadily grew larger and created bigger lending platforms, the emphasis in originations moved away from bank branches to third-party originators, such as mortgage brokers and smaller lenders. Brokers do not lend any of their own money, but present themselves as a fiduciary that seeks the best possible mortgage for the potential borrower. Unlike financial advisors who sell insurance and securities products, mortgage brokers lack comprehensive and meaningful regulatory oversight. California, one state that regulates over 35,000 mortgage brokers, has no requirement that mortgage brokers place the borrower's economic interests ahead of their own.[7] Of the 53 state agencies that regulate mortgage brokers, only 17 require testing, 32 require continuing education, and 41 have criminal background checks.[8] In response to the crisis, the U.S. Treasury has proposed new rules for oversight of mortgage originators, including minimum standards for licensing of individuals and review of state standards.

It has been suggested that the compensation scheme for mortgage broker practices creates moral hazard; the higher the rate sold to the borrower, the higher the compensation paid to the broker. The practice is known as yield spread premium (YSP). The lender pays the broker for selling a loan with a higher-than-prevailing rate. For example, if the prevailing rate is 6 percent and the broker convinces the borrower to accept 6.5 percent, the lender may pay the broker up to 2 percent of the total loan proceeds.[9] Because banks abhor interest rate risk, they will typically offer higher YSP payments on adjustable rate mortgages, encouraging brokers to steer borrowers into these products. The premiums on subprime mortgages tended to be higher than comparable prime mortgages, which also resulted in steering.[10] Interestingly, lenders must disclose YSP only on the HUD-1 settlement statement, not the initial Good Faith Estimate. Borrowers rarely see the HUD-1 until a few days before the closing, and they often do not see it until closing. This settlement practice means that borrowers may not know how the lending institution compensates the broker.

Beyond broker-originated loans, smaller banks and finance companies originated a disproportionate amount of poor-performing loans. Without access to securities underwriting, these smaller institutions originate loans, hold them for a very short period of time, and then sell them to a larger lender or investment bank. Seller agreements typically hold the selling bank liable for representations and warrants that they adhered to the underwriting guidelines of the purchasing bank. Should the purchasing institution discover any mistakes in the selling lender's underwriting, the seller may be required to repurchase the loan. When loan defaults were low, the sellers were able to avoid this problem. However, when borrowers began defaulting within repurchase windows, larger lenders required more repurchases. Faced with mounting repurchases and cut off from credit lines, many sought bankruptcy protection. Since the height of the subprime lending boom in 2006, 298 mortgage lenders or origination channels have either declared bankruptcy or ceased lending activities.[11] Small mortgage lenders and finance companies comprised the majority of these failures.

With the exception of repurchase agreements, compensation schemes for smaller lenders resemble mortgage broker compensation. The mortgage purchaser pays the seller based upon the interest rate of the loan, paying a premium for higher rates. In the event of a repurchase, the selling bank must repay that premium.

Unsurprisingly, the smaller lenders that proliferated over the course of the 1990s and into the twenty-first century lacked banking oversight.[12] Most mortgage lenders participating in the third-party market were capitalized by heavy borrowing. Only deposit-taking institutions require the additional scrutiny of the Federal Deposit Insurance Corporation. Lacking deposits, many institutions were almost completely unregulated. Many were able to choose their regulator, often applying for separate state and federal charters.

To facilitate loan originations, purchasing lenders provided sellers with detailed underwriting standards and loan approval guidelines. Given the compensation structure for third-party originators, including mortgage brokers, this has presented a great problem to the buyers. Oftentimes, the buyer does not have any contact with the actual borrower because the third-party originator provides all the documents necessary for approval. Given that the loan originator has access to the approval guidelines, he has the ability and incentive to falsify documents to ensure approval.

IN THE FRONT DOOR, OUT THE BACK

Although it has been alleged that large banks were the unwitting victims of cheating and fraud perpetuated by underregulated and unscrupulous originators, by 2006, the size of the U.S. mortgage securities market eclipsed the treasury market almost twofold, reaching $6.5 trillion.[13] As banks grew larger, so did the proportion of mortgages sold into securitizations. When the Fed began raising rates in 2004, lenders began looking at less-than-prime borrowers as a source to replace the refinance transactions that filled their coffers when interest rates were at historic lows. As housing prices continued to soar and defaults remained low, banks expanded the range of available products and their willingness to accept loans not meeting traditional underwriting standards.

Residential lending has and always will be a staple of banks and the financial system. Over the last decade, more than 130 million home loans have been made.[14] High-rate mortgages have accounted for a great deal of growth in lending.[15] The *Wall Street Journal* analyzed Home Mortgage Disclosure Act (HMDA) data covering 2004 to 2006, and found that "more than 2,500 banks, thrifts, credit unions and mortgage companies made a combined $1.5 trillion in high-interest rate loans."[16] Over the same time frame, high-rate mortgages grew from 16% to 29% of mortgages issued.[17] The expansion of the secondary markets and capital from foreign savers created the liquidity to support the growth in the market.

Securitization of residential mortgages is not a new thing. Created by Fannie Mae, mortgage securitization began in the 1970s, grew through the 1980s and 1990s, and now fluctuates between 50 and 60 percent of the total market.[18] Securitization enables the funding lender to offload the risk of the loan and create additional liquidity by selling it as part of a package of loans in the secondary market, and profits through the sale of the security. The most common instrument for transforming a loan portfolio into a tradable security is the Mortgage Backed Security (MBS), essentially a bond backed by residential mortgages. A mortgage servicer collects principle and interest payments from mortgagors and pays those sums forward to the owners of the MBS. While lenders used to hold high-rate mortgages in a higher proportion than prime loans, by 2006 they were offloading them in MBSs at a higher rate than all loans, 73 percent to 67 percent.[19]

Traditionally, investment banks dominated the securitization and secondary markets. The passing of the Gramm-Leach-Bliley Financial Services Modernization Act in 1999 codified the deregulation of the financial markets that occurred over the 1990s.[20] The act repealed the Glass-Steagall Act of 1933 that prevented commercial deposit–taking banks from owning investment banks. By repealing Glass-Steagall, GLBA vertically integrated lending institutions and securitizers, thereby allowing banks to fund loans one day and sell them the next.

GLBA allowed commercial banks to cut into significant profit centers for investment banks. With branches and networks of loan officers, commercial banks could now leverage their existing positions within the mortgage industry by tapping the secondary market for additional capital. As of 2004, MBS comprised 28 percent of bank assets, compared to just 10 percent in 1987.[21] Fearing loss of market share, investment banks went on a buying spree of mortgage originators. Now in bankruptcy, Lehman Brothers lent subprime lender First Alliance $500 million despite a Lehman vice president's description of the firm as a "sweat shop" where employees left "their ethics at the door."[22] Lehman went on to build its own subprime lender, Finance America, and purchased Alt-A lender Aurora Loan Services and subprime lender BNC Mortgage. Despite growing mortgage defaults and slowing home price appreciation in 2006, Merrill Lynch and Morgan Stanley purchased subprime lenders First Franklin and Saxon Capital Inc. for $1.3 billion and $706 million, respectively.[23] The acquisitions allowed them to outpace Lehman as the largest securitizer of subprime mortgages in 2007.[24] Driven by acquisitions by the big players in the business, Wall Street dominated the mortgage market in 2006 with a 60 percent share.[25]

Not to be outdone by the investment banks, commercial banks grew their operations through acquisition. Commercial banks bought up smaller banks, rivals, and mortgage lenders with increasing frequency throughout the 1990s and 2000s. In 2003, 227 bank acquisitions or mergers were announced.[26] At the end of 2002, there were 7,887 government-insured commercial banks, compared to 12,347 in 1990.[27] Critics have argued that bank consolidation results in higher incidence of predatory lending, due to change in regulation. When a national bank purchases a state bank, regulation changes from the state to the Office of the Comptroller of the Currency (OCC). Consumer rights advocates argue that the OCC cannot effectively regulate national banks effectively because it has only 1,800 bank examiners (see Table 11.1).[28]

Irrespective of the regulatory gaps created by bank growth and consolidation, the acquisition sprees of both commercial and investment banks beginning in the late 1990s created lending behemoths that were heavily dependent on economies of scale. The mortgage industry relies

Table 11.1 Capital Requirements for Banks

U.S.	2.5%
UK	8%
BASEL requirements	8%

Source: Freshfields Bruckhaus Deringer LLP, *A Rethink of Capital Requirements for Asian Banks?* (November 2008).

heavily on expensive technology and human capital. Loan origination platforms cost millions of dollars in technology and investment. A single loan transaction may rely upon a dozen people to complete, depending on factors such as type of transaction, location of real property, and type of origination. In a vertically integrated firm encompassing a loan originator and security underwriter, the cost is even greater. Given these high fixed costs, loan originators' profits relate more to volume than to quality.[29] Given the highly competitive market, originators face great pressure by securitizers to continue feeding their highly profitable bond trading desks with new deals.

Lax monetary policy through 2003 resulted in low interest rates that fed the mortgage origination machine. In 2002, the refinance boom peaked at $1.44 trillion.[30] Countrywide, the country's largest loan originator by volume, hired more than 6,000 people to continue the operation.[31] While most banks responded to rising interest rates by laying off staff and curtailing marketing activities, many began to push into the subprime arena. This came as no surprise to those familiar with residential lending; after refinance boom years, lenders typically turn to alternative lending and lowered underwriting standards to maintain profits. In 1995, the FHA loosened its underwriting guidelines amid predominately strict monetary policy.[32] In 1999, banks such as U.S. Bancorp, Chase Manhattan, and Norwest Mortgage Corp. began actively courting and marketing to the subprime sector. Loosening standards and aggressive lending in previous cycles likely did not have the impact that we have seen in the current cycle because prior cycles did not see the financial innovation seen in the recent cycle (see Table 11.2).

Table 11.2 Capital Requirements in the United States

1990	10%
2005	2.50%

Minimum capital requirements for Freddie Mac and Fannie Mae were 2.5%.
Source: §12 U.S.C.S. 4612.

Innovation in mortgage lending can be characterized as expansion of traditionally prudent underwriting practices into imprudent avenues. This occurred both in the primary market for mortgages and the secondary markets of securitization. Lenders and securitizers increasingly relied on increases in property values in lieu of rational lending standards.[33] Years of increasing home prices masked poor underwriting quality; only the retreating tide of the collapsing secondary market revealed the abusive practices from years prior.

Banks expanded their underwriting standards because they felt they could effectively mitigate the increased risk by charging a higher rate to higher risks. The theory went that, if done effectively, the losses created by lending to the less than creditworthy would be offset by the additional revenue from higher rates. Problems arose when the pricing adjustments failed to capture the multiplicative effect of layering of risk and the possibility that loan originators use as adjustments to qualify mortgagors who would not otherwise obtain a loan.

Lenders soon began relaxing underwriting and loan approval guidelines to capture a bigger part of a shrinking pie. The stated-income loan is perhaps the most talked-about improper extension of credit, pursuant to which lenders would extend credit without verifying the borrower's income. These loans were traditionally extended to borrowers who could not verify their income because they were self-employed or did not want to produce income tax returns for personal reasons. Lenders began abusing these standards by allowing borrowers with easily verified income, including fixed income, to forego verification.[34] Absent an overweening moral objection to income verification, many borrowers seeking this type of financing would very likely have been unable to verify enough income to qualify for the loan. Lenders seemed to acknowledge the abuse of these so-called "liar's loans." BNC Mortgage, a subprime lender owned by Lehman Brothers, developed two separate pricing models.[35] The company charged one rate to self-employed borrowers seeking a subprime loan, while they charged borrowers with verifiable income a higher rate for the same loan. Essentially, BNC charged a higher rate for the right to lie.

Banks went further with stated asset loans, no-ratio loans, and no-documentation loans. A prime loan generally requires verification of assets to cover 2, 6, or 12 months' worth of mortgage payments to be available to the borrower. With a state asset loan, the borrower need only state the amount of assets, not verify them. In a no-ratio loan, the borrower does not disclose income; rather, the underwriter determines whether the person's business, job title, and tenure suggest they can repay the loan. These type of loans were designed for people who chose to spend a higher-than-usual amount of their income on housing expenses, or those who did not want to outright lie on their loan application. No-documentation loans are probably the most baffling, as the borrower does not even state his occupation and the underwriting decision is made based entirely on credit history and collateral. Aside from unemployment or criminal activity, there are few reasons why a borrower would refuse to declare even their occupation or source of income.

Where lenders did verify borrower income, they allowed the borrower to take on increasingly higher debt payments. Previously, a loan guaranteed by Fannie Mae would not allow the principal, interest, tax, and insurance payment of a loan to exceed 28 percent of gross income, and total debt could not exceed 36 percent.[36] In 2006, lenders were willing to lend up to 55 percent debt-to-income.[37]

Beyond creativity in underwriting guidelines, lenders extended credit to marginal borrowers through innovation in loan products and features. Financial innovation typically follows periods in which housing became unaffordable. Prior to the creation of long-term financing, mortgages were short term and had to be rolled over if not paid off in full. The 30-year fixed-rate mortgage is the legacy of the Great Depression and the New Deal's recognition of the failure of capital markets. The long-term mortgage made homes affordable to the multitude.

Layering of risk occurred where the lender extended credit at a high debt-to-income ratio and failed to account for affordability features such as interest-only payments and adjustable rates. The lender extended credit by basing the qualifying ratios on the initial payment, not an inevitable reset. These features were widespread and varied. Borrowers and pundits alike use the terms interchangeably, often obscuring their meaning and importance.

In an interest-only loan, the borrower pays only the interest due, plus taxes and insurance if escrowed. Interest-only loans, whether adjustable or fixed rate, offer a lower payment for the first 5 or 10 years. Lenders designed these loans for people with fluctuating income sources, such as self-employed business owners or sales people. As home prices soared, the features quickly became affordability products. Accordingly, interest-only loans accounted for 30 percent of subprime originations in 2005.[38] With an interest-only loan, the payment necessarily increases after the interest-only period expires.

For example, a $200,000, 6 percent, 30-year fixed-rate mortgage with a five-year interest-only period would have an initial payment of $1,000 per month. After five years, the payment increases nearly 29 percent to $1,288.60. For a marginal borrower, this increase could mean the difference between making a payment and putting food on the table.

In an adjustable-rate mortgage (ARM), the rate may be fixed anywhere from 2 to 10 years. The most widespread subprime ARMs were 2/28 and 3/27 loans, where the initial rate is fixed for only the first two or three years, respectively. These short-term loans were developed as credit repair loans, offering borrowers the opportunity to refinance revolving and high-interest-rate debt into an affordable mortgage, allowing the borrower two to three years to establish a better payment history and higher corresponding credit score. In a rising home price market, the plan works infallibly, allowing the borrower to refinance before the ARM resets.

When an ARM resets, the bank bases the new interest rate on an underlying interest rate, typically Libor,[39] plus a margin. Subprime ARMs distinguish themselves from prime loans by charging an extremely high margin. An ARM eligible for delivery to Fannie Mae can carry a margin of no greater than 2.25 percent over Libor, whereas a subprime ARM margin can be as high as the lender desires, typically between 6 and 8 percent.[40] Prior to the freeze-up of debt markets in 2008, a prime borrower with a 6 percent, five-year ARM adjusting in 2008 saw her interest rate decrease to as low as 5.25 percent. In an identical subprime loan with a 6 percent margin, the rate increased to 9 percent. Assuming a fully amortized loan with a 30-year term and initial amount of $200,000, the monthly payment increased from $1,199.10 to $1,561.81, a $362.71 or 30 percent increase. As of November 2007, Bank of America anticipated $362 billion of subprime ARMs and $152 billion of other mortgages would reset in 2008, close to 8 percent of all outstanding securitized mortgage debt.[41]

Perhaps the most aggressive affordability product unleashed was the pay option ARM. An option ARM gives a borrower between three and four payment options each month. The first option is a minimum payment, based on either a minimum interest rate (say 1 percent) or the actual interest rate minus a spread, usually between 3 and 4 percent. The next payment is an interest-only payment, a 30-year amortizing payment, and, ironically, a 15-year amortizing payment. When making a minimum payment, the borrower defers a portion of the interest due, which the lender adds back into the loan. The loan balance and payment increase correspondingly. Surprisingly, the pay option ARM qualifies as an Alt-A, not a subprime mortgage.[42]

As a matter of course, a borrower making the minimum payment each month will soon receive a significant payment shock. With certain loans, the payment increases each month with a change in interest rate. Other loans have a fixed period in which the payment does not change. Both types of loans ultimately cap the total amount of negative amortization (deferred interest), generally at 110–115 percent of the original loan balance. For a borrower making the minimum payment each month, she generally reaches the cap within three years of starting the loan. At that point, she no longer has the option of the minimum payment, and must make the interest-only or greater payment on the new, larger loan balance. For a borrower with a 6 percent rate, 3 percent minimum rate, $200,000 initial balance, and 115 percent cap, the payment will increase from $500 per month to $1,150 on or around 42 months into the loan. Much like traditional ARMs, lenders qualified borrowers based on the initial payments, not the inevitable increase.

Despite the inevitable growing loan balance, lenders allowed borrowers to purchase homes with a pay option ARM and less than 20 percent down payment. In 2005, 22 percent of pay option ARM borrowers put less than 20 percent down.[43] For a borrower with less than 10 percent down, the property would be underwater within three years, assuming home prices remain constant.

Beyond traditionally recognized underwriting criteria such as debt-to-income ratios and loan-to-value analysis, lenders became increasingly reliant on credit scoring to determine eligibility. Although Fannie Mae and Freddie Mac later dropped credit scores as a factor in underwriting, the mortgage giants pioneered the use of credit scoring as a determinant of loan performance in 1996.[44] When lenders were at their most aggressive, many offered 100 percent financing on investment properties with a 620 FICO score.[45] The average FICO score in America hovers around 710, depending on scoring methodology.

Most surprising, lenders stopped requiring down payments even on prime loans. Even when home prices began to slide into 2007, many still had programs for borrowers to purchase or refinance with no down payment. Lenders accomplished this several ways. For loans with no second lien, the lender either required borrower-paid private mortgage insurance, or charged a higher interest rate to obtain it later. Mortgage insurance pays the lender a portion of the loan balance in the event of a default. Next, they split loans into two pieces, a standard first-lien mortgage at a typical rate, and a second-lien mortgage with a higher interest rate. Generally, the lender either sold the second lien or used the excess interest from the second-lien mortgage to obtain lender-paid mortgage insurance on the loan, usually without the borrower's knowledge. Beginning in 2007, private mortgage insurers tightened their guidelines and pulled back on high loan-to-value transactions.

In addition to establishing extremely liberal and foolish guidelines, lenders frequently violated their own rules to push up loan volume. At Lehman's BNC Mortgage, "several ex-employees said, brokers or in-house employees altered documents with the help of scissors, tape and Wite-Out."[46] When employees complained about underwriting practices, management chastised them for "not wanting to be creative about making deals work."[47] Former employees of Ameriquest Mortgage claimed their jobs included "deceiving borrowers about the terms of their loans, forging documents, falsifying appraisals and fabricating borrowers' income to qualify them for loans they couldn't afford."[48] The terrible performance of 2006 and 2007 vintage subprime loans demonstrates the poor controls at subprime lenders. According to UBS, "some 65% of subprime loans originated in 2007 will end up in default compared with about 45% of those originated in 2006."[49] Freddie Mac indicated that 1.38 percent of mortgages it purchased in 2007 are in serious default after 18 months, compared to 0.38 percent for 2006 vintage loans.[50]

COLLAPSE OF THE SECONDARY MARKET

The collapse of debt markets can be broken into two periods, pre– and post–Bear Stearns. Prior to the collapse of Wall Street's two smallest investment banks, debt markets outside of nonprime mortgage continued to function normally. After Bear Stearns, credit markets seized up and ultimately resulted in the collapse of Lehman Brothers, the acquisition of Merrill Lynch by Bank of America, the conversion of Goldman Sachs and Morgan Stanley to commercial banks, the takeover of Fannie Mae and Freddie Mac by the government, and the $130 billion bailout of American International Group. The calamity can best be understood by examining the securitized products and derivatives that these companies created and looking at the risk they took on by owning them.

The mortgage-backed security is the simplest and most well-known securitized product, although it varied significantly in characteristics and quality between issuances. A large investment bank purchases millions of dollars of mortgage loans and pools them by common characteristics. Generally, the majority of loans have been originated by one or two large banks using uniform underwriting standards. Although there may be deviations, most of the loans will conform to a general level of creditworthiness. The underwriter issues certificates of various denominations and classes specifying an expected level of interest to be paid to the holder. These certificates represent different tranches with varying credit qualities. In the prospectus, the underwriter outlines how and when principal and interest will be paid to the various certificate holders, with the highest-class tranches being paid interest first and the lower classes last. This is often referred to as a "mezzanine," since the payments flow down to the lowest bondholders. The highest tranche, often called super-senior or higher than AAA, may have claims on the first 70–80 percent of cash flows from the mortgages, and protection from the first 20–30 percent of defaults. Credit rating agencies follow the mezzanine structure with their ratings, rather than rating the issuance as a whole. Each step down from the super-senior tranche rates lower than the higher tranche. The lowest tranche may not receive any cash flows, but is usually priced lower than par, meaning that it will appreciate in value as the mortgages are repaid. This tranche often received a prime rating, albeit the lowest available. A prime rating is extremely important because most of the largest bond purchasers, pension funds, mutual funds, and insurance companies can only purchase prime debt.

At the MBS level, the security is transparent. The issuer has outlined the types of loans within the trust, the general underwriting standards and the basis for exceptions to those standards, and the risks unique to the issuance. The securities become more opaque when they are sold into collateralized debt obligations (CDO). A CDO follows the same structure as a MBS, but whereas mortgage loans represent the underlying asset in an MBS, almost anything can be packaged into a CDO: pools of mortgage loans, car loans, commercial mortgages, credit card debt, accounts receivable, and even unpaid parking tickets. When a debt issue contains all of the above, assessing its relative risk becomes difficult if not impossible. The Federal Reserve has acknowledged that two-layer securitizations are exposed to a credit event with great potential for loss.[51] Given the additional opaqueness and risk, it does not appear to make sense to repackage a package, but the reason becomes obvious when one considers the 1.0–1 percent commission earned by investment banks on the resale of MBSs in CDOs.[52] Despite the additional layer of risk presented by a CDO, ratings agencies provided the highest tranches AAA ratings and investment grade to the mezzanine. This willingness of credit agencies allows banks to take previously low-rated debt, and through credit enhancement, turn it into investment grade.

Perhaps the most contrived CDO is the synthetic CDO, an issuance in which the underlying security is a credit default swap (CDS). A CDS is a credit derivative that resembles an insurance contract on a financial product in the event of a credit event such as bankruptcy or default. In exchange for a premium, a CDS seller guarantees to pay the buyer an amount if the credit event occurs. For example, a holder of Lehman Brothers' debt may agree to pay AIG an annual premium in exchange for payment in the event of Lehman Brothers' default or bankruptcy. Since this contract guarantees to pay out to anyone in the event of default, the contract need not be held by a holder of Lehman debt. If it appears that Lehman may default, the value of the contract rises in value, allowing speculators to profit from default. The same applies for any type of CDS on any debt issuance, including CDOs and MBSs. As debt products became more opaque, the market for CDSs grew to over $62 trillion in notional value in 2007, but decreased to $55 trillion in 2008.[53] By purchasing a synthetic CDO, a buyer can hedge against broad credit events, so long as the seller remains solvent.

FAILURE OF THE SYSTEM

The fall of housing prices pierced the veil of the securitization market, exposing the problems inherent to the system. Credit ratings agencies failed to accurately capture the quality of securities and overrated many issuances. As defaults grew, the agencies downgraded many issues, creating a selling frenzy by investors required to hold only investment-grade debt, and resulting in tremendous downward pressure on prices and erosion of liquidity. After seeing the systematic risk posed by bank defaults, the government intervened and propped up many of the institutions necessary to provide for financial market solvency.

The purchasers of MBS and other credit products relied heavily on credit ratings provided by the agencies, which were not required to disclose the method by which they rated the issuance. The agencies failed because they did not pick up on the systemic risk created by falling home prices. Credit ratings agencies are one of the few businesses in which the seller, not the buyer, pays for the appraiser.[54] Judging by the high overall level of defaults, they likely based their ratings more on the credit enhancement provided by mezzanine structure rather than the underlying mortgagor's ability to repay the loan. They did not recognize that originators did not adhere strictly to the underwriting standards outlined in the prospectus. Recognizing the poor performance of the previously highly rated debt, Standard and Poor's downgraded or took other negative action on over 8,000 different mortgage bonds or collateralized debt obligations in 2008.[55]

Although the system works to distribute risk, banks failed to do so with regard to the super-senior tranches of CDOs. First, underwriters sold some of the risk to off-balance-sheet vehicles, but they also provided explicit or implicit liquidity backstops to the vehicles. Much of this risk came back onto banks' balance sheets when liquidity pressures emerged in the second half of last year. Second, underwriters chose to retain some of the super senior exposure, in some cases reportedly because they met some resistance when they attempted to sell them at very slim spreads.[56] Although banks profit most when they can sell debt, they often faced tight spreads with regard to super-senior tranches of CDOs, and chose to keep them on their books.[57] They assumed they would always be able to sell them later, since they were ordained investment grade by the ratings agencies. Risk managers failed to learn from the structured credit turmoil created by the downgrade of General Motors debt in May 2005. When this occurred, the value of super-senior tranches of CDOs decreased while the noninvestment grade tranches increased in value.[58] Third, they failed to properly assess the risk posed by holding the CDOs. They underestimated the risk of a nationwide decline in home prices, assuming incorrectly that they would be protected behind the lower tranches of the CDO.

THE COLLAPSE OF BEAR STEARNS AND THE BEGINNING OF THE END

Credit markets began to freeze in early 2007 when many of the most aggressive subprime lenders began to shut their doors amid growing foreclosures and decreasing home prices. The failure of two hedge funds at Bear Stearns, the High-Grade Structured Credit Strategies Enhanced Leverage Fund and its sister fund, the High-Grade Structured Credit Strategies Fund, marked the transition of the credit crisis from residential mortgages to structured finance and the credit market as a whole.

The two Bear funds were emblematic of the hedge fund industry and finance as a whole. The funds enhanced investment returns in subprime securities by borrowing heavily in short-term credit markets. The hedge funds pledged their securities as collateral with counterparty in exchange for short-term borrowing, which is typically liquid and lower in rate. The funds used the proceeds of the short-term loan to purchase more securities. When the value of the pledged securities decreased, the counterparty, in this case Merrill Lynch, required the funds to either post more collateral or repay the loan. Bear could not liquidate the securities it held to repay the loan, so Merrill began to seize the assets posted as collateral. On June 20, Merrill started selling the seized collateral only to find that there were not many buyers, even for the highly rated super-senior tranches of debt.[59] In July, Bear Stearns management sent a letter to investors stating that the funds, which were worth $925 million and $638 million in March, essentially had no value left.[60]

The collapse of the two hedge funds had implications beyond just the investors who lost their money and the impact on Bear's reputation as a savvy risk manager. Because CDOs are traded over the counter rather than on an exchange, price history is spotty, and a sharp change in valuation can have a far-reaching effect. Merrill fetched lower-than-anticipated prices for the securities held as collateral, even the AAA-rated super-senior tranches. This meant that many banks had overvalued similar assets in their mark-to-market books. The Merrill liquidation set a price floor and indicated that holders of the debt will have to mark it down to similar levels. Additionally, there were few buyers for the debt. For any future liquidation, there may not be any buyers willing to purchase the debt at any level, which created fear for counterparties holding mortgage-related debt as collateral.

The problems for Bear Stearns did not end when the hedge funds collapsed. Although the smallest of the five independent Wall Street investment banks, Bear had the most subprime exposure, which caused its liquidity position to erode in a little under a week. On Monday, March 11, the company stood on roughly $18 billion in cash, but by Thursday had little over $2 billion.[61] Although most of Bear's loans were secured by collateral, the previous quarter's illiquidity lead many lenders to believe that if they seized that collateral, it would not be worth the debt outstanding. Consequently, many lenders refused to renew their loans.[62] The following day, the Fed stepped in to offer emergency 28-day funding until it could arrange a suitor. While the money prevented Bear from defaulting on overnight repurchase agreements, clients continued to pull money out of the institution, and lenders refused to do business with a bank reliant on short-term, emergency funding from the Fed. On March 17, 2008, J. P. Morgan announced it would be purchasing Bear Stearns at a price of $2 per share, later upped to just over $10. To complete the deal, the Federal Reserve extended a $30 billion loan to J. P. Morgan, which brought the most toxic of Bear's subprime mortgages onto the Fed's balance sheet.[63]

Bear could not continue to exist because it relied on short-term funding to maintain its balance sheet. When short-term funding dried up, it found it could not sell its mortgage assets to raise capital, and as confidence in the firm sank with its share price, it could not issue new equity.

Post Bear Stearns, credit markets continued to seize up, and the crisis began to spread beyond holders of subprime securities. Fannie Mae and Freddie Mac became the next companies to fall due to fear and illiquid markets. Throughout the 1990s and into the twenty-first century, critics pointed to the Government Sponsored Entities high-leverage ratios as an indicator of impending doom. At Fannie, the company regularly held only 2.5 percent capital for each dollar of equity, approximately one-third the average.[64] Fannie maintained this highly leveraged position by carefully managing financial risk, preventing perverse incentives from taking on unnecessary risk, and receiving implicit backing by the government. The company managed its finances by carefully matching the duration of assets to liabilities so that long-term obligations funded long-term assets, rather than funding and refunding long-term assets with short term borrowing.[65] The company incentivized employees through the overall performance of the loan portfolio, rather than through increases in volume.[66] Finally, given their charter, many investors simply assumed the government would step into the entities' shoes in the event of default.

As housing prices continued to depreciate and Fannie lost additional market share to private securitizers, the company began taking on additional risk. Many have pointed to HUD's enforcement of affordable housing goals as a reason for the company's exposure to the meltdown.[67] The majority of Fannie's losses stemmed from its guaranty book of business. In exchange for a fee, Fannie agrees to shoulder the burden of any credit losses from a pool of loans. It does so by exchanging its own debt for the pool of mortgages, moving the risk from the selling bank to Fannie. At some point in 2005, Fannie began purchasing Alt-A and, to a lesser extent, subprime mortgages. In September of 2008, the company owned $2.94 trillion in its guaranty book of business. As of September 30, 2008, Fannie Mae's total guaranty book of business was $2.94 trillion.[68] Its losses for the first three quarters of 2008 totaled $18 billion, $17 billion of which came from the guaranty book.[69] Alt-A loans accounted for 70 percent of losses attributable to Fannie's single-family home book of business, even though the loans accounted for only 11 percent of the portfolio as a whole.[70] Subprime represented one-third of 1 percent of the portfolio, and accounted for 2 percent of those losses.[71] Large numbers of defaults signaled to mortgage investors that subprime could be spreading into prime, and those investors started selling Fannie debt and equity, increasing its funding costs and limiting its access to capital.

With similar problems mounting at Freddie Mac, the Treasury and Fed took notice that the companies were in jeopardy of becoming insolvent. In July, the Treasury extended a credit line to the GSEs to maintain solvency. Rather than calming investors, the plan signaled to equity investors in the companies that in the event of a government takeover, the government would wipe out equity holders.[72] As their stock prices fell, the companies found themselves unable to raise capital equity markets to fund their mission of purchasing mortgages. As the ratings agencies cut all but their highest-rated debt, both companies saw their borrowing costs skyrocket, driving up interest rates for mortgages on the primary market. Seeing the failure of the previous plan, on September 7, Treasury Secretary Henry Paulson announced that the two GSEs had been placed into conservatorship by their regulator, the Federal Housing Finance Authority (FHFA).

The conservatorship had an immediate impact on housing markets. As the government finalized financial backing of the two giants, the yield spreads between their MBSs and comparable government treasuries narrowed, lowering mortgage costs in the primary market. Additionally, the FHFA relaxed some of the GSE's underwriting standards, which had been greatly restricted in an effort to lower funding costs. The FHFA felt that the standards were restricted more than necessary, and that relaxing them would benefit homeowners with little marginal risk to the government.[73] Furthermore, the conservators initiated the winding down of both GSEs, which had been greatly called for in the previous 15 years. They set a maximum cap of directly owned mortgages of $850 billion each, allowing the two companies to continue providing liquidity to the markets until they will begin reducing each company's portfolio by 10 percent per year until they fall under $200 billion.[74]

The conservatorship essentially stabilized the prime end of the market and served a critical role in continuing housing finance, given that the two companies provided nearly 70 percent of all mortgage transactions in 2008.[75] The takeover was not without losers. In exchange for continued funding, the Treasury received stock warrants to purchase up to 80 percent of the company at a nominal value, essentially wiping out the equity holders. The government purportedly structured the transaction this way to prevent "moral hazard," or rewarding the equity holders for investing in a company that took excessive risks. Unfortunately, a large number of equity holders were smaller regional banks. State and federal bank regulators allowed banks to hold Fannie and Freddie stock in their Tier 1 capital requirement, which means that many banks may become undercapitalized and end up in some form of receivership.

BEAR STEARNS, AGAIN

As the crisis at Fannie and Freddie mounted, problems similar to those at Bear Stearns mounted at the smallest remaining investment bank, Lehman Brothers. Lehman bet heavily on both subprime and Alt-A loans, greatly increasing its exposure by doing so with borrowed money. In the second and third quarters of 2008, the firm recognized losses totaling $6.7 billion, mostly from bets on real estate.[76] While Lehman's collapse was ultimately its own doing, the manner by which it occurred demonstrates how vicious and fearful the market had become by September.

Lehman followed much the same course as Bear Stearns in its collapse, but faced a much more public erosion of confidence. As the company spiraled towards insolvency, longtime CEO Dick Fuld waged a very public battle over the possibility that hedge funds and other investments were intentionally spreading false rumors over the financial health of the company, in hopes to benefit from short selling the company stock. Beginning in May, David Einhorn, manager of hedge fund Greenlight Capital, publicly disparaged the firm to institutional investors, stating that the company hid losses by over-marking the value of its real estate portfolio.[77] Fuld went so far as to call Lloyd Blankfein, CEO of Goldman Sachs, to discuss whether Goldman traders had been talking down Lehman stock.[78]

Whether the rumors and criticisms brought to bear by hedge funds and traders were entirely correct or merely contributed to the collapse remains to be seen. Amid the disparagement, Lehman sought desperately to raise capital, despite having raised $6 billion in early June.[79] By September, the pessimism surrounding the firm likely made raising capital either impossible or on such unfavorable terms that doing so would be imprudent. Since August, the firm had attempted to sell a stake of the company to the Korean Development bank, for around $4–6 billion. On September 9, those talks publicly fell apart, sending the company stock price reeling.[80] Lehman also floated plans to spin off its troubled real estate investments and to sell performing assets, such as its prized ownership of asset manager Neuberger Berman. While the real estate plan never got off the ground, buyers waited until Lehman went into bankruptcy and the sale of Neuberger plunged from a reported $10 billion to $2.5 billion.[81]

By the end of the week, the company was out of options to raise capital and faced a ratings downgrade that would have forced it to put up more collateral that it did not have. Sensing failure, the firm looked to the government to arrange another shotgun marriage like that of Bear Stearns to J. P. Morgan. This time, the Treasury refused to back the troubled assets held by the investment bank, a precondition for any bank interested in buying Lehman. Without a deal to be purchased, the bank collapsed and filed for bankruptcy on September 15. At the time it failed, Lehman had $630 billion in assets, five times greater than WorldCom's assets at the time of its collapse in 2002.[82]

At the same time as the Lehman bankruptcy or shortly thereafter, each independent investment bank disappeared. Merrill Lynch sold itself to Bank of America, an erstwhile Lehman purchaser. Morgan Stanley and Goldman Sachs both became commercial banks to access more favorable funding from the Fed, but subjecting themselves to greater oversight.

BEYOND MORTGAGE DEBT

The Lehman collapse impacted the global financial structure greater than the Treasury had originally surmised and caused the crisis to spread beyond just the financial sector into the broader credit markets. The most pronounced disruption occurred in the CDS market, where the Lehman bankruptcy introduced the idea of counterparty risk into the market, creating the fear that in the event of default on the bond, the insurer may not be able to pay up. Over the weekend of the collapse, average cost of insurance on $10 million in debt for five years went from $152,000 on Friday, September 12, to $194,000 on the following Monday.[83] Increases in CDS premiums create losses for sellers of insurance, who in turn must post additional collateral to their counterparties to cover the increased risk of default. Those sellers then begin offloading assets to cover their trading positions, creating additional downward pressure in all markets, debt and equity.

As the largest seller of insurance in the CDS market, American International Group faced massive capital calls. At the end of June, AIG had a notional exposure of $441 billion in the CDS market, $58 billion in subprime.[84] Throughout 2008, counterparties required the company to post additional collateral against these positions, eroding AIG's base. As liquidity dried up, the ratings agencies cut AIG's credit ratings, requiring additional collateral to be posted. Finally, on September 16, the Treasury announced they had extended an $85 billion credit line in exchange for warrants to purchase 79.9 percent of the company. Ultimately, AIG captured over $150 billion in bailout loans and capital injections.

The Treasury likely rescued AIG due to its importance in maintaining regulatory capital levels for banks. CDSs guarantee the value of assets held on banks' books, thereby freeing up additional money to be lent in credit markets.[85] Additionally, the contracts insulate the buyers against disruptions at other companies, decreasing risk. A default by the biggest player in the market would further freeze the credit markets and expose banks to untold risk.

BEYOND THE FINANCIAL COMPANIES

After Bear Stearns, Lehman, AIG, Fannie, Freddie, and a rash of record-setting bank failures, credit slowed to a mere trickle among financial companies. Credit losses for mortgage-related securities amounted to $760 billion by the end of the third quarter.[86] As fear of additional bank collapses spread through the market, banks demanded a higher yield on money lent, and investors flocked to the safest investments available, short-term treasuries. The yield on short dated treasuries dropped to less than 0.10 percent, sometimes negative, and the three-month London Interbank Offer Rate (LIBOR), a critical measure of lending between financial companies, spiked from 2.8 percent prior to the Lehman collapse, to over 4.6 percent.[87] Typically, three-month LIBOR tracks less than 10 basis points (1 basis point = 0.001%) over the Fed's funds rate. Post Lehman, the spread exceeded 200 basis points.

The difficulty in lending in the interbank market quickly spilled over to the commercial market. Companies with all but the most spectacular balance sheets experienced difficulty in the short-term lending markets. In September, the spread on investment-grade debt over the comparable treasury increased to 283 basis points, 88 percent higher than the five-year average.[88] Shut out from bank lending, many companies turned to commercial paper markets to meet short-term financing needs. Issuance of highly rated commercial paper with durations of 10 days or less more than tripled in September, as lenders were unwilling to take on longer-term risk.[89] AT&T reported that over a two-day period following the Lehman collapse, it was unable to issue anything other than overnight paper.[90] GE, perhaps the largest issuer of commercial paper, saw three-month yields on its borrowing increase from an average of 2–3 percent to over 5 percent.[91] With over $90 billion in paper outstanding, that created an additional annual cost of $360 million.[92]

Beyond the impact on corporate borrowing, the spike in Libor further hindered recovery in housing markets. Many lenders base their purchase and refinance rates on the index; an increase in Libor translates directly into increased borrowing costs for potential purchasers, decreasing affordability and availability of mortgages. Additionally, most banks base their adjustable-rate mortgage reset rates on Libor, potentially increasing rates on existing mortgages due to reset in October. While subprime loans typically always reset higher, lower Libor rates had the potential to ease costs for existing prime and Alt-A borrowers, where loan ARM margins are lower.

GOVERNMENT ACTION

Sensing that credit markets had gone from frozen to crumbling, the Federal Reserve and the Treasury began taking broad approaches to systematically address the problems rather than dealing with crises as they arose. To stem the outflows from money market mutual funds, which were threatening to collapse the commercial paper market, the Fed temporarily guaranteed fund balances. To decrease corporate borrowing costs, the Fed implemented a temporary lending facility to enable banks to purchase commercial paper and created another facility to purchase longer-dated commercial paper when those markets become illiquid.

The moves made by the Fed opened up short-term credit markets, but the government had not yet addressed the problems underlying the crisis: diminishing liquidity and toxic assets at banks. On Friday, September 19, Treasury Secretary Paulson announced an aggressive $700 billion plan to systematically address these two issues.

The plan sought relief through two major initiatives. First, the Treasury would recapitalize banks by purchasing equity; specifically, nonvoting preferred shares in "banks and thrifts of all sizes."[93] Doing so would provide the banks with cash while providing the Treasury with an attractive yield and a stake in the success of the banks. Second, the Treasury would take the most toxic and illiquid assets off the banks' balance sheet by purchasing them directly through market mechanisms.[94] Banks had been reluctant to move the bad assets off their balance sheets for several reasons. In many cases, nobody wanted to purchase the assets, or, if there was a bid, it was too low for the banks to accept. Selling the assets at depressed prices would cause the bank to take a larger write down than previously acknowledged, creating the need for further credit downgrades and balance sheet pressure. Finally, many banks simply did not know how to value the assets left on their books, given the opacity and lack of a common market mechanism.

To accomplish this goal, the Treasury planned to hire money managers to assess the value of the assets and then provide a minimum bid in a reverse auction. By providing a bid, the Treasury hoped to unlock the frozen market for subprime securities and act as a buyer of last resort. Problems with this plan immediately surfaced. First, the money managers to be hired would inevitably come from the firms holding these securities. This creates a huge conflict of interest with respect to using taxpayer money to purchase private assets, as the manager could favor assets and prices that favored his firm. Second, the complexity of the instruments and the rate at which they were deteriorating would prevent the Treasury from acting quickly. Nobody really knew what these securities were worth, and any attempt to discover what lies beneath a two-tier securitization would inevitably take a tremendous amount of time.

The proposed Emergency Economic Stabilization Act (EESA) and appurtenant Troubled Asset Relief Program (TARP) immediately became a lightning rod for criticism. Perhaps the combination of the two approaches to fixing the system, recapitalizing banks and buying troubled assets, led to the impression that the government was rewarding the foolishness of Wall Street bankers who made fortunes in the process. Republicans criticized the bill as anti–free market and creating a giant burden on the taxpayers, tantamount to socialism. Democrats characterized the bill as a bailout for tycoons that did very little to help struggling homeowners. On September 29, the House of Representatives rejected the legislation by a vote of 228–205.[95] Markets reacted immediately, with investors fleeing equities and driving the returns on short-term treasuries negative. The Dow Jones Industrial Average (DJIA) dropped 777.68 points, or 7 percent, the largest one-day point drop since the markets reopened following September 11, and the 17th-largest percentage drop in DJIA history.[96]

Although the bill failed in its initial form, a newly revamped bill came to a vote by that Friday. Despite the Treasury's initial desire to keep the legislation simple and prevent it from becoming a Christmas tree, the proposal sprawled from the three-page outline to a 451-page behemoth.[97] In order to muster additional political support, the bill expanded FDIC insurance and included everything from caps on executive pay to "tax relief provisions for disaster victims; research and development tax credits; a hybrid car tax credit; and tax breaks for teachers who spend their own money on school supplies."[98] After a tense week, the bill passed, 263–171.

THE ROAD TO RECOVERY

Following passage of the bill, the Treasury quickly went to work recapitalizing banks by making direct investments in preferred shares. The plan quickly departed from the initial strategy of taking toxic assets off bank balance sheets. On November 12, Paulson announced that the Treasury would not buy mortgage-related securities, but would focus exclusively on making equity investments. With the first $350 billion tranche, the Treasury made $250 billion in direct investments in banks, $40 billion went to AIG, $25 billion to Citigroup, $20 billion in other lending, and the remainder went to automakers to prevent their imminent collapse.[99]

The EESA has made limited and indiscernible progress in unfreezing credit markets. On the one hand, short-term lending and commercial lending markets have returned to pre-Lehman levels, with investors moving from ultra-safe treasuries back into commercial paper. Aided by additional rate cuts by the Fed, as well as new credit facilities, the three-month Libor decreased to 1.26 percent.[100] The market for new issuance has continued to be tight, with only GE testing the market since September and paying a hefty 100-basis-point premium over secondary and 400 basis points over treasuries for $4 billion, 30-year bonds with FDIC backing.[101]

The government has made the most significant progress in decreasing the funding costs for new and refinanced loans. Aside from the aforementioned benefit accrued from a decreasing Libor rate, the Fed has directly lowered mortgage costs by purchasing $500 billion in mortgage-backed securities.[102] This program, announced in December, has driven prime mortgage rates down to an average of 5.03 percent by the beginning of 2009, from highs of over 6.5 percent in 2008.[103] The problem with programs targeted at lowering interest rates is that they do not target borrowers who lack credit, capacity, or collateral. Given the accelerating rate of price decreases, many homeowners have been shut out of the market because the amount of their mortgage exceeds the value of the property. Those with blighted credit histories cannot qualify for a prime loan, and the Alt-A and subprime markets simply do not exist.

Despite the Herculean efforts to jumpstart lending markets, very little has been done to address the fundamental problem creating turmoil in credit markets: homeowners facing foreclosure. By the end of the 3Q 2008, the number of homes in foreclosure or default had risen 11 percent increase from the prior year.[104] The biggest push to help homeowners with adjustable-rate mortgages has been to modify those loans, resetting the interest rates and changing the terms of the loan to make it affordable to the borrower. The success of this has been extremely limited. First, mortgage servicers do not have explicit authority to modify the terms of a mortgage held in trust by a mortgage-backed security. To modify the loan, the servicer, often a bank, must seek approval from the trustee, creating costly delays and credit impairment for the borrower, who may already be in arrears. Second, there is growing evidence that modification does not prevent foreclosure. In December, the Office of the Comptroller of the Currency and the Office of Thrift Supervision issued a report that indicated that over half the loans modified in the first quarter of 2008 slipped back into default within six months of modification.[105] This indicates what few have been willing to admit; abusive subprime lending practices contributed less to the crisis than borrowers simply unable to afford homes at any rate.

To deal with the growing failure of previous attempts to curb foreclosures, the FDIC has taken the most aggressive and comprehensive measures to address the problems. Under the direction of Chairman Sheila Bair, the FDIC developed a program to systematically address mortgage affordability at Indy Mac Federal Savings Bank, which was taken over by the FDIC on July 11.[106] Like any other mortgage servicer, Indy Mac Federal is limited to addressing loans held solely on its books, or where servicer agreements allow the bank to take measures to proactively address a borrower in default. Additionally, the bank can only enter a workout agreement where the potential recovery to the investor exceeds the cost of foreclosure.[107] Working with a pool of 60,000 loans in default 60 days or more, the plan targets to achieve a borrower debt-to-income ratio of less than 38 percent of gross income.[108] To accomplish this, the bank can first lower the loan interest rate to 3 percent for up to five years, after which the rate climbs by 1 percent per year until it reaches a maximum of just under 6 percent.[109] If this does not make the loan affordable, the bank can then "extend the amortization term of the mortgage or defer payments on a portion of the principal."[110] Deferring a portion of the payment effectively creates a "silent second" mortgage. A political compromise, the deferred balance eliminates payment on the debt without actually eliminating the debt. After the principal loan balance is repaid at the end of the loan term or by sale of the home, the lender may require repayment of the debt or forgive it altogether.

Through the actions at Indy Mac, the FDIC hopes to accomplish two things outside of home retention: maximization of value for mortgage investors, and adoption of the program as best practice for other mortgage servicers. Nonperforming loan portfolios typically yield 32 percent of book value, while performing portfolios have yield 87 percent in auction sales.[111] By transforming defaults into partially performing loans, the servicer unlocks value by preventing a foreclosure, putting tax, insurance, and maintenance costs back on the homeowner, and maintaining property values. If servicers universally adapt this process, investors will be able to more adequately value the securities that hold these loans, and that will perhaps unlock the frozen securities market.

ASSESSING THE CAUSES

Amid the massive government response to the crisis, many looked to the government as a cause of the declination in underwriting standards and prudent lending decisions. A major target for blame was the Community Reinvestment Act (CRA) of 1974. Congress enacted the act in response to deterioration in the quality of life in cities and the scarcity of credit amongst the urban poor. The act required FDIC-insured lenders to extend credit in the communities from which they derived their asset base and to create lending programs for low-to-moderate income earners. Critics argue that the act resulted in banks extending credit to less-than-creditworthy borrowers.

The CRA did have a prominent role in expanding credit to under-served communities, evolving from the partnering of covered institutions with community groups to stricter enforcement of community lending goals by Congress. Initially, the act had little enforcement and oversight. Through the 1980s, a renewed focus on fair lending practices resulted in some banks partnering with community groups to create new mortgage products and expanded underwriting criteria to meet the needs of the community.[112] In 1989, the Financial Institutions Reform, Recovery, and Enforcement Act (FIRREA), along with greater enforcement of bank regulation, resulted in greater oversight of community lending activities and public disclosure of CRA compliance.[113] The additional emphasis on bank regulation resulted in regulators applying the strongest sanction available under the act, denial of mergers due to noncompliance.[114] Despite the renewed efforts, greater interest community lending had little effect during a time of little bank consolidation.

The CRA lacked a prominent position in bank manager's decisions until the passage of the Gramm-Leach-Bliley Financial Modernization Act of 1999. GLBA made explicit that before any bank or bank holding company could acquire or engage in any financial service activity made legal by the act, it must be in compliance with the CRA.[115] It also strengthened ratings criteria and increased the frequency of review. However, changes to the Act prior to GLBA had weakened the enforcement criteria. For example, changes in 1995 allowed banks to choose whether or not to include the activities of affiliated mortgage companies.[116] Further, regulators allowed banks to include loans based on loan characteristics rather than if they served a covered community.[117] These two provisions allowed banks to essentially pick and choose the loans favorable to receiving a satisfactory CRA rating.

The CRA also failed to keep up with the changing nature of mortgage lending. Mortgage companies, not covered or selectively covered, originated the majority of all mortgage loans starting in 1997. As securitization became the dominant source of funding over deposits, covered areas began to shrink. Additionally, subprime mortgage originators tended to be private companies and independent finance companies, funding by debt and not FDIC-insured deposits.[118]

Apologists for the CRA and its regulatory progeny have claimed that the performance of loans made under the CRA is not consistent with the hypothesis that the act contributed to the crisis. First, they point out the loans made by covered institutions tended to be prime loans with expanded underwriting criteria, developed specifically to serve the needs of a unique community.[119] These loans were fully underwritten, often had requirements beyond the typical credit, capacity, and collateral, and include financial and homeowner training. Secondly, covered banks were "significantly less likely than other lenders to make high cost loans ... [and] [t]he average APR on high cost loans originated by CRA Banks was appreciably lower than the average APR on high cost loans originated by other lenders."[120] Statistically, they further note, there is a high correlation between the concentration of high-cost loans and foreclosure rates.[121] Ninety-six percent of all subprime refinance loans, the poorest performing of all loans, were made by non-covered mortgage companies.[122] Finally, the apologists note that CRA lenders retained a higher proportion of originated loans than non-CRA lenders, more closely aligning the performance of the bank with the long-term performance of the loan.[123]

However, while these claims are by and large accurate as far as they go, they miss the essential point—namely, that the CRA, and in particular the mid-1990s regulations that put enforcement teeth into CRA, reinforced the perception among all banks (and not just banks formally covered by the CRA) that housing prices were sure to rise and the bubble continue to expand; for only in the belief that housing prices would continue to rise would regulators and policy makers feel secure enough to pressure lenders to lend to marginal buyers.

12

The Federal Reserve

It has been alleged that the easy-money polices of the Federal Reserve in the aftermath of the 2000–2001 stock market collapse played a significant role in the final stages of the housing bubble "blowoff," culminating in the collapse of 2007–2009.

Although many factors must be reviewed cumulatively when analyzing the housing market, all purchases come down to money, and any conversation about money is incomplete without a focus on the U.S. Federal Reserve. It has been said that the central bank of the United States is to the world of finance and economic policy what the Supreme Court is to the law.[1] Just as the Supreme Court is the final arbiter concerning the law, the "Supreme Court of Finance" is the "lender and economic policy maker of last resort."[2] The Federal Reserve has several policy tools that it utilizes to affect economic activity and inflation.[3] The most well-known tool by which the Federal Reserve accomplishes this goal is the federal funds rate, which in essence sets short-term interest rates.[4] The federal funds rate ultimately trickles down to the price at which consumers pay to borrow money. Although not directly linked, this rate effectively dictates the price at which potential homeowners can obtain the biggest obstacle standing in the way of the American dream: money!

Another tool by which the Federal Reserve affects monetary policy is by acting as regulator and supervisor of the money that it lends. As the price of borrowing decreased, banks offered more creative financing options and loosened the requirements for who became the recipients of home mortgages. The Federal Reserve, however, remained unconcerned for some time at these developments, since loose loan standards seemed to be serving the political goals of revitalizing an economy that was recovering from a stock market crash and the terrorist attacks of September 11, 2001. The Federal Reserve operates to control inflation and prevent deflation, and the housing market bubble provided the necessary air to the economy after the stock market crash. As investors turned their attention from stocks to houses, the stage was set for the bursting of another bubble. The only question is, what role did the Federal Reserve play in "Blowing the Housing Bubble"?

In order to better understand what role the Federal Reserve played in the housing bubble, it is necessary to first understand what the Federal Reserve is by examining a brief history of the central bank of the United States. We will then examine what the Federal Reserve does and how it does it, followed by when and why the Federal Reserve's implementation of its policies affected the housing market. Although the extent to which Federal Reserve policy played a role in the housing market crash is debatable, there is no denying the role that the Federal Reserve played in supplying the air to the housing bubble.

HISTORY OF THE FEDERAL RESERVE

The most powerful central bank in the world was not born overnight, but rather developed as a response to the needs of the American economy. The Federal Reserve System was conceived by Congress in the form of the Federal Reserve Act of December 23, 1913, as a direct response to the failures of the national banking system.[5] The proverbial straw that broke the camel's back came in 1907, when, for the third time in just over 30 years, banking panics threatened to cripple the economy.[6] In its most desperate hour, the void of financial leadership was filled by one man, John P. Morgan (the elder). Having made millions off the misfortunes of the U.S. Treasury a decade prior, Morgan became a "One-man Federal Reserve System and Reconstruction Finance Corporation."[7] As the adage goes, "He with the most gold makes the rules," and J. P. Morgan made the rules, deciding who would benefit from his help and who would be left to fend for himself. Realizing the "vast and growing concentration of money and credit in the hands of comparatively few men,"[8] Congress went to work. The final version of the Federal Reserve Act struck a balance between a central bank ran by bankers and one run by the government. For fear that one central bank would too closely resemble the developing money trust, the newly elected Democratic Senate leader, Carter Glass of Virginia, made changes.[9]

Because monetary policy breeds political conflict, the Republicans sought to ensure that the Federal Reserve was shielded by government, and the Democrats sought to ensure that it would not be a bankers' bank. In a nutshell, the Federal Reserve was "a public board supervising quasi-private reserve banks, a board free from congressional appropriations and presidential oversight, a board composed of officials exercising Congress's monetary powers yet possessing great autonomy and broad flexibility."[10]

The Federal Reserve Act created a bank more decentralized than its predecessors. A bank that "precluded all ideas of a central bank,"[11] and one that "generally diffuses control instead of centralizing it."[12] The nation became 12 subdivided subsets, each with its own Federal Reserve Bank. The 12 banks were governed by 7 members appointed by the president of the United States, who formed the Board of Governors. Twelve men appointed by each of the 12-member banks formed the Federal Advisory Council, who assisted the Board of Governors.[13]

Although initially independent and decentralized, the Federal Reserve has slowly adapted and developed its role since its inception. From 1933 to 1935, Congress passed four different banking reforms that became turning points in the federal banking system.[14] Although these acts had other objectives, they had a lasting effect on the powers of the Federal Reserve System. These four acts were: the Banking Act of June 16, 1933; the Securities Act of May 27, 1933; the Securities and Exchange Act of June 19, 1934; and the Banking Act of August 23, 1935. These acts wrought three major changes to the powers of the Federal Reserve Board.[15] First, the Board became the Board of Governors of the Federal Reserve Board and no longer had the secretary of the treasury or comptroller of the currency as governor. The power of the other reserve banks became more centralized in the Federal Reserve Board, which was now centered in Washington, D.C. A Federal Open Market Committee (FOMC) was created using the seven members on the board and five other members from the 12 reserve banks. Of those five, one always serves as president of the New York Federal Reserve Bank, while the other four members rotate. The FOMC was given more control over open market policy decisions. Lastly, the Federal Reserve Board was given more control in using reserve requirements as well as authority to set margin requirements on investments.

Although the treasury secretary was no longer a member of the board, the next 16 years in the Federal Reserve's history were marked by a battle for the Federal Reserve's independence from the Executive Branch (namely the Treasury and the president). The debates were often heated and intense.[16] The Federal Reserve argued that in order to properly enact monetary policy, it must be free from political influence and independent of the Treasury's decisions. The Treasury argued that an independent Federal Reserve would be detrimental to a system of democracy as well as to the economy. Under this theory, the Treasury coerced the Federal Reserve into fixing the price of Treasury paper and buying whatever was sold. This agreement foundered in the early 1950s when the Korean War started to send the nation into a deep deficit. In 1951, the Federal Reserve finally rebelled. This was "the most important moment in the history of central banking, first stirring of the idea that a central bank should and could be an instrument of governance separate from the legislature that created it and the executive that appointed its leaders."[17]

Thus, the Federal Reserve became an independent central bank with the authority to influence the economy like no other before it. The "accord" of 1951 has since been modeled by several other countries.[18]

The history of the Federal Reserve can be separated into increments of 18–20 years. The next generations of the Federal Reserve were defined by its chairman; starting in 1951, William McChesney Martin Jr. manned the helm for 19 years. Although, "the job of the Fed has thus come to be the politically sensitive task of balancing three different goals: 'keeping long-term growth as high as possible, keeping unemployment as low as possible, and keeping prices as stable as possible.'"[19]

Martin helped define what would become the basic tenet of the Federal Reserve, fighting inflation. When speaking of inflation, Mr. Martin stated that "No greater tragedy, short of war, could befall the free world to have our country surrender to the easy delusion that a little inflation, year after year, is either inevitable or tolerable. For that way lies ultimate economic chaos and incalculable human suffering that would undermine faith in the institutions of free men."[20]

In speaking of how the inflation process works, Martin stated, "A spiral of mounting prices and wages seeks more and more financing. It creates demands for funds in excess of savings and since these demands cannot be satisfied in full, the result is mounting interest rates and so-called tight money. If the gap between investment demands and available savings should be filled by creating additional bank money, the spiral of inflation which tends to become cumulative and self-perpetuating would be given further impetus."[21]

Although there were other monetary goals of the Federal Reserve, keeping inflation low became its mission. In defining the balance of these goals, Paul Volcker, Fed chairman from 1979 to 1987, stated, "A basic premise of monetary policy is that inflation cannot persist without excessive monetary growth, and it is our view that appropriately restrained growth of money and credit over the longer run is critical to achieving the ultimate objectives of reasonably stable prices and sustainable growth."[22]

Creating expansion and preventing inflation are essentially the two most important tasks and are the basis of monetary policy.[23] Thus, the Federal Reserve's goal is really one of price stability, a continuous balancing act between prices that are too high and those that are too low.[24] In order to keep stability, the Federal Reserve must first know if the economy is heating up or cooling down. This is done by examining the four major policy variables: inflation indicators; indicators of business expansion; money and credit aggregates; and conditions in the foreign exchange market and domestic financial markets.[25]

From its inception and through the growth of its powers via Congress, the Federal Reserve became armed with several weapons or tools to achieve its monetary objectives and enforce its monetary policy. The Federal Reserve has four primary tools in particular: the discount rate; open market operations; regulation and supervision; and setting reserve requirements.[26]

Open market operations and regulation will be the primary focus of this chapter, but a brief understanding of each is necessary. The discount rate is essentially how much it costs to borrow money from the Federal Reserve and is largely symbolic. Second, the open market operations consist of buying and selling government securities and are under the control of the Federal Open Market Committee (FOMC).[27] The FOMC, established through the Bank Act of 1933, consists of the seven members of the Federal Reserve Board, the president of the Federal Reserve Bank of New York, and four other members that rotate between heads of the other 11 regional Federal Reserve banks. The committee meets every five to eight weeks. The tightening and loosening of money through the open market is reflected in the federal funds rate. The federal funds rate is the overnight rate charged when banks borrow from each other. The federal funds rate and the discount rate usually move together.

Third, the Federal Reserve has regulation and supervision over the banks within its control, and will be discussed in more detail later. The last and least used—but still powerful—of the tools is the ability of the Board of Governors to restrict available cash by changing the minimum reserve requirement that banks must keep on hand.[28]

A large caveat exists to the Federal Reserve's use of tools to control the economic outlook of the United States as well as the global economy. The implementation of monetary policy is by no means a science, but rather one of art. The battle of the Federal Reserve since its creation has been to foster an atmosphere conducive to allowing it to freely work within its framework to try to outguess the economy.

WHEN AND WHY

In the world of homeownership, the mortgage rate plays a key role. Although other factors determine one's ability to secure financing, such as credit history, job history, and the ability to furnish a down payment, the price it will cost to borrow money is a deal breaker. The mortgage rate not only determines if a home purchase is a viable option for a potential home buyer, but often decides how large a home a potential home buyer may purchase. The easier it is to obtain cheap financing, the greater the number of expensive homes that will be sold.

After the crash of the "dot-com bubble," investors looked not only at securing a piece of the American dream, but for a safe, easy return on their money. What place better to turn than to a market where the sky is the limit? A utopian—but illusory—world where values only appreciate, and where buying low and selling high is more than a buzz word, it is a mantra. Because of the financial burdens of real estate investing, making money in real estate previously required already having it. For those who did not already have money, the availability of cheap funds became a determining factor in one's ability to purchase real estate in hopes of making a profit. Mortgage rates are the fuel that drives the housing market, not only for first-time home buyers, but for investors as well. It is only common sense that the more fuel there is, the bigger the fire. If mortgage rates are the fuel that keeps the fire going, or the air in the bubble, what is the driving force behind the rise and fall of mortgage rates?

THE LINK BETWEEN LONG-TERM MORTGAGES AND
THE FEDERAL FUNDS RATE

In theory, the short-term interest rates controlled by the Federal Reserve should have no direct effect on long-term interest rates, which are set by the private market for long-term securities including treasuries. But as loan requirements loosened in the early 2000s in order to accommodate the quotas set by the CRA and its regulatory progeny, fewer loans were 30-year fixed, and more were "adjustable" based on short-term rates. Because of this development, Federal Reserve policy began to have an even greater effect on the housing market and the expansion of the bubble.

The answer to this question is not simple and is no way straightforward. But by examining the Federal Reserve's use of short-term interest rates as a monetary tool and its relation to long-term rates, one can see how the Federal Reserve plays a critical role in determining long-term mortgage rates, and how as a result it allowed the over-availability of easy credit. As will be discussed, the ability of more American people to purchase their homes directly influenced rising home prices and exacerbated the housing bubble.

At an investment education symposium, then-Governor Ben Bernanke stated that the FOMC "has no direct control over the key interest rates and asset prices"; rather, the focus is on "the Committee's target value for an otherwise obscure short-term interest rate, the federal funds rate."[29] Bernanke is right that the Federal Reserve does not directly affect long-term interest rates or asset prices. But the Federal Reserve's use of the federal funds rate, albeit a means of affecting short-term interest rates, has indeed affected long-term interest rates.

Empirical evidence shows a link between short-term interest rates and long-term interest rates on 10-year Treasury notes.[30] In the same address, Bernanke further explained the connection between the federal funds rate and long-term interest rates, stating that "the more important means by which monetary policy affects Treasury yields is through the effect of policy on the expected future path of short-term interest rates."[31] Bernanke explained that investors' expectation of what the Federal Reserve will do with the funds rate in the future will affect the price of long-term interest rates because an investor can choose between investing long term or making repeated short-term investments. In short, "the long-term rates that really matter for the economy depend not on the current short-term rate but on the whole trajectory of future short-term rates expected by market participants."[32] The link between 30-year interest rates and 10-year Treasury notes is a more direct connection. But the link between 10-year Treasury notes and the funds rate is, as Gus Faucher, an analyst for Moody's, stated, "For loans like the 30-year fixed mortgage, what really matters is what lenders think is going on with inflation, since that can reduce the value of the loans they're making."[33] Thus, the Federal Reserve indirectly controls mortgage rates.

The understanding of the connection between short-term interest rates and long-term mortgage rates helps to explain how the Federal Reserve affects the housing market. The year 2001 was not an easy one for the morale of the United States as well as its economy. Following the bursting of the dot-com bubble and the toll that the tragedy of September 11 had on the financial markets, the Federal Reserve feared a recession. In a last-ditch effort to boost the economy, the Federal Reserve did what it does best. From 2001 to 2002, it lowered the interest rate over four percentage points, leaving it below 2 percent at the beginning of 2002.

By the fall of 2003, the interest rate hit an all-time low of 1 percent, where it would remain for well over a year. In the middle of 2004, the Federal Reserve raised the rate, and continued to gradually do so, over the next two years. By 2002, the U.S. economy technically was no longer in a recession; however, interest rates remained at an all-time low.

Although the funds rate is not directly linked to the 30-year fixed mortgage rate, the 30-year conventional mortgage rate over 1999–2008 dropped nearly 2 percent during the same time the funds rate experienced a 4 percent drop. The data demonstrates a convincing link between the two rates from 1999 to 2003. The difference comes in 2003, when the Federal Reserve began raising interest rates while the mortgage rate stayed low and did not rise in conjunction with short-term interest rates. The data also presents two pertinent questions related to housing prices: Why did the Federal Reserve keep interest rates so low, and why did the mortgage rates not respond to the rise in interest rates? By examining these two questions separately, the Federal Reserve's role in the housing bubble becomes more clear.

THE FEDERAL FUNDS RATE AND THE "TAYLOR RULE"

As addressed previously, the Federal Reserve's use of monetary policy is an art, not a science. That the Federal Reserve's use of the federal funds rate can have a wide-ranging effect on the economy has been previously discussed. But the Federal Reserve does have certain methods that it uses to decide how and when to act. One such method is the Taylor Rule:

> The "Taylor rule," named after the prominent economist John Taylor, is another guide to assessing the proper stance of monetary policy. It relates the setting of the federal funds rate to the primary objectives of monetary policy—that is, the extent to which inflation may be departing from something approximating price stability and the extent to which output and employment may be departing from their maximum sustainable levels . . . If inflation is picking up, the Taylor rule prescribes the amount by which the federal funds rate would need to be raised or, if output and employment are weakening, the amount by which it would need to be lowered. The specific parameters of the formula are set to describe actual monetary policy behavior over a period when policy is thought to have been fairly successful in achieving its basic goals.[34]

The Taylor Rule is one of the mechanisms that has been used with a high level of success since the early 1980s and that have allowed the Federal Reserve and, namely, Alan Greenspan, to garner worldwide praise for keeping inflation under control. During the period from 2003 to 2006, the Federal Reserve deviated from the Taylor Rule in keeping interest rates low from 2003 to 2004. In a speech at a symposium in Jackson Hole for the Kansas City Federal Reserve, Taylor discussed how the Federal Reserve's adherence to the Taylor rule would have had a different result. According to Taylor, the interest rates should have been raised in the second quarter of 2002, taking a steeper slope to the actual rate in 2006. Taylor stated, "A higher federal funds rate path would have avoided much of the housing boom, according to this model. The analysis also suggests that the reversal of the boom and thereby the resulting market turmoil would not have been as sharp."[35] This analysis indicates that the Federal Reserve's decision to keep interest rates low was an ad hoc decision as a response to the declining economy, and, in hindsight, it likely was the wrong decision.

In an oft-quoted speech to the American Bankers Convention in California in September 2005, Greenspan himself stated that, "we can have little doubt that the exceptionally low level of home mortgage interest rates has been a major driver of the recent surge of homebuilding and home turnover and the steep climb in home prices," and further stated that in "the United States, signs of froth have clearly emerged in some local markets where home prices seem to have risen to unsustainable levels." Unwilling to call the rise of home prices to unsustainable levels a "bubble," Mr. Greenspan referred to what was occurring merely as "signs of froth." Acknowledging that low interest rates were feeding the fire, the FOMC continued raising interest rates from 2004 until 2007. In an unexpected development, the Federal Reserve found that as it started to raise interest rates to curb inflation, including that of the housing market, the long-term mortgage rates stayed down instead of increasing with the short-term interest rates. In his semiannual monetary report to the Senate in February 2005, Greenspan explained this phenomenon as the "bong yield conundrum."

Greenspan stated that, "[i]n this environment, long-term interest rates have trended lower in recent months even as the Federal Reserve has raised the level of the target federal funds rate by 150 basis points. This development contrasts with most experience, which suggests that, other things being equal, increasing short-term interest rates are normally accompanied by a rise in longer-term yields." The fact that the chairmen expected long-term rates to rise when short-term rates increased is evidence of the connection between short-term and long-term rates. Greenspan further stated that "[h]istorically, though, even these distant forward rates have tended to rise in association with monetary policy tightening ... For the moment, the broadly unanticipated behavior of world bond markets remains a conundrum.[36]

Greenspan, as well as other top economists, has zealously attempted to explain the "conundrum." Financial globalization and an increase in savings fueled by Asian economies top the list of such explanations. But evidence exists to suggest that this change in trends was in fact caused by Federal Reserve actions taken well before 2005. In a working paper for the Federal Reserve Bank of St. Louis, Daniel L. Thornton explains the "conundrum" on the Federal Reserve's fundamental switch in how it utilized the funds rate. He stated, "The FOMC switching from using the funds rate as an operating target to a policy target"—an example of Goodhart's Law. Once the Fed began using the funds rate as a policy target, the behavior of the funds rate necessarily differed from what it would have been had it not been constrained by the Fed's policy targeting procedure.[37]

Theorizing that Federal Reserve monetary policy created the "conundrum," Taylor believed that the Federal Reserve's deviation from normal policy was at fault: "A key lesson here is that large deviations from business-as-usual policy rules are difficult for market participants to deal with and can lead to surprising changes in other responses in the economy."

In sum, no one factor can explain why the housing markets artificially skyrocketed in pricing during the last five years of the bubble. Nevertheless, the Federal Reserve's lowering of interest rates, accompanied by an expectation that long-term rates would decrease and short-term rates and mortgage rates would both decrease as well, is the reason why the Federal Reserve was quiescent as home values rose sharply, as did consumer spending, and started to make the economy look healthier. As home prices rose, the Federal Reserve was not the only group happy to see such low interest rates. As interest rates dropped, so did lenders' standards regarding who should get loans and how much should be lent. Although the Federal Reserve did not have the necessary powers to intervene and regulate all of the banks and mortgage brokers that were fueling the fire, it did have some power to regulate and supervise, through its power over short-term rates if nothing else. By examining the Federal Reserve's regulatory and supervisory powers, one can see the role that regulation (or lack thereof, as the case may be), played in the boom and bust of the housing market.

REGULATION AND LACK OF INTERVENTION

While real estate prices surged upward, homeowners began using their homes' equity as their own personal piggy banks to fuel the economy. The Federal Reserve failed to intervene because the surging prices made them look better. Also, the Federal Reserve's current system provided a safety net that more or less encouraged banks to take risks under the assumption that they were "too big to fail."

As mentioned above, one of the tools that the Federal Reserve possessed was the ability to regulate financial institutions. The change in the powers of the Federal Reserve since its inception has already been discussed; however, these powers continued to grow well into the close of the twentieth century. By examining the acquisition of these new powers as well as the capabilities of the old, we will see what the Federal Reserve was able to do and what they could have done to slow what quickly became risky lending on the part of lenders, causing prices to go higher as more people who ordinarily would not have had access to suitable financing became beneficiaries of creative lending practices. One purpose of the Federal Reserve is to restore confidence in the economy as a whole. The Federal Reserve is worthless if it has no ability to keep banks and speculators from making risky investments. We will first examine why the banks regulate, what the regulatory powers of the Federal Reserve are, how it has grown in the last 14 years, what the problems were that created a need for regulation, and how the Federal Reserve failed to exercise its powers.

WHY REGULATE BANKS: SAFETY NETS AND TOO BIG TO FAIL

The government's very success in virtually eliminating the risk of bank runs in the United States has led to a second major reason for supervising and regulating banks. Deposit insurance, the discount window, and Federal Reserve payment system guarantees—the very things that have eliminated bank runs—create what is called a "safety net" for banks. The existence of this safety net gives the government a direct stake in keeping bank risks under control, just as a private insurance company has a stake in controlling the risks of policyholders. Because deposit insurance and other parts of the safety net can never be fully and accurately priced, it is necessary to monitor and sometimes act to control bank risks in order to protect the potential call on taxpayer funds. An equally important, if unintended, consequence of the safety net is that it creates what economists term "moral hazard" incentives for some banks to take excessive risks. That is, the safety net creates incentives for banks to take larger risks than otherwise, because the safety net, and potentially taxpayers, may absorb most of the losses if the gamble fails. Such incentives are especially strong if the bank is close to failure, since at this point, bank stockholders have virtually nothing to lose. Moral hazard likely is not much of a problem when banks are healthy and bank capital ratios are high. But back in the late 1980s, when over 200 banks were failing each year, moral hazard was a serious concern.[38]

In October 2002, Ben Bernanke, then one of the governors of the Federal Reserve Board, gave a speech specifically addressing the issue of asset-based bubbles and the use of the Federal Reserve's policy. Bernanke addressed monetary policy and supervisory powers as two ways of controlling asset price bubbles such as the housing bubble. Bernanke contended that for a number of reasons, monetary policy, namely interest rates, is not the proper means of controlling bubbles, because there is no way of safely "popping" such bubbles. In reference to the Federal Reserve's regulatory powers, Bernanke stated:

> The Fed has a range of powers with respect to financial institutions, including rule-making powers, supervisory oversight, and a lender-of-last

resort function ... In particular, alone and in concert with other agencies, the Fed should ensure that financial institutions and markets are well pre-pared for the contingency of a large shock to asset prices. The Fed and other regulators should insist that banks be well capitalized and well diversified and that they stress-test their portfolios against a wide range of scenarios. The Fed can also contribute to reducing the probability of boom-and-bust cycles occurring in the first place, by supporting such objectives as more-transparent accounting and disclosure practices and working to improve the financial literacy and competence of investors ... A far better approach, I believe, is to use micro-level policies to reduce the incidence of bubbles and to protect the financial system against their effects.[39]

Although the ability of the Federal Reserve to affect the housing bubble with interest rates remains debatable, Bernanke's remarks serve as prima facie evidence of the Federal Reserve assuming responsibility for preventing asset price bubbles through the use of its regulatory and supervisory powers.

FEDERAL RESERVE REGULATORY POWERS

The Federal Reserve shares its supervisory and regulatory responsibil-ities with several other institutions, including the Office of the Comp-troller of the Currency (OCC), the Federal Deposit Insurance Corporation (FDIC), the Office of Thrift Supervision (OTS), and others at the state level.[40] Although regulation and supervision are closely related, they must not be confused. Regulation refers to the ability to set the rules and guidelines, and supervision refers to the inspection and enforcement of the rules.[41] The Federal Reserve can write regulations for all lenders but can only supervise and enforce those regulations with banks in their supervisory jurisdiction.[42]

In order to understand which institution has authority over which bank, it is necessary to first understand that banks essentially come in one of five flavors based on the chartering authority.[43] Banks chartered by the state government are known as state banks and are supervised by either the Federal Reserve (state member banks) or the FDIC (state non-member banks). All national banks are supervised by the OCC, while the OTS supervises savings associations, and the supervision of foreign banks is shared among several groups. It should also be noted that most companies are owned by another company, known as a holding company, and it is the Federal Reserve that has authority over all holding companies regardless of the type of subsidiaries that exist under the holding company umbrella.

Thus, the regulation of banks is not divided into equal shares, but can be viewed better as intertwined and overlapping circles. In order to prevent complete chaos, the Federal Financial Institution Examination Council (FFIEC) was formed by Congress in 1978.[44] Essentially, a representative from each of the organizations discussed above, including the National Credit Union Administration, compose this council. Its responsibility is to coordinate the regulation and supervision of all of the separate entities. The list of practices allowed by the regulatory and supervisory agencies leading up to the collapse of the housing market is long. Who had the power and authority to end those practices? Because the FFIEC is a combination of all organizations with authority to regulate individual spheres, it is more than likely that it had the most power to change things.

Overall, the Federal Reserve has regulatory and supervisory powers over bank holding companies, state member banks, and many of the activities of foreign banks. Debating who could have and who should have prevented the bursting of the housing bubble is futile. Despite the passing of HOEPA in 1994, the Federal Reserve still was reluctant to get its hands dirty, and exercised its powers only on a couple of occasions.[45] This is evidenced by the Federal Reserve's actions after the housing bubble burst. In July 2008, the Federal Reserve passed a rule that amended the Truth in Lending Act (regulation Z), which was part of HOEPA, and which was intended to solve many of the problems stemming from unfair and deceptive lending practices.[46] Federal Reserve chairman Bernanke said that "The proposed final rules are intended to protect consumers from unfair or deceptive acts and practices in mortgage lending . . . [i]mportantly, the new rules will apply to all mortgage lenders, not just those supervised and examined by the Federal Reserve."[47] Enacted in 1994, HOEPA strengthened provisions of the Truth in Lending Act that require creditors to inform borrowers about the cost of credit for consumer transactions. HOEPA triggers these disclosure requirements for home equity loans whenever the lender's rates or fees exceed the yield on Treasury bills by 10 percentage points or more. In addition, HOEPA prohibits the use of certain conditions, including balloon payments, in loan agreements and bars creditors from relying solely on a consumer's home as the source of debt repayment.

HOEPA grants the Federal Reserve broad powers to "prohibit acts or practices in connection with refinancing of mortgage loans that the Board [of Governors] finds to be associated with abusive lending practices or that are otherwise not in the interest of the borrower." HOEPA specifically authorizes the Federal Reserve to lower the trigger point for truth-in-lending disclosures to eight points over the Treasury yield. HOEPA also requires the Federal Reserve to hold periodic hearings to review HOEPA's effectiveness. The central bank conducted its first set of HOEPA hearings in 1997.[48]

Under the Graham Bliley Act of 1999, the Federal Reserve's supervisory powers became one of umbrella supervision. The Federal Reserve is the primary bank regulator of only 5 of the largest 25 banks; the large, complex and internationally active banks that are the major sources of systemic risk. The Federal Reserve is able, nevertheless, to maintain a flow of information about the risk profiles and risk management practices of all large banking organizations through its responsibilities as exclusive supervisor of all bank holding companies. It is for this reason that the Federal Reserve places such a great emphasis on maintaining its role as supervisor of bank holding companies.[49]

PROBLEMS THAT NEEDED REGULATING

Alan Greenspan, in March 2000, stated the Federal Reserve's concern regarding "abusive lending practices that target specific neighborhoods or vulnerable segments of the population and can result in unaffordable payments, equity stripping, and foreclosure. The Federal Reserve is working on several fronts to address these issues and recently convened an interagency group to identify aberrant behaviors and develop methods to address them."[50]

FAILURE TO REGULATE, OR OVER REGULATION?

In October 2008, Greenspan informed the House Committee on Oversight and Government Reform that "[t]hose of us who have looked to the self-interest of lending institutions to protect shareholders' equity, myself included, are in a state of shocked disbelief." Representative Henry A. Waxman of California, chairman of the committee, responded tartly that "[y]ou had the authority to prevent irresponsible lending practices that led to the subprime mortgage crisis. You were advised to do so by many others. Do you feel that your ideology pushed you to make decisions that you wish you had not made?" Greenspan conceded: "Yes, I've found a flaw. I don't know how significant or permanent it is. But I've been very distressed by that fact."

In sum, the myriad of regulations promulgated under Mr. Greenspan did little to slow the expansion of the housing bubble, and indeed may have exacerbated it. In lieu of the thousands of pages of regulations and documents heaped on hapless house buyers at closings, a simple warning as follows might have served far better:

> I understand that my monthly payment may double in six months, and that my interest rate may triple by next year. I further understand that, statistically, given my low down payment and unsatisfactory credit history, my chances of losing my home to foreclosure within three years exceeds 90 percent.

13

Tax Policy

A primary contributing factor in creating the American housing bubble has been U.S. tax policy which awards the highest subsidies, in the form of tax deductions of up to a million dollars[1] to the wealthiest one third of Americans willing to buy the grandest and most expensive houses, while denying subsidies to the bottom two thirds of American income earners who either can't afford a house at all or who can't take advantage of the housing deduction because for them it does not exceed their standard deduction given to all taxpayers.[2]

For a country whose first comprehensive income tax code was premised on the social engineering premise of a graduated tax placing a higher burden on the wealthy than the poor, it is ironic that the American housing bubble finds its roots in one of the most regressive tax provisions ever to be implemented in any tax code by any nation in human history.

Perhaps the ultimate irony is that the tax provision which contributed most to the American Housing Bubble (and thus also to its ultimate collapse) came about by an historical accident now lost to the collective memory. The shameful story of how this came to be is an extraordinary one, yet it appears to have had a benign beginning.

On the eve of the First World War, it became apparent that the U.S. government would require wider sources of revenue that went beyond the collection of tariffs and taxes on liquor and tobacco. The last major war fought by the U.S. had been the Civil War in which the federal government had been compelled to impose an income tax of 3 percent on all incomes in excess of $800 per year.[3] At the time the exigencies of war precluded any serious constitutional challenges to the power of congress to impose such a tax. Only after the Civil War came to an end was this experiment in imposing income taxes allowed to lapse, thus preempting any constitutional challenge.[4]

The first post-Civil War income tax code, passed by Congress in 1913,[5] imposed only a modest tax on the highest income earners, though rates were later increased in the 1916 Revenue Act to a maximum rate of 15 percent for the highest income brackets. Although rates continued to be graduated 1918 Congress had increased for those in the lower brackets to 6–7 percent. Even so, however, only 5 percent of Americans had incomes high enough to incur tax liability.[6]

With the first income tax code only running to a few pages, there were few detailed provisions for deductions other than directed primarily toward businesses since the code was intended only to tax business profits, not business revenue. Since major companies often had to borrow money to purchase capital, a deduction for the interest paid on these loans was therefore considered to be appropriate. However, the actual language of the first code made no distinction between interest paid on loans to finance business ventures, and interest paid on any other type of loans. So deductions were permitted for interest across the board for all types of loans. The significance of this deduction for potential homebuyers who wanted to borrow money to buy a house was not realized at this time since less than 5 percent of taxpayers incurred any tax liability at all, and those who did tended to buy their houses for cash. Lower income citizens had very limited access to home mortgages as Building and Loan Associations required down payments of 20–50 percent,[7] and banks rarely lent money for terms longer than two or three years, though insurance companies sometimes lent money for terms of six to eight years, and Building and Loans for terms as long as eleven years for those with outstanding credit.[8] Nevertheless, even under loan terms which would surely be considered onerous today, and with the a home mortgage deduction under the income tax code which was virtually inconsequential in its impact, almost half of all Americans owned their own home.[9]

Today, of course, the home mortgage deduction is touted as a benign and necessary incentive to achieve the "American Dream" of owning a home, despite the fact that other major industrialized countries achieve higher rates of home ownership without giving million dollar subsidies to their richest citizens. For example, compared to the one million dollar subsidies offered in the form of tax deductions to wealthy Americans for the purpose of buying homes, the United Kingdom offers zero subsidies to homebuyers in the form of home mortgage deductions, as to do Germany and France.[10] Nevertheless, even without such subsidies to the rich, home ownership rates in the United Kingdom are far higher than that in the U.S. In the UK, home ownership rates exceed 70 percent, and in Greece exceed 85 percent.[11] Home ownership rates in the U.S. by contrast, have fallen from a peak of 69 percent at the peak of the housing bubble in 2006, to closer to 67 percent in 2010.[12] Even the million dollar subsidies handed out to the richest one third of Americans has failed to achieve the home ownership rates enjoyed by countries which provide no such subsidies at all to their richest citizens (see Table 13.1).

In 2008, the U.S. lavished over $80 billion on the top third of American income earners to buy the biggest and most extravagant houses they could afford.[13] Nor surprisingly, the average size of an American home has risen from 949 square feet in 1900 to 2436 square feet in 2005.[14] With the government providing such sums to buy houses for rich Americans, the effect on home prices has indeed been dramatic. Such prices have risen from a median of $2938.00 in 1940 to $240,200.00 in 2005, far exceeding the rate of inflation,[15] thereby putting homes beyond the reach of millions of Americans.

We return then to the story of how an inconsequential provision for interest deduction in the 1913 tax code ballooned into the $80 billion dollar subsidy program in 2008.

Despite a common perception that it was the New Deal Policies of President Franklin Roosevelt which first fostered the notion of home ownership as the ultimate national ideal, it was in fact Herbert Hoover who in 1932 pushed through the Federal Home Loan Bank Act of 1932 with the purpose of "providing liquidity" to mortgage lenders.[16]

The sad story of how this first major step on the road to the kind of "securitization" that led to the ultimate disconnect between borrowers and lenders—the creation of the FHA, Fannie Mae and Freddie Mack— and which ended catastrophically in the collapse of the housing market in 2007 is documented in previous chapters. IN any case, however, by 1984 the "accidental origin" of the home mortgage deduction has been largely lost to the collective memory, and politicians began spinning the myth that these subsidies were part of the American dream to own gigantic houses. As Ronald Reagan proclaimed that year, "(W)e will preserve that part of the American dream which the hone mortgage interest decision symbolizes."[17] It may be recalled that included in the Republican agenda in 1984 was a plan to simplify the American tax code by eliminating a number of

Table 13.1   Comparison of Home Ownership between Various Developed Countries

Country	Tax Deduction for Housing	Home Ownership Rate	Growth in Real Home Prices	Notes
U.S.	Yes	69%	9.50%	Mortgage interest up to $1 million deductible
UK	No	71.70%	18.10%	Abolished taxes in a number of steps (1983, 1988, 1991, 2000)
Germany	No	43.60%	−2.40%	Abolished 1986
France	No	63.10%	9.90%	Gradually abolished from 1991 to 2000.
Italy	Yes	76%	10%	Tax credit of 19% mortgage interest

Source: Tiffany Chaney & Paul Emrath, U.S. vs. European Housing Markets: In-Depth Analysis (May 5, 2006), http://www.nahb.org/generic.aspx?genericContentID=57411&print=true (last visited Oct. 1, 2010).

tax deductions (such as the deduction for interest on credit cards) while at the same time reducing the tax rates in all income brackets. While this plan did indeed succeed in both simplifying the tax code while reducing tax rates, it left largely untouched the 800 pound gorilla tax deduction in the form of the home mortgage deduction (see Table 13.2).[18]

By 1997, the myth of home mortgage interest deduction as a "symbol" of the American dream was so ingrained in the public psyche that real estate and other interest groups felt comfortable complaining about having to pay capital gains on the windfall profits

Table 13.2   U.S. Real Estate Tax Deduction Expenditure (in Billions)

2000	21
2001	22
2002	24
2003	22
2004	21
2005	23
2006	24
2007	26

Source: HousingEconomics.com.

Table 13.3   Mortgage Interest Expenditure (in Billions)

2000	70
2001	71
2002	70
2003	64
2004	66
2005	68
2006	72
2007	76
2008	80

Source: NAHB/Housing Economics, National Association of Home Builders.

that they had enjoyed during the run-up in home prices caused by the government's annual 80 billion dollar subsidies. To cater to these groups, Congress passed the "1997 Taxpayer Relief Act,"[19] which consisted mainly in waiving the already low capital gain tax on profits from sales of homes up to a half a million dollars for couples. This gave yet another shot in the arm to home prices as homes now became an even more attractive investment vehicle for speculator eager to find a reliable tax haven (see Table 13.3).

By 2002, the myth of the home mortgage deduction has been elevated from its status as myth to political orthodoxy, as George Bush proclaimed official government policy: "[W]e want *everybody* in American to own their (sic) own home."[20] Thus echoing Herbert Hoover's famous ill-fated promise: "A chicken in every pot."

But even $80 billion in annual subsidies was not considered enough incentive to buy homes, and government soon followed with such acts as the Community Reinvestment Act[21] which set quotas for lending to those with marginal credit histories and threatening sanctions on banks who did not meet the quotas. Because many of these marginal buyers with questionable credit histories had no money to put down on a house, banks seeking to meet their quotas were driven to create exotic financial instruments such as "Collateralized Debt Obligations" and "Structured Investment Vehicles."[22] Despite the esoteric sounding names, however, they were all designed to for just one purpose— namely to increase leverage. At the home borrower level, this kind of extreme leverage was manifested by loans which required little or no down payment. Borrowers and lenders alike, even financial planners justified such extreme leverage by assuming as an economic law that housing prices would always go up—forever. Thus even borrowers who put no money down could look forward to building equity as the value of their homes soared over time. In turn, this equity would constitute the homeowner's own private piggy bank which could be raided for purchases of luxury goods and vacations.

As a result of such policies, homebuyer-speculators, and just pure speculators, were driven to a wild frenzy of speculation. Finance advisors calculated that the U.S. government tax policies essentially amounted to the government giving out free homes to the wealthiest Americans. Here's how the calculation worked:

A borrower with no money to put down on a house could simply "borrow" the down payment (if one was even required) in the form of a second deed of trust. With the money borrowed, the buyer could then buy a $1,000,000.00 house at an interest rate of say 5 percent. If, as expected, the home increased in value by 5 percent a year (and many homeowners expected much higher rates of annual increase in value, up to 50 percent a year in some parts of California at the height of the bubble) the increase in value compensated the borrower for the 5 percent he had paid in interest, and the tax savings on a deduction of a million dollars served as the equivalent of a cash subsidy to the homeowner above and beyond getting the house for free. The higher the income of the homeowner, the greater the tax deduction, up to a million dollars.

It was the closest thing to a governmental policy of taking tax dollars and simply dropping hundred dollar bills out of an airplane for anyone to pick up.

Of course the bubble created by policies could not go on forever. Like a Ponzi scheme, the only question was not whether it would collapse, but when it would collapse. What is most surprising is not that the housing bubble was created, but that it lasted so long before bursting. In part it lasted as long as it did because every time there were signs that the bubble might burst and housing prices might actually fall to the level at which an American earning a median income might actually be able to afford one, the government stepped in to prolong the bubble by threatening banks that didn't lend money to marginal buyers (as it did in the Community Reinvestment Act and later in the housing regulations promulgated in the mid-1990s which put real teeth into the CRA), and in the 1997 granting of an additional tax exemption for windfall housing profits.

Finally, when the bubble did finally collapse in 2007 (despite all the billions squandered by government in its ill-fated campaign to inflate housing prices), and it began to look like housing prices might actually fall to affordable levels, the government then stepped in again in 2009 in a desperate attempt to keep the bubble going by handing out $8000.00 subsidies to qualified homebuyers in order to keep home prices as high as possible.[23] Even media pundits joined this government campaign, proclaiming again and again variations on the theme that it would "be a tragedy if home prices were allowed to fall to levels at which people could actually afford to buy them."

America, and to a large extent the entire world, is now paying the price for the government's bubble economics and its role in inflating housing prices. As even credit rating agencies began to buy into the premise that investing in the housing bubble was a "sure thing", and began awarding triple A ratings to securities comprised of slices and dices of underlying mortgage obligations, the stage was set for international financial collapse.

Most disheartening is that the appropriate lessons have not been learned from the international economic collapse. Without those lessons learned, there remains the risk of future economic catastrophe.

14

Real Estate Practices

Throughout history, there have been various procedures and numerous changes regarding real estate practices in the United States. In early times, buying and lending practices were simple and straightforward. This may seem to some as a beneficial method. However, this simple method often resulted in foreclosure and default mortgages due to unforeseen circumstances and failure to ensure payment by the mortgagee. In addition, in the past, there were a great number of individuals who purchased their houses with cash, never involving a lender or bank. As time went on, mortgages became more prominent and involved a complex number of factors. Mortgages are now adaptable and interchangeable to custom-fit the buyer and allow for larger loans. However, this also presents a problem in that it allows for a higher level of risk coupled with the consequence of default and foreclosure.

In the 1800s, when an individual purchased a home, a bank would lend money directly to the new homeowner. There was no middle man, and transactions were completed rather smoothly. To contrast, banks often did not require a down payment that was adequate in relation to the amount of the loan and the value of the house. In addition, the credit history of a possible home buyer was not thoroughly verified. However, most loans made were based solely on the discretion of bank employees, and there was no force placed on banks by the American government to perform precarious loans. During this time, since loans were made directly from the bank to the consumer, if the homeowner defaulted on the mortgage, the loss went directly to the bank, and the bank felt the consequences first hand of a default on a mortgage.

In the period leading up to the Great Depression, most lenders were mandating higher margins on loans. The reason for this was because the banks were protecting themselves from real estate explosions, speculative homeowners, and the large margin of fluctuating land values as a result of the growth in American urban areas.[1] As a result, banks devoted a modest amount of attention to pertinent risk factors such as a consumer's ability to pay and the current amount of equity in the home.[2] In addition, at that time many appraisers did not take the profession seriously, and often appraisals were performed quickly and hastily. To add to this problem, many mortgages were executed with little or no down payment.[3]

During this time there were two categories of American citizens. The first class paid for the entire home or paid a substantial amount down.[4] The second class merely purchased homes as a speculative venture.[5] During this period, the majority of mortgages were short term, lasting somewhere between 5 and 10 years. Following the end of the 5- to 10-year period, the buyer could either pay the entire remaining balance in one lump sum or refinance the balance. The second class of citizens, those in the speculative market, usually hoped that at the end of the 5- to 10-year period, the house could be sold for a profit. During this time, lenders would often offer a mortgage with a low down payment followed by a second mortgage containing a manipulative rate.[6] Due to this style of real estate practice, many homeowners were forced into foreclosure. Additionally, since there was such a wide span of interest rates across the country, real estate capital could not easily surge. For example, in 1931 alone, interest rates ranged from 5.9 percent to 10 percent.[7] As a result, many Americans rented during this period.

During the Great Depression, the years between 1929 and 1941, the state of real estate took a downward twist. In turn, foreclosure rates increased significantly.[8] This was due to widespread unemployment and increased sales of real estate due to failure to pay taxes. In conjunction, lenders retained the foreclosed properties instead of selling them in an effort to retain assets. In 1933, more than 50 percent of America's mortgage was in debt.[9]

Following this, legislation attempted to offer some relief to home-owners. However, this did not prove effective. President Roosevelt then tried to protect consumers from foreclosure. As a result, the Homeowners' Loan Corporation (HOLC) was enacted. The HOLC operated by providing bonds to mortgage lenders. As a result, the consumer received a lower interest rate.[10] The HOLC is partially responsible for putting into practice a uniform system of real estate appraisal.[11] The HOLC also set in motion the process of long-term mortgages. As a result, foreclosures decreased and recovery began.

CURRENT REAL ESTATE PRACTICES

The creation of the Federal Housing Administration (FHA) also helped to stabilize real estate in the United States by taking the first steps toward "securitization." The FHA invited private mortgage lenders to base loans on certain criteria.[12] As a result, interest rates became more uniform and borrowers were allowed to make lower monthly payments. The FHA also provided homebuilders with various services.

Recently, government has passed legislation that has permitted homeowners to borrower against the equity in their homes. In addition, Congress has also encouraged home equity mortgage markets.[13] Secured by second mortgages, home equity loans became increasing popular. As a result of these home equity loans, the amount of home equity debt increased greatly.[14] Home equity loans have caused half of all foreclosures in the recent years.[15] The reason for this is because the home equity loans are not being used to purchase a home.

PREDATORY LENDING

The housing bubble triggered a great expansion in the practice of predatory lending.[16] For the most part, predatory lending occurs between the borrower and a mortgage broker.[17] Predatory lending is most common in the refinancing of homes and the extension of home equity loans. Factors involved in predatory lending include excessive fees, excessive interest rates, lending without the ability to repay, loan flipping, prepayment penalties, and balloon payments.[18]

One characteristic involved in predatory lending is prepayment penalties on mortgages.[19] Many times, mortgage holders attempt to pay off a mortgage early in an effort to avoid balloon payments; however, when prepayment penalties accompany the loan, it discourages individuals from paying off the mortgage completely. Studies have illustrated that mortgages that contain prepayment penalties have a 52 percent greater risk of default compared to mortgages that do not contain a prepayment penalty.[20]

A second characteristic of predatory lending is that often, homeowners that possess these types of mortgages owe more on the balance of the mortgage than the home is actually worth.[21]

Prospective buyers play a major role in predatory lending. This is because the belief is reinforced that mortgage brokers are acting in the best interest of the consumer, when in fact many mortgage brokers are merely attempting to guide borrowers into higher interest rates and fees.[22] Lenders in the practice of predatory loans often target minorities and the elderly.[23] Predatory loan holders often have substantial equity in their homes due to rising real estate prices.

The effects of predatory loans are often damaging to victims and result in consumers paying too much toward fees and interest.[24] In some cases, homeowners end up paying too much in fees, while others ultimately lose their homes. As a result, foreclosures occur, and there is an eventual negative impact on neighborhoods due to vacant homes resulting in decreased property values.[25]

MORTGAGE REFORM AND THE ANTI-PREDATORY LENDING ACT OF 2007

The Mortgage Reform bill was created in an effort to respond to the aggressive subprime lending practices.[26] Initiated by the House Financial Services Committee, this bill attempted to discourage prepayment penalties and unacceptable incentives.[27] The first part of the bill provides for licensing and registration of mortgage brokers, and imposes a duty of care on mortgage brokers, including a duty to fully examine whether the homeowner will be able to repay the loan based on relevant factors. Brokers are also required to provide full disclosure to buyers.

One section of the bill requires that lenders make reasonable inquiries to reflect that the consumer will be able to repay the loan and will also result in a benefit to the consumer. The bill also prohibits numerous high-cost mortgage loans and expands on other certain protections that are in place under HOEPA.[28]

SUBPRIME MORTGAGES

Subprime mortgages became very popular between 2000 and 2005.[29] Subprime mortgages are loans in which only interest on the loan is paid for a period of time, or the borrower is given the option of only paying a portion on the principal of the mortgage. Subprime mortgages often imposed lax loan standards, and often required little income verification or credit check.[30] As a result, foreclosures increased because these homeowners were never prepared to pay such costly mortgages and therefore defaulted quickly. In the past, subprime mortgages were afforded only to wealthy borrowers who were disciplined enough to benefit from lower monthly payments. However, lenders began offering subprime mortgages to ordinary buyers. Consequently, housing prices have increased because those people who in the past could not attain a mortgage were now able to obtain these subprime loans.

With the development of secondary markets, lenders began to get into the practice of selling mortgages to investors. As a result, the lender suffers no consequences when the borrower defaults on the mortgage.[31] This practice creates a disconnection between the individuals who make particular lending decisions and the individuals who ultimately bear the risk of default. When lenders make loans without any consideration of the consequences, loans often end in default and houses in foreclosure.[32]

In today's society, most subprime loans are still configured to result in refinancing, debt consolidation, or simple consumer credit.[33] For the most part, subprime loans are not predatory, but most predatory loans are subprime.[34]

THE ROLE OF THE INTERNET IN REAL ESTATE PRACTICES

During the last decade and primarily the last few years, the Internet has played a huge part in the practice of real estate. Across the country, prospective home buyers are using the Internet to endeavor in their home search.[35] In the past, individuals used the Internet as an initial search tool, which was followed by the assistance of a real estate agent. In today's society, the Internet serves as a primary tool. Eighty-four percent of home buyers now use the Internet as a source of information for future purchases.[36]

The Internet can be a good tool for perspective home buyers in order to establish ideas and thoughts. However, currently prospective home buyers are using the Internet as a purchasing tool versus a research tool. In addition, there are also various aspects and features in communities that cannot be viewed by simply logging on to the Internet. To compare, the Internet now offers comparable price analysis, finance and title insurance, property tax amounts, building inspector information, and access to real estate lawyers.[37]

Even those individuals interested in selling their home may utilize the Internet by posting ads and photos of their homes. Virtual tours can also be performed online to further assist buyers and sellers.

15

Credit Rating Agencies

Rating agencies continue to create (an) even bigger monster—the CDO market. Let's hope we are all wealthy and retired by the time this house of cards falters.[1]
— 2006 Internal Email from Standard and Poor Rating Agency.

The role of the credit rating agencies in the creation of the housing bubble is the subject of heated current debate.

John Moody initiated credit rating agencies in the United States in 1909.[2] Moody's bond rating innovation came along rather late, considering Dutch investors had been buying bonds for three centuries, English investors for two centuries, and American investors for one century.[3] Thus, investors had been successfully purchasing bonds without any type of credit rating system for quite some time.

In the United States, the expansion of the railroad system triggered the growth in the corporate bond market, which eventually led to the need for a credit rating agency.[4] Typical corporations of the United States were banking, insurance, transportation, and manufacturing enterprises.[5] Railroad corporations began swelling into unsettled territories, where few banks and investors could finance them.[6] "The solution to the problem of financing U.S. railroads was the development of a huge market, both domestic and international, in the bonded debt of the U.S. railroad corporations."[7] The U.S. railroad bond market spread like wildfire to the rest of the world, but the U.S. corporate bond market was "several magnitudes larger than that of any other country."[8]

Original credit ratings were bonded for the debts of U.S. railroads.[9] Information on the properties, assets, and liabilities of railroads was collected for publication.[10] The statistics of major railroads were reported for several years, and the publication was recognized as an authoritative source.[11] Moody was the first to begin ratings of railroad bonds,[12] followed by the Poor Company, which soon merged with Standard Statistics to form Standard and Poor's.[13] Eventually, the three independent credit rating agencies that had formed, Moody's, Standard & Poor's, and Fitch, came up with a way to rate "prospective quality measures" that was useful to investors.[14] Subsequently, the quality rating measures proved to be successful over time. U.S. bank regulators, along with insurance companies, pension funds, and money market funds, insisted that securities were "investment grade."[15] Thus, the importance of credit ratings increased in the corporate bond market.

Additional expansion of credit rating agencies began in the 1970s.[16] The three main credit rating agencies all still had the same concept, but naming of their systems was a little different. The agencies began selling the reports to subscribers, mostly issuers of securities.[17] Staff of the agencies increased substantially to keep up with the demand.[18] Thus, globalization of credit rating agencies had begun.[19]

Expansion of the credit rating agencies was not the only thing that has changed over the years. The dynamics of the credit rating agencies have also morphed into a different structure[20]—namely, the way the agencies make their revenue.[21] When Moody first established the ratings in 1909, the business model was "investor pays."[22] However, in the midst of the expansion in the 1970s, all three main credit rating agencies changed their business model to an "issuer pays."[23] The issuers were more motivated to pay for the ratings because they had to reassure nervous investors of the quality of their securities.[24]

There is speculation as to why the shift in the business model occurred. One theory was that in the 1970s, the use of copy machines became widely used, and agencies feared that investors would copy the manuals, which would decrease their revenue.[25] Another theory was that agencies realized that it was the issuers that needed the ratings to sell their bonds and thus, they were the ones that would be willing to pay for the rating.[26] Thus, charging the issuers for the ratings guaranteed their revenues more so than charging the investors for it.

In a bond, the bond investor parts with his money.[27] At the same time, the borrower promises to make scheduled payments.[28] Credit rating agencies "claim that their ratings provide [investors] with an indication of [the borrower's] ability (and willingness) to live" up to their end of the deal.[29] However, the problem in the cycle occurs because the self-regulated credit agencies are paid by the very same party they rate.[30]

It is clear that Standard & Poor's, Moody's, and Fitch all profited from granting positive ratings during the credit bubble.[31] However, the trust in the ratings has been lost, and investors are looking for other ways to research bonds.[32] Additionally, lawmakers have become upset with the way the agencies have performed and want to see them held accountable.[33] They are frustrated that the same three credit rating agencies continue to dominate the market when they have failed.[34] Unfortunately, the U.S. Treasury refuses to step in and ensure that the credit rating agencies are reliable.[35] This leaves lawmakers to try to find a way to restore the trust and confidence in the rating systems.[36]

It remains unclear as to why the rating of securities has been left entirely to the private sector. Inspection of aircraft is not left to private inspection agencies controlled or beholden to the airlines, but rather, to the Federal Aviation Agency. Likewise, meat inspections are not left to private inspection agencies beholden to meat packers. While private credit agencies will doubtless have a role in rating the soundness of securities, a neutral government agency rating securities would be an invaluable tool in protecting investors from the kind of conflicts of interest between rating agencies and those entities whose securities are being rated. Had such a government agency been in existence prior to the housing bubble, there might have been a very different outcome.

16

Appraisers

By 2007, the housing bubble had begun to burst, and home prices were in steep decline.[1] By 2009, the value of residential real estate continued to plummet.[2] The question many people are asking is, where did all the value in residential real estate go? Considered in this chapter is role of the home appraisal process played in the housing bubble collapse.

APPRAISAL DEFINED

An appraisal is: "[An opinion of [t]he most probable price, as of a specified date, in cash, or in terms equivalent to cash, or in other precisely revealed terms, for which the specified property rights should sell after reasonable exposure in a competitive market under all conditions [for a] fair sale, with the buyer and seller each acting prudently, knowledgeably, and for self-interest, and assuming that neither is under undue duress."[3]

Every parcel of real estate, regardless of whether is residential or commercial, has a monetary value. It is the job of the real estate appraiser to formulate an opinion of that value by attempting to pinpoint what a typical buyer would pay to a typical seller of a similar property.

The home appraisal process requires several stages. The first stage is to walk through the property to be appraised. At this stage, an appraiser will notice such things such as recent upgrades or remodeling. The appraiser is also looking to gauge the overall quality and condition of the property. While the appraiser is not an inspector, they do also consider potential issues such as water in the basement or cracked foundations. The appraiser will measure, take pictures, and walk the perimeter of the property. Following this walk-through, the appraiser will have a good idea of what characterizes the property, the neighborhood, and the overall appeal of the subject property.

The actual appraisal is prepared by comparing a subject property home to other similar, recently sold, homes in the same neighborhood. Then, after considering differences between the homes, the appraiser will make adjustments to the sales price of the similar homes, or "comps." This is a key stage of the process because the comps will ultimately define the value of the subject property. If the appraiser picks comps that sold on the high end, then the subject property will end up with a higher appraised value. If the appraiser picks lower priced comps, then the value of the subject property will be lower. This is where the appraiser's experience, technique, and prudence are critical. This is also where the temptation to use high-value comps comes into play. If an appraiser picks comps based on a sales price, rather than comparability, the appraisal will be inflated. After picking the comps and making the adjustments, the appraiser comes up with a final opinion of value.

PROBLEMS WITH APPRAISALS

A number of different factors can go into compiling an appraisal. In considering all the stages and steps of an appraisal, one can appreciate how mistakes, sloppiness, and lack of foresight can have a big impact on the final result. And, of course, the final result is what the bank depends on to make a considerable financial decision.

A predominate cause of an appraisal being called into question is a belief that the property has been overvalued.[4] Most often, the client will assert that they paid too much for a property due to a bad or a negligent appraisal. Less frequently, an appraiser is sued for undervaluing the property. For example, in *Gay v. Broder*, an appraiser evaluated the value of the property to be less than the purchase price, which prevented the appellant from obtaining a VA loan.[5] This forced the homeowner to obtain conventional financing, to his disadvantage. The homeowner sued the appraiser, claiming negligence, recklessness, and breach of the appraisal agreement.[6] In another case, pending as of this writing, a bank filed suit against a real estate appraiser for allegedly inflating values on appraisals and then passing on the appraisals to the bank who then closed the loans on the properties in question.[7] The homes went into foreclosure shortly after the closings and the bank lost approximately $630,000.[8]

Simple errors can cause an appraisal to be called into question. Most appraisers use software that will help guide them through the actual writing of the report. However, there is still plenty of room for errors, such as putting the wrong date on an appraisal. This error, understandable as it may be, can have a tremendous influence on the subsequent transaction.

Improper zoning can also be an issue. If an appraisal indicates that the zoning is single family residential but it turns out to be commercial, the entire opinion contained in the appraisal will most likely be way off. For example, in *Sadtler v. Jackson-Cross Co.*, a homeowner hired a real estate appraiser to assess some land.[9] In his appraisal, the appraiser misclassified the proper zoning of the property, gave an incorrect opinion as to how many tracts could be subdivided, and was sued due to that error.[10]

The use of comparables that are dissimilar to the subject can lead to a faulty appraisal. In *Barry v. Raskov*, the property being appraised was a residence.[11] The first comparable did not exist, and the second was a nursery school that was sold for its value as a business. The third comparable was stated as being 3,000 square feet and listed as having sold for $375,000.[12] It was later determined that this third property was half the size claimed and that it sold for only $175,000.[13]

Drive-by appraisals also pose a problem. Occasionally, an appraiser will be ordered to simply do an exterior inspection from a public street.[14] This becomes problematic because in order to complete an appraisal of this type, the appraiser has to make a number of assumptions that are critical to the final outcome of the appraisal.

Since a number of computations are required to complete an appraisal, the potential for error is often high. It is the responsibility for the appraiser to double check their work; however, no one is perfect, and even small errors can have big consequences.

Most of the time, an appraiser will do a walk-through and be able to make the necessary observations. However, if there are obstructions present, then the appraiser will have no way to inspect the full property. The appraiser should do everything in their power to fully inspect; however, it is not always possible. Moreover, if there are material defects in the property that are obstructed, then the appraisal could be faulty.

Also, most of the time, residential properties are subject encroachments, such as utility easements or governmental right-of-ways. These are typical and rarely have an impact on value. However, sometimes the easements or encroachments are significant and do impact the final result. If the appraiser does not address these issues, then the appraisal could be faulty.

Not recognizing external obsolescence can also be an issue. Anything that could be a detriment to value that lies outside the property and cannot be fixed in considered incurable external obsolescence. Examples would include freeway noise, an unpleasant view (such as a parking lot), or even a persistent odor from a factory or sewer.

The appraisal process is designed to consider as many aspects of a property and then come to a supportable opinion of value. It is clear that is process is complicated and contains many different moving parts. During the housing bubble, many appraisal errors were attributed to oversight. However, New York state attorney general Andrew Cuomo "has accused appraisers of helping fuel the nation's foreclosure crisis by pumping up home values at the behest of lenders and other real estate professionals."[15]

APPRAISERS, REGULATIONS, AND HOUSING BUBBLES

Historically, the appraisal process worked quite well for the home buyers, home sellers, and the banks who loaned the money. However, that changed over time. During the 1980s, the savings-and-loan (S&L) disaster was eerily similar. In the S&L crisis, 2,912 federally insured financial institutions with combined assets of $924 billion failed over a 15-year period.[16] The S&L crisis was not very different from the crisis we face today.[17] It was widely assumed at the time that a large portion of those gigantic losses experienced was due to poor, sloppy, and sometimes fraudulent appraisals. "Recognizing the breakdown in credit and appraisal processes as root causes, the federal banking agencies during the S&L crisis started to send a message to the nation's lending institutions that they must improve their credit and appraisal procedures."[18]

In an effort to avoid a similar situation in the current crisis, the federal government undertook sweeping regulations aimed specifically at appraisal practices. The final product of this effort was the Financial Institutions Reform Recovery and Enforcement Act of 1989 (FIRREA).[19] The primary goal of this legislation was to regulate the banks, mortgage brokers, and appraisers and stop the over-valuation of real estate. The primary tool it used was the Uniform Standards of Appraisal Practice. These standards require, among other things, that individual states develop and enforce uniform appraisal licensing practices. A key component of the licensing standards was a requirement that the appraisers agree to a code of conduct requiring that they remain objective and do not manipulate the value of their appraisals.

With such stringent new regulations, one might think that the appraiser would be the last person to turn to for unprofessional or fraudulent work, since if an appraiser is found to be engaging in sloppy or fraudulent work, he may lose his license. However, because appraisers are often the only link in the real estate transaction chain that has this licensing obligation, the act has proved to be ineffective.

THE REAL ESTATE DEAL

Because of this imbalance in licensing requirements, it becomes important to understand the relationships within a typical real estate deal. The home buyer hires a banker or mortgage broker from which to borrow the money. The banker in turn hires the appraiser to tell the bank how much they should lend, using the property as collateral. If the appraisal does not meet or exceed the agreed-upon sales price, the transaction often will not close. Typically, this failure is due to the fact that the buyer would have to make up the difference in cost with a cash payment at the closing. Because few can afford to bring substantial amounts of money to a real estate closing, an appraisal for less than the contract price would often kill a deal, thus depriving agents of their commissions as well as disappointing the buyer.

If an appraisal does not come in at the purchase price, or above it, the banker has a problem, which quickly becomes the appraiser's problem as well. This results in what some appraisers call "pressure" to "hit" the value.[20] The pressure to push for higher values is not limited to purchase transactions. The issues involved with refinancing mortgages are even more problematic in two significant ways. First, mortgage brokers are typically compensated by the fees,[21] so that there is an incentive to push values higher. Second, there is no opposing party to the sale. This is important because in a sales transaction, there are competing interests regarding the price—the buyer wants a low price, and the seller wants a high price. Through negations, the final price is fixed even before the appraiser does his job.

In refinancing, there is only one party to the transaction, the homeowner (and his banker) and his only interest is in how high the appraised value can go. The more the value on a refinancing appraisal, the more the homeowner can borrow,[22] thus the more the banker can profit.

In the past, none of this posed much of a systematic threat to the integrity of the U.S. housing stock, because ultimately the bank was responsible to their shareholders for the amount of monies they lent. But, with the advent of securitization (banks selling their loans in bundles in the form on bonds), banks were no longer on the hook for losses due to defaults, and were free and clear once that loan was resold.[23]

APPRAISERS AND PRESSURE

With the housing market in a steep correction,[24] the obvious question is, how did the values become so out of whack in the first place?

Appraisers have started to talk about the pressure from lenders to "make the deal." Some suggest that appraisers are being asked to create fiction in regards to home values. "Brokers, real estate agents and banks asked appraisers to do a lot of pretending during the housing boom, pumping up values while ignoring defects."[25] One appraiser who "was examining a suburban home a few years ago discovered 5 feet of water in the basement. The mortgage broker arranging the owner's financing asked him to pretend it wasn't there."[26]

Being asked to overlook significant defects is only one way appraisers get pressured. Appraisers are also simply expected to "hit the number." As stated by Susan Wachter, professor of real estate at the Wharton School of the University of Pennsylvania: "There's always pressure for appraisers to 'hit the number,' but in the past cycle it became extreme. There are many stories of appraisers pressured to certify that the price a buyer was willing to pay for a particular property was what the property was actually worth."[27] This pressure can be subtle and come in the form of simply finding that they stop receiving work from the lender.[28] Without work, a license to appraise real estate does little to put food on the table.

"The honest appraisers saw that the situation was helping to drive housing prices beyond reason."[29] Such appraisers were soon warning "the potential for great financial losses to the economy if the penalties for pressuring appraisers were not enforced. The petition also complained that honest appraisers were being blacklisted. It drew 11,000 signatures."[30] The problem of inflated values has only grown because appraisers select recently sold properties on which to base their appraised values. So when recent comps that have been inflated are used in new appraisals, the new appraisal will also be inflated. So the problem not only continues, it snowballs out of control until there is an avalanche of overpriced homes and no one to buy them.

CURRENT ISSUES

With the benefit of hindsight, the damage inflicted by inflated values is easily discernible. Vast numbers of homes are in foreclosure, entire neighborhoods are in decline, and a huge number of properties are "underwater." "It is reported that more than 8.3 million U.S. mortgages or 20% of all mortgaged properties were saddled with negative equity at the end 2008, according to Loan Performance, a company that tracks mortgage data."[31]

The U.S. Treasury agrees, recently acknowledging that "[w]hile this crisis had many causes, it is clear now that the government could have done more to prevent many of these problems from growing out of control and threatening the stability of our financial system."[32] Beginning on May 1, 2009, a new set of regulations aimed at safeguarding appraisals has been adopted by Fannie Mae and Freddie Mac. The new code bars loan officers, mortgage brokers, or real-estate agents from any role in selecting appraisers.[33] Without access to the appraisers, these individuals no longer can apply pressure, subtle or not.

These new regulations raise the question of whether real estate agents or mortgage lenders are to choose the appraisers. One method the banks are using is the outsourcing of the appraisal process, utilizing appraisal management companies (AMCs). Sometimes these AMCs are owned by the banks that are using them.[34] The AMCs maintain a list of appraisers whom they hire directly and then oversee during the entire appraisal process. It has been contended that the AMCs do serve some useful ends; however, they can potentially cause a decline in appraisal quality.[35] This is true because AMCs get as much work out of the appraisers as they can for as little fee as possible. This is a good business decision for the AMCs, but some allege the practice leads to the use of inexperienced and unqualified appraisers because they have to travel long distances to complete the appraisal. This is because the experienced appraisers in the immediate area will not work for 60 percent of their typical fee. "Many appraisers are struggling to survive on the fees paid by the AMCs," says Bill Garber, a spokesman for the Appraisal Institute, a trade group based in Chicago. Appraisers are being asked to work faster even as their fees are cut, and that conflict with the goal of getting reliable appraisals, he says.[36]

17

Accounting

As in the case of auditors during the collapse of Enron in mid-November 2001, investors have sought to bring auditors to account for their role in the housing collapse.[1] While the terrorist attacks of September 11, 2001, contributed substantially to the economic problems of the time, politicians and the mainstream media had found yet another villain to attack—Enron. Enron was at one time considered one of the most innovative companies in the United States, until their fraudulent accounting practices were uncovered and the company subsequently went bankrupt. Several other major companies would soon follow in Enron's footsteps for similar reasons, causing many investors across the country to lose their life savings.

DEVELOPMENT OF OBJECTIVES OF FINANCIAL REPORTING

In order for self-regulated markets in a capitalistic society to exist, some form of recordkeeping is essential to provide stakeholders at all levels with the means to evaluate the performance of business enterprises. Owners and executives working within organizations desire timely and accurate information to assist them in making business decisions. Current and potential investors use financial statements in order to make educated investment decisions. Creditors use financial information to determine the solvency and cash flow status of potential borrowers. The Internal Revenue Service and other regulatory organizations rely on financial reporting for both legal and economic considerations, providing them with a means to account for, among other things, federal, state, and local income taxes; employment and unemployment taxes; sales taxes; insider trading; price gouging; and leverage ratios, among others. Financial reporting plays such a significant role in the business community on both a micro and a macro scale, yet so few people really understand how the process works.[2]

There is no doubt that the accounting profession currently faces numerous issues in financial reporting. In the aftermath of the housing bubble collapse, the major issues facing the accounting profession can be divided into four main categories: mark-to-market accounting; off–balance sheet financing; the increasing complexity of financial instruments; and the relevance of regulation on the financial markets.

With regard to mark-to-market or "fair-value" accounting, it has been observed that "[b]laming fair-value accounting for the credit crisis is a lot like going to a doctor for a diagnosis and then blaming him for telling you that you are sick."[3] Perhaps the leading charge against the financial reporting system is the seemingly new practice of mark-to-market accounting. First and foremost, mark-to-market accounting is in no way new to the current financial crisis. Conversely, the process of marking certain investments in debt and equity securities to fair value originates all the way back to May 1993.[4]

Not only has fair value been used to adjust asset value for quite some time, but the debate in the accounting profession over what assets should be valued at fair value versus historical cost has gone on for decades. This valuation debate is the same debate that is currently widely publicized in the mainstream media. Historically, accountants have generally favored the principle of conservatism in financial reporting. Accordingly, assets and liabilities on the balance sheet have been valued at cost. Cost is the purchase price that an entity pays to obtain an asset. On the other hand, fair value measures what an asset could be sold for in an orderly transaction. The principle of conservatism historically favors the cost approach in reporting value because of the uncertainty in measuring a hypothetical fair value.[5]

By way of illustration, assume that XYZ Company purchases a machine to be used in its operations for $100,000 on January 1, 200X. At the end of the year, it must be determined what value is to be recorded on the balance sheet. Advocates of the cost approach argue that the machine should be reported at cost, or $100,000. Throughout the following years, a systematic reduction in the value of the machine is recorded, otherwise known as the process of depreciation. For example, if the useful life of the machine was determined to be 10 years before it would have to be disposed, then at the end of years 1, 2, 3, etc. the machine would be worth $90K, $80K, and $70K, respectively—i.e., $100,000 divided by 10 years of service, or a $10,000 reduction in value per year. Moreover, an expense of $10,000 would be recorded each year on XYZ's books.

On the other hand, advocates of fair value would argue that the machine should be recorded on the balance sheet at what it could be sold for in an orderly transaction, rather than some systematic approach that is arbitrary to what the machine could actually be sold for. Assume that at the end of the year 1, the machine is still worth $100K. A fair-value approach would list the machine on the balance sheet at $100K, with no related expense. Further, assume that the machine actually increased in value to $150,000. Under this scenario, the machine would be listed on the balance sheet at $150K, with a gain of $50K reported on the income statement. In contrast, if the machine was worth only $50K at the end of year one, then the machine would be listed at $50K, and an expense of $50K would be reported.

Although the provided example illustrates the debate between fair value and cost in its most rudimentary form, it helps to have a basic understanding of the difference between the two concepts to understand why this is such a difficult issue to resolve. While this may not seem to be too difficult of an issue after reading over the preceding example, the issue becomes increasingly difficult to understand when one considers more complex scenarios involving various investments—most notably for our discussion, the infamous mortgage-backed security.

Companies have been able to use fair-value estimates in preparing their financial statements for certain debt and equity investments since 1993. Under this accounting standard, investments were to be classified as either trading securities, available-for-sale securities, or held-to-maturity securities based on management's intent. Trading securities were defined as "securities that are bought and held principally for the purpose of selling them in the near term," while available-for-sale securities are merely those securities that are not trading securities. While trading and available-for-sale securities reported at fair value at year end (marked to market), only the change in value in trading securities is reflected in earnings. Held-to-maturity securities are not reported at fair value at year end, but are kept on the books at amortized cost. Moreover, only debt investments can be classified as held to maturity because equity investments do not have a maturity date.[6]

This accounting standard enabled management to manipulate earnings through classifying similar investments into different categories based on their "intent." To illustrate, assume that XYZ Company makes a $1 million investment in some stock. At the end of the year, the stock has declined in value for whatever reason and is now worth only $500,000. If XYZ classified the stock as either available for sale or trading securities, then the investment would be written down and reported on the balance sheet at $500,000. Now, even though the investment has not been sold, the XYZ would recognize a $500,000 loss in earnings if the investment was classified as trading securities, rather than available-for-sale securities, simply based on management's intent. This example illustrates one of the primary problems associated with mark-to-market accounting.

It is important to note that SFAS 115 only applies to *certain* investments in debt and equity securities, and the mark-to-market approach has not overshadowed as much of the balance sheet until the recent passing of SFAS 157 and 159.[7] SFAS 157, Fair Value Measurements, was enacted to help clarify fair-value measurement procedures for assets and liabilities in both liquid and illiquid markets.[8] The big issue with fair value accounting today is grounded in the passing on SFAS 159, the Fair Value Option Standard.[9] Generally, SFAS 159 allowed financial institutions to reexamine their balance sheets, and to elect to reclassify debt and equity investments from held to maturity and available for sale to trading securities. Additionally, it expanded the scope of financial assets and liabilities available for fair value valuation. This election became available for years beginning after November 15, 2007.[10]

A major charge against fair value accounting was illustrated in the *Economist*, concerning fair value's contribution to "procyclicality." Bankers argued that when the economy is doing poorly, the fair-value approach requires them to recognize losses on these investments, impairing their capital structure, which in turn further reduces the value of their investments, which would have to be written down again.[11] Moreover, in March 2007, AIG and other companies argued that fair-value accounting should be suspended in times of economic downturn because of the inability of accurate valuation, forcing them to make large write-downs of investments.[12]

While opponents of fair-value accounting have legitimate concerns, they ignore several issues inherent in fair value accounting. First, the belief that fair-value accounting is some new phenomenon is not true. Fair value has been available in valuing investments going back to 1993 with the enactment of SFAS 115.[13] SFAS 159 merely expanded the scope of fair value's applicability.[14] Another myth of SFAS 159 is that it forced companies to value their investments at fair value. In fact, the ability to reclassify current investments and expand the scope of other investments available for fair value valuation was *optional*.[15] The spread of the use of fair value was widely dispersed.[16]

One of the major issues overlooked by the fair-value opponents is precisely what accounting is supposed to provide—independence and greater transparency for users of financial statements. After the Enron debacle, one major fear of investors was that accountants were not independent from the companies they were auditing, and therefore financial statements could not be relied upon.

SFAS 157 enacted three levels of valuation for investments, from those that can be traded in an active market (highly liquid) to those that no longer have an active market (highly illiquid). If there is no active market to base valuation, companies are allowed to use other valuation methods to determine their fair value.[17] While this may be more difficult to determine, the alternative to revert to their original cost would be misleading and further hinder transparency.

In reference to Japan's financial disaster of the 1980s, Japan's minister for financial services, Yoshimi Watanabe, asserts that Japanese banks exacerbated their country's economic problems by "avoiding ever facing up to its losses."[18] If nothing else, mark-to-market accounting at least prevents banks from doing what Japanese banks did during the 1980s.

Although the case can be made that mark-to-market accounting provides greater transparency and more accurately reflects a company's financial position than the cost method, there is still a major problem to the valuation of present-day investments. Valuation becomes increasingly difficult when complexity of some financial instruments is considered. While common stock can be classified as equity, and a loan can be classified as debt, financial and complex financial instruments contain components of both debt and equity. For this reason, it is often difficult to classify them. Fundamental financial instruments consist of evidence of an ownership interest in an entity, both: (1) imposes on one entity a contractual obligation to deliver or exchange financial instruments to a second entity, and (2) conveys to a second entity a contractual right to receive or exchange other financial instruments with the first entity.[19]

Fundamental financial instruments can be classified into six basic forms. They consist of unconditional receivable (payable), conditional receivable (payable), forward contract, option, guarantee or other conditional exchange, and the equity instrument.

The unconditional receivable (payable) is an unconditional right (obligation) to receive (deliver) cash or another financial asset on or before a specified date. This can be seen as a future one-way transfer.

Examples of these instruments are trade accounts, notes, and loans and bonds receivable (payable). In contrast, a conditional receivable (payable) is a right (obligation) to receive (deliver) cash or another financial asset dependent on the occurrence of an event beyond the control of either party involved. It is a potential one-way transfer. Interest rate caps are examples of conditional receivables (payables). Under an interest rate cap, a company could have a floating rate loan in which they don't want to pay more than 8 percent. The company would purchase an interest rate cap from a speculator that would ensure a fixed rate of 8 percent. If the floating rate increased to 9 percent, the speculator who sold the interest rate cap is obligated to pay the difference in interest.[20]

A forward contract involves two entities that have unconditional rights (obligations) to exchange other financial instruments with the other entity on potentially favorable (unfavorable) terms. These are similar to unconditional receivable (payables), except forward contracts include more than one entity that must make the future exchange. Forward purchase-sale contracts and futures contracts are examples of forward contracts. These transfers cannot be for metals, grains, and other goods because the items in the exchange must be financial instruments. Similar to conditional receivables (payables) are guarantees or other conditional exchanges. These involve a contract between two entities in which an exchange of financial instruments must take place if an event outside the control of either party occurs. An example of this situation would involve a performance bond.[21]

One of the most well-known financial instruments is the equity instrument. An equity instrument is just evidence of an ownership interest in an entity. The most basic example of this is common stock. Finally, the last type of fundamental financial instrument is the option. Options are contracts in which the option writer is obligated to exchange financial instruments with the option holder if an event within the control of the holder occurs. There are both call options and put options. Call options give the holder the right to buy financial instruments at a future time at a specific price. On the other hand, put options give the holder the right to sell financial instruments at a future time at a specific price. These are advantageous to the holder because if prices rise or fall, the holder can choose to buy or sell depending on which would be favorable. It is also important to note that options are common features of compound financial instruments.[22]

This set of six fundamental financial instruments is subject to change. Complex financial instruments combine two or more fundamental financial instruments, such as debt and equity.[23] The main classifications consist of convertible bonds, callable bonds, mortgages and mortgage backed securities, and interest rate swaps.

Convertible bonds are a type of bond that can be converted into shares of stock in the issuing company. These bonds combine debt with the option to convert.[24] Combing these two features creates volatility of equity and debt because the issuer does not know if the holder will use the bond for interest payments (debt) or for ownership interest (equity). Management's speculation of the holder's intent is purely subjective, and would be difficult to estimate on the financial statements. Callable bonds combine an unconditional payable and a call option held by the issuer.[25] So, the holder of the bond has the unconditional right to receive interest payments on the bond, unless the issuer decides to exercise the right to call the bond. This allows the issuer the ability to buy back the entire amount of debt when it may be advantageous for them to do so.

Mortgage and mortgage-backed securities are composed of a combination of a series of required cash flows (each an unconditional receivable-payable contract) with the privilege of prepaying the principle balance at any time (financial option held by the homeowner). These could also include a guarantee, except that there would be recourse provisions.[26] The final type of complex financial instrument outlined is the "interest rate swap." These create both components of debt and equity between companies involved and the market lender. The best way to understand interest rate swaps is through an example. Assume that two separate companies want to raise capital through a loan. Company A wants a floating interest rate, while Company B would prefer to borrow under a fixed rate. The two companies would decide to work together under an interest rate swap. Company A would pay a floating rate to Company B, while Company B would pay a fixed rate to Company A. Simultaneously, Company A borrows in the fixed market, while Company B borrows in the floating market. By doing this, both companies maximize their comparative advantages, creating a more desirable situation for both parties.[27]

The Financial Accounting Standards Board (FASB) provides that the recognition and measurement of complex financial instruments should be approached by analyzing them in terms of their fundamental financial instrument components, and that there must be distinction between the liability and equity components.[28] Liabilities create interest expenses, which reduce net income. Equity instruments entail dividend payments, which do not reduce net income but decrease equity.[29]

On July 25, 2002, Congress voted 422–3 in the House, and 99–0 in the Senate, for a complete overall of the regulatory structure of the accounting profession through the Sarbanes-Oxley Act. In the years following its enactment, many in Congress and the regulatory community have boasted of the success of Sarbanes-Oxley. In the aftermath of the housing bubble, accounting practices and standards appear to have been a symptom rather than a cause of the collapse. In the end, however, Sarbanes-Oxley failed to detect the impending economic downturn.

Fallout: The Litigation Mess

(We've) sold more crap (CDOs) to Pursuit (hedge fund).[1]
—E-mail cited by Connecticut court judge in the 2009 case filed by
Pursuit Partners, LLC against UBS AG, claiming that UBS sold its CDOs
to Pursuit after gaining inside knowledge that the market for debt obligations collateralized by home mortgages was about to collapse.

In the aftermath of the housing bubble collapse, the confidence of nearly
all market participants was shattered as losses accumulated in virtually
every segment of the economy. With an estimated 63 percent of subprime mortgages securitized,[2] the subprime mortgage crisis created a
ripple effect that impacted other areas of the mortgage industry and
the corporate world. The International Monetary Fund estimates that
the crisis will cost about $945 billion.[3] It is therefore not surprising that
a litigation explosion has occurred. This litigation has left plaintiffs,
defendants, politicians, government agents, journalists, and society at
large clamoring to find the causes of the financial crisis and, perhaps
more importantly, whom to blame. Although identifying causes is difficult, litigation is illuminating which market participants were aware of
the bubble before it occurred, and hence, which participants are likely
to be the most vulnerable to lawsuits.

Plaintiffs in pending cases have alleged that many investment bankers were aware of the impending housing bubble collapse, and used
that knowledge to unload their mortgage-backed securities on unsus-
pecting buyers. In the case of *Pursuit Partners v. UBS AG*, Connecticut-
based hedge fund Pursuit Partners alleged that UBS created and sold
investment-grade debt securities knowing they were about to be downgraded.[4] Pursuit's complaint alleged that "UBS, in a bid to dominate
fixed-income sales markets, made a push into the sales of CDOs

underpinned by mortgage loans only to later incur billions of dollars in losses that contributed to an overhaul of bank management and a loss of investor confidence in the bank." In a ruling in that case, Connecticut court judge John F. Blawie ordered UBS to set aside $35.5 million "to cover potential judgment against it." The court further noted that there was "sufficient evidence to satisfy the probable cause standard with respect to [Pursuit Partners'] claim that UBS was in possession of superior knowledge that was not readily available to Pursuit." Given that the evidence presented showed UBS employees had called the debt securities "crap" and "vomit," the judge probably had little doubt there was sufficient evidence to satisfy the probable cause standard.

Similarly, in a July 2008 U.S. Securities and Exchange Commission report,[5] the SEC quoted correspondence among rating agency employees that showed individuals within the agencies had knowledge of the looming bubble bursts. The report purported to reveal that agencies had insufficient resources to accurately rate residential mortgage-backed securities, engaged in poor disclosure, and maintained conflicts of interest. The report also cited e-mails suggesting that the senior management knew that the CDOs were heading for problems. Among the e-mails, one analyst allegedly "expressed concern that [her agency's rating] model did not capture 'half' of the deal's risk, but that 'it could be structured by cows and we would rate it.'" In another e-mail, an agency manager allegedly wrote a senior agency manager saying the rating agencies continue to create an "even bigger monster—the CDO market" and said, "let's hope we are all wealthy and retired by the time this house of cards falters."

Indeed, as the pieces come into place, virtually every market participant in the securitization process has been named a defendant. The following is a compilation of common plaintiffs and defendants that have arisen in suits so far.

SHAREHOLDERS AND THE GOVERNMENT VERSUS RATING AGENCIES

Credit rating agencies have come under fire politically and legally from shareholders. The three biggest agencies, Moody's Investors Service (Moody's), Standard & Poor's (S&P), and Fitch Ratings Ltd. (Fitch), have faced or are currently facing suits from shareholders who claim the agencies "assigned bonds high ratings without disclosing they were backed by subprime mortgages," applied lax rating criteria to maintain revenue streams, were too close with issuers who paid for their ratings, failed to conduct due diligence in the evaluation process, or generally misled investors.[6]

In addition to civil liability, key employees within financial agencies may be at risk for criminal prosecution. Credit agency employees may also be subject to prosecution under the Credit Rating Agency Reform Act of 2006.[7] The act provides a means for criminal prosecution of agencies that gave favorable ratings to investment banks in return for ongoing business.[8] The failure to disclose ratings may serve as evidence of a criminal conspiracy that is prosecutable under the law. As described by William R. Martin and Kerry Brainard Verdi in *The Subprime Mortgage Crisis: Somebody Has to Pay,* credit rating agencies "generate fees from investment banks, which seek favorable ratings for the asset-backed securities.... Some of the biggest agencies reportedly generated almost half their fees from rating investment bank products. Nearly 80 percent of all subprime loans that were syndicated were given AAA ratings—the highest rating. If the agencies gave favorable ratings to subprime-mortgage-backed securities in return for a continuing stream of business from the investment banks, this may constitute a violation of the Credit Rating Agency Reform Act of 2006."[9]

SHAREHOLDERS, CUSTOMERS, INSTITUTIONAL INVESTORS, REI TRUSTS AND THE GOVERNMENT VERSUS INVESTMENT BANKS

Shareholders, customers, institutional advisers, and real estate investment trusts have promulgated suits against investment banks. Shareholders are suing banks in their capacities as advisers, underwriters, parties to repurchase agreements, and publicly traded companies.[10]

Investment bankers may be held criminally liable for securities fraud if they "knowingly failed to disclose that asset-backed securities are backed by portfolios full of loans that fail to meet minimum lending standards."[11] In this instance, Section 10(b) and Rule 10b-5[12] of the Securities Exchange Act permits prosecution of investment bankers who failed to disclose to potential investors that the asset-backed securities were backed by portfolios with loans that did not meet minimum lending standards.

FINANCIAL INVESTORS AND STATES AND MUNICIPALITIES VERSUS FINANCIAL INSTITUTIONS

Financial institutions have become litigation targets for financial investors. Institutional investors have sued companies that sold them mortgage-backed securities.[13] In one case, Citigroup shareholders sued Citigroup, alleging the CEO "blatantly ignored the [subprime] industry crumbling around it."[14] The suit followed a Citigroup announcement that the company would write down up to $12 billion in previously undisclosed and unaccounted-for losses related to sub-prime mortgage-backed assets. The shareholders complaint alleges that the CEO "stood recklessly defiant in the face of the subprime mortgage crisis and increasing delinquency rates among subprime borrowers."

These institutions also are increasingly facing regulatory suits initi-ated by states and municipalities seeking to recover for losses suffered by their citizens.[15] Attorney generals from states such as Massachusetts and New York have filed suit seeking civil penalties, restitution, and injunctions to recoup the losses of some of their state's citizens and pre-vent further harm from occurring. Municipalities have filed suit against financial institutions alleging that their subprime lending practices have cause a public nuisance because the high rate of mortgage foreclosures has led to blighted neighborhoods and have resulted in disproportion-ately high foreclosure rates in black neighborhoods.[16]

INVESTORS VERSUS HEDGE FUNDS

Hedge funds have become litigation targets as well. As described by Brian E. Robison in *Litigation in the Wake of the Subprime Lending Collapse: What Has Happened and Where We Are*, if a hedge fund "had invested heavily in mortgage-backed securities that are now virtually worthless due to high default rates, investors in those funds may allege that the hedge fund managers failed to conduct adequate due diligence before investing in those securities, failed to disclose the risks of those holdings to investors in the fund or failed to account for the risk of default on their books." To date, several large hedge funds are in financial distress, or have declared bankruptcy, due to their overreliance on securities backed by subprime loans.[17] Plaintiffs have alleged that funds did not adequately disclose risks, and those funds did not maintain sufficient loss reserves to endure an economic downturn. They may also consider claiming the funds failed to follow internal investment guidelines, or did not follow or implement proper risk-management procedures.[18]

BENEFICIARIES VERSUS BOND TRUSTEES

As of April 3, 2008, attorneys for Jenner & Block LLP reported that their research revealed at least 30–40 suits targeting trustees or company-sponsored retirement plans (usually either company executives or third-party financial institutions). These suits often allege that plan trustees failed to manage plan assets prudently in accordance with their fiduciary duties by investing in subprime mortgage-backed securities.[19] Many of these suits allege that trustees failed to disclose risk undertaken by the investment in subprime mortgages.

SHAREHOLDERS, BORROWERS, AND ISSUERS V. MORTGAGE LENDERS

Subprime mortgage lenders have been sued by shareholders, borrowers, and issuers. One study found that while nearly every participant in the subprime collapse has been sued, mortgage lenders make up the highest percentage of defendants at about 32 percent.[20] Shareholders have sued claiming a failure to disclose and properly account for the surge in forced repurchases of subprime loans and "misrepresentations and material omissions relating to valuations, accounting methodologies, and poor underwriting."[21] Others have sued alleging lenders failed to reserve amounts necessary to cover their risk.[22] Borrowers of subprime lending have brought hundreds of suits alleging, misleading loan documents, misleading representations by mortgage brokers, fabrications of credit information, collection of illegal or otherwise improper interest, and overcharges for settlement services.[23] They also frequently allege predatory lenders have taken advantage of unsophisticated borrowers who do not understand the implications of the loan terms.[24] In addition, lenders are facing lawsuits from issuers for failure to buy back loans. The plaintiffs allege negligence as well as lack of due diligence on, and misrepresentations about, the quality of the underlying mortgages.[25]

Mortgage lenders may also be susceptible to criminal prosecution for continuing a financial criminal enterprise and criminal conspiracy under 18 U.S.C. § 225. If the lenders have defrauded banks or financial institutions by making false representations and appraisals about a property to a bank or financial institution, they could be held liable under the law. Moreover, prosecution under 18 U.S.C. § 225 is a "likely avenue for government to pursue, since the Racketeer Influenced and Corrupt Organizations Act (RICO) ... is now a favorite charging scheme of the government in a myriad of situations, including financial crimes."[26]

19

Conclusions

In order to prevent a repeat of the housing bubble collapse that occurred in 2007–2009, U.S. policy makers must focus on the factors that contributed to the creation of the housing bubble rather than on the factors that contributed to the collapse of the bubble once the bubble was created.

In order of importance, the most important factors in creating the bubble were:

1. U.S. income tax policy, which gave the top third of American income earners vast sums of money through which to increase demand for housing and so pump up the price to levels not affordable to the average American.
2. Social policy, as reflected in the Community Reinvestment Act, which put pressure on banks to lend to marginal borrowers, reduce lending standards, and reinforce the perception that housing prices would always rise.
3. Lack of education in our public schools about economic history and economic theory and practice.
4. The 1983 decision by the U.S. Bureau of Labor Statistics to delete housing prices from the Consumer Price Index, thus creating the impression to investors that the real inflation rate was far lower than it actually was. This in turn left the Federal reserve with a perceived opening to lower interest rates without undue risk of inflation, thereby triggering demand by marginal borrowers to buy houses with low or no down payment and instead to rely on future appreciation as the sole path to achieving equity.
5. The exclusionary practices of local communities, which restrict the supply of houses by imposing lot size requirements and excluding multifamily housing.

RECOMMENDATIONS FOR FUTURE POLICY FOLLOW FROM RECOGNITION OF THE FACTORS CONTRIBUTING TO THE HOUSING BUBBLE:

1. *Eliminate the home mortgage deduction.* Although this action would be politically difficult to accomplish, widespread dissemination of certain facts would make it more palatable to voters—namely, that only one-third of the richest Americans benefit from the home mortgage deduction; that the richest Americans who need the deduction the least benefit the most; and that the bottom two-thirds of Americans, including one-third who own their own homes, subsidize the most extravagant homes of the rich. Dissemination of the fact that many European nations achieve a higher percentage of citizens who own their own homes without the benefit of a tax subsidy may also contribute to the acceptance of this action.

2. *Discontinue the practice of attempting to implement social policy through the use of threats of punishment against banks and lending institutions who fail to meet lending quotas to marginal buyers.* Instead, focus on enforcing laws against racial discrimination according to the Civil Rights Act and other laws available to punish racially discriminatory practices.

3. *Institute courses in the public schools designed to educate students about economic history and economic theory.*

4. *Reinstate the price of houses in the Consumer Price Index in order to advise all investors, particularly bond and montage investors, of the real rate of inflation.*

5. *Restrict the power of local communities to impose exclusionary zoning and lot size policies designed to promote urban sprawl and restrict the supply of affordable housing.*

Glossary

Adjustable Rate Mortgage (ARM) – A long-term loan in which the interest rate is adjusted at specific times based on one of the publicly reported indexes.[1]

Asset-backed Securities (ABS) – A financial security that is backed by an asset such as a loan, lease, or receivable. It is not backed by real estate or mortgage-backed securities.[2]

Collateralized Debt Obligations (CDO) – An investment-grade security that is backed by a combination of bonds, loans, and other assets.[3]

Credit Default Swap (CDS) – A type of swap that "transfers the credit exposure of fixed income products between parties." The buyer of the swap is protected, and the seller guarantees the credit worthiness of the product.[4]

Credit Derivative – A derivative whose value is derived from the credit risk on an underlying bond, loan, or other financial asset. In this way, the credit risk is on an entity other than the counterparties to the transaction itself.[5]

Derivatives – A hybrid investment that is based on the value of an underlying investment. Types of derivatives include investments such as futures contracts, options, or mortgage-backed securities.[6]

Gross Domestic Product (GDP) – The total value of all the goods and services that are produced within the boundaries of a country.[7]

Hedge Fund – An investment partnership that is available to institutions and wealthy individual investors. It uses a variety of investment strategies including "hedging against market downturns, ... investing in derivatives, using arbitrage, and speculating on mergers and acquisitions."[8]

Historical Cost – In accounting, it is the measure of value of an asset based on its original cost when it was first acquired.[9]

Inverse Floater – A type of bond or other type of debt instrument used in finance whose coupon rate has an inverse relationship to short-term interest rates (or its reference rate). With an inverse floater, as interest rates rise, the coupon rate falls. As short-term interest rates fall, both the market price and the yield of the inverse floater increase.[10]

Investment Grade – A rating given to a bond that indicates its low risk of default.[11]

Itemized Deduction – A deduction that consists of money spent on certain goods and services in the taxable year. It includes expenses such as gifts, state and local taxes, medical expenses, etc.[12]

London Interbank Offer Rate (LIBOR) – A benchmark for the short-term interest rate in which the most preferred borrowers, like banks, are able to borrow money. It is an average of the "most creditworthy banks' interbank deposit rates for larger loans."[13]

Mark-to-market Accounting – In accounting, it is recording a security's price or value to match its current market value.[14]

Mortgage-backed Security (MBS) – A bond that is backed by real estate mortgages and guaranteed by a government agency. They are self-amortizing because the earnings are based partly on interest and partly on the repayment of the underlying mortgage's principal.[15]

Shadow Banking System – All financial intermediaries who facilitate credit across the financial system but are unregulated and regulated institutions' unregulated activities.[16]

Standard Deduction – A base amount of income that is not subject to tax when the itemized deduction method is not used to calculate taxable income.[17]

Structured Investment Vehicles (SIVs) – A pool of investment assets that seeks to "profit from the credit spread between short-term debt and long-term structured finance products."[18]

Synthetic Collateralized Debt Obligation (or BISTRO) – A collaterlaized debt obligation (CDO) in which the underlying credit exposures are taken on using a credit default swap rather than by having a vehicle buy physical assets. They generate income selling insurance against bond defaults in the form of credit default swaps. Sellers of credit default swaps receive regular payments from the buyers, which are usually banks or hedge funds.[19]

VA Loan – A mortgage loan program that helps veterans and their families obtain financing for a home.[20]

Yield Spread Premium (YSP) – The amount earned by a mortgage broker when the interest rate sold to a borrower is above the borrower's qualifying par rate.[21]

Selected Bibliography

BOOKS

Baker, Dean. *Plunder and Blunder: The Rise and Fall of the Bubble Economy.* Sausalito, CA: Poli Point Press, 2008.

Brands, H. W. *Traitor to His Class.* New York: Doubleday, 2008.

Bookstaber, Richard. *A Demon of Our Own Design.* New Jersey: John Wiley & Sons, 2007.

Burdekin, Richard, and Pierre Siklos, eds. *Deflation: Current and Historical Perspectives.* Cambridge: Cambridge University Press, 2004.

Cohan, William D. *House of Cards: A Tale of Hubris and Wretched Excess on Wall Street.* New York: Doubleday, 2009.

Cooper, George. *The Origin of Financial Crises.* New York, Vintage Books, 2008.

Egan, John J., John Carr, Andrew Mott, and John Roos. *Housing and Public Policy: A Role for Mediating Structures.* Cambridge, MA: Ballinger Publishing Company, 1981.

Ferguson, Niall. *The Ascent of Money: A Financial History of the World.* New York, New York: Penguin Press, 2008.

Fischer, David Hackett. *The Great Wave.* New York: Oxford University Press, 1996.

Green, Richard K., and Stephen Malpezzi. *A Primer on U.S. Housing Markets and Housing Policy.* Washington, DC: The Urban Institute Press, 2003.

Keynes, John Maynard. *The General Theory of Employment, Interest and Money.* Hamburg, Germany: Management Laboratory Press, 2008.

Kindleberger, Charles P., and Robert Aliber. *Manias, Panics, and Crashes.* 5th ed. New Jersey: John Wiley & Sons, 2005.

Krugman, Paul. *The Return of Depression Economics and the Crisis of 2008*. New York: W.W. Norton & Company, 2009.

Kunstler, James Howard. *The Geography of Nowhere: The Rise and Decline of America's Man-made Landscape*. New York: Touchstone, 1993.

Miles, David. *Housing, Financial Markets, and the Wider Economy*. New York: John Wiley and Sons, 1994.

Mitchell, J. Paul, ed. *Federal Housing and Policy Programs: Past and Present*. New Brunswick, NJ: Center for Urban Policy and Research, 1985.

Olney, Martha L. *Buy Now, Pay Later: Advertising, Credit, and Consumer Durables in the 1920s*. Chapel Hill: University of North Carolina Press, 1991.

Parker, Randall E. *The Economics of the Great Depression: A Twenty First Century Look Back at the Economics of the Interwar Era*. Greenville, NC: Edward Elgar Publishing, 2007.

Posner, Richard A. *A Failure of Capitalism*. Cambridge, MA: Harvard University Press, 2009.

Selmi, Daniel P., James A. Kushner, and Edward H. Ziegler. *Land Use Regulation: Cases and Materials*. 3rd ed. New York: Aspen, 2008.

Shiller, Robert J. *The Subprime Solution*. Princeton, NJ: Princeton University Press, 2008.

Shleifer, Andrei. *Inefficient Markets: An Introduction to Behavioral Finance*. New York: Oxford University Press, 2000.

Soros, George. *The New Paradigm for Financial Markets*. New York: Perseus Books Group, 2008.

Tett, Gillian. *Fool's Gold: How the Bold Dream of a Small Tribe at J. P. Morgan Was Corrupted by Wall Street Greed and Unleashed a Catastrophe*. New York: Free Press, 2009.

Zandi, Mark. *Financial Shock*. Upper Saddle River, NJ: FT Press, 2009.

PERIODICALS

"A Century of Progress, America's Housing 1900–2000." National Association of Home Builders.

"A Mortgage Fable." *Wall Street Journal*. September 22, 2008.

"A Rethink of Capital Requirements for Asain Banks." Freshfields Bruckhaus Deringer. November 2008.

Adams, Kristen David. "Homeownership: American Dream or Illusion of Empowerment." *South Carolina Law Review* 60, no. 3 P. 573 (Spring 2009): 573.

Adams, Peter. "Gambling, Freedom, and Democracy." Routledge, 2007.

Adelson, Mark, and Jacob, David. "ABS/MBS Litigation Outlook." *Asset Securitization Report*, November 19, 2007.

"America's Debt to Income Ratio as Compared with Other Countries." Article from the Credit Blog section Credit Loan, available at http://www.creditloan.com/blog/2008/10/30/americans-debt-to-income-ratio-as-compared-with-other-countries/, October 30, 2008.

Apgar, William C., and Duda, Mark. "The Twenty-Fifth Anniversary of the Community Reinvestment Act: Past Accomplishments and Future Regulatory Challenges." June 1, 2003, available at http://www.newyorkfed.org/research/epr/. Federal Reserve "Artificially Inflated House Prices Caused the Crisis." October 14, 2008, available at http://online.wsj.com/article/SB122394498830631193.html. Wall Street Journal.

Avery, Robert B., Paul S. Calem, and Glen B. Canner. "The Effects of the Community Reinvestment Act on Local Communities." *Division of Research and Statistics, Board of Governors of the Federal Reserve System*, March 20, 2003.

Bank of New York Economic Policy Review 9 (June 1, 2003): 169.

Bajaj, Vikas. "Inquiry Assails Accounting Firm in Lender's Fall." *New York Times*, March 27, 2008.

"Bank Shot." *New Republic* 238, no. 4829 (February 13, 2008).

Barta, Patrick. "E-Commerce: A Consumer's Guide-Mortgages-Apply Yourself: If You're Going to Play the Online-Mortgage Game, It Helps to Know the Rules." *Wall Street Journal*, January 14, 2002.

Barta, Patrick. "Fannie Mae, Freddie Mac Are Chided on Low Income Homeownership Effort." *Wall Street Journal*, November 30, 2000.

Barta, Patrick. "Loan of Your Own: Maverick Lenders Try to Lure Home Buyers with Custom Pricing-Mortgage Industry Follows Trafel, Insurance, Autos in Tailoring its Rates-Minorities, Poor May Suffer." *Wall Street Journal*, January 5, 2001.

Barta, Patrick. "Loan Stars: Why Calls Are Rising to Clip Fannie Mae's Freddie Mac's Wings—The Worry is Economic Risk as They Buy Own Debt and Subprime Mortgages—Hard to Argue with Success." *Wall Street Journal*, July 14, 2000.

Been, Vicki, Ingrid Ellen, and Josiah Madar. "The High Cost of Segregation: Exploring Racial Disparities in High-Cost Lending." *Fordham Urban Law Journal* 36, no. 3 p. 361 (April 2009): 361.

Bernanke, Ben S. "At the Federal Deposit Insurance Corporation's Forum on Mortgage Lending for Low and Moderate Income Households." *Financial Regulation and Financial Stability*, July 8, 2008.

Bernanke, Ben S. "Community Development Financial Institutions: Promoting Economic Growth and Opportunity." *Federal Reserve*, November 1, 2006.

Bernanke, Ben S. "Fostering Sustainable Homeownership." *Federal Reserve*, March 14, 2008.

Bernanke, Ben S. "Risk Management in Financial institutions." *Federal Reserve*, May 15, 2008.

Bernanke, Ben S. "Stabilizing the Financial Markets and the Economy." *Federal Reserve*, October 15, 2008.

Bertschi, Scott F. "Courts Will Dilute Liability among Participants in Subprime Mortgages." In *First Focus: The Subprime Crisis—A Thomson West Report*, ed. Jodine Mayberry, 73. Andrews Publications, 2008.

Black, Barbara. "The SEC's Role in the 2008 Financial Meltdown." (The Fallout From the Bailout: The Impact of the 2008 Bailout on Lending Regulation, Securities Regulation and Business Ethics, Dayton, OH), March 20, 2009.

Bleak Houses; Finance and Economics. February 15, 2007. http://www.economist.com/finance/PrinterFriendly. *Bleak Houses, The Economist*, Feb. 15, 2007.

Bosack, Sean O. "Will Proposed Predatory-Lending Legislation Hurt the Mortgage Industry?" In *First Focus: The Subprime Crisis—A Thomson West Report*, ed. Jodine Mayberry, 177. Andrews Publications, 2008.

"Boom to Bust." *Global Agenda*, July 26, 2008, 79.

Branson, Douglas M. "The Credit Crisis: Taking the Long View." (The Fallout From the Bailout: The Impact of the 2008 Bailout on Lending Regulation, Securities Regulation and Business Ethics, Dayton, OH), March 20, 2009.

Braunstein, Sandra F. "The Community Reinvestment Act." *Federal Reserve*, February 13, 2008.

Braunstein, Sandra F. "Subprime Mortgages." *Federal Reserve*, available at http://www.federalreserve.gov/newsevents/testimony/braunstein 20070327a.htm. March 27, 2007.

Brenner, Reuven. "Gambling and Speculation; A Theory, a History, and a Future of Some Human Decisions." Cambridge: Cambridge University Press, 1990.

Brescia, Raymond H. "Part of the Disease or Part of the Cure: The Financial Crisis and the Community Reinvestment Act." *South Carolina Law Review* 60, no. 3 P. 617 (Spring 2009): 617.

Bryce, Martin C. "Baltimore Sues Wells Fargo in the Latest Fallout From the Subprime Crisis." FIRST FOCUS: The Subprime Crisis – A Thomson West Report p. 149, 2008.

Canova, Timothy A. "Legacy of the Clinton Bubble." *Dissent Magazine*, Summer 2008.

Carswell, John. "The South Sea Bubble." Stanford, CA: Stanford University Press, 1960.

"CD Oh No! Credit Markets." *Economist*, U.S. edition, November 10, 2007.

Cho, David. "Fed Takes Aim at Deceptive Home Lending Practices." *Washington Post*, December 19, 2007.

Clark, Kim. "Through the Roof." *U.S. News and World Report* 138, no. 21 (June 6, 2005): 41.

Cohen, Laurie. "Citigroup Feels Heat to Modify Mortgages—Nonprofit Groups Press for Subprime Relief; Deciding Who Gets Help." *Wall Street Journal*, November 26, 2007.

"Confessions of a Risk Manager: A Personal View of the Crisis." *Economist*, U.S. edition, August 9, 2008.

"Cracks in the Façade—America's Housing Market." *Economist*, U.S. edition, March 24, 2007.

Craig, Susanne, Matthew Karnitschnig, Annelena Lobb, and Carrick Mollenkamp. "Lehman Races to Find a Buyer—Bank of America Is Said to Be in Preliminary Talks; U.S. Plays Matchmaking Role." *Wall Street Journal*, September 12, 2008.

Craig, Susanne, Matthew Karnitschnig, Serena Ng, and Randall Smith. "Lehman Faces Mounting Pressures—Stock Drops 45% as Capital-Raising Talks Falter; Firm Discusses Sale of Assets." *Wall Street Journal*, September 10, 2008.

Craig, Susanne, Kate Kelly, Aaron Lucchetti, and Jeffery McCracken. "The Weekend That Wall Street Died—Ties That Long United Strongest Firms Unraveled as Lehman Sank Toward Failure." *Wall Street Journal*, December 29, 2008.

Crane, Agnes T. "S & P Won't Rate Some Mortgages." *Wall Street Journal*, January 20, 2003.

Dennis, Brady, and Robert O'Harrow Jr. "A Crack in the System." *Washington Post*, December 30, 2008, A01.

"Dilemma for Fannie and Freddie: Serving 2 Masters." *New York Times*, September 8, 2008.

Dickerson, A. Mechele. "Over-Indebtedness, the Subprime Mortgage Crisis, and the Effect on U.S. Cities." *Fordham Urban Law Journal* 36, no. 3 p. 395 (April 2009): 395.

England, Robert Stowe. "Inside the Market Correction." Mortgage Bankers Association of America, May 1, 2007.

Enrich, David, and Damian Paletta. "Failed Lender Played Regulatory Angles—Red Flags Flew but Lamb's Banks Kept Pouring Out Loans, Til They Collapsed." *Wall Street Journal*, October 3, 2008.

"Fast and Loose, How the Fed Made the Subprime Bust Worse." *Economist* 385 (2007): 16–20.

Federal Reserve press release. July 14, 2008.

"Few Stand to Gain on This Bailout, and Many Lose." *New York Times*, September 8, 2008.

"The Finger of Suspicion; Mortgage Industry Lawsuits." *Economist*, U.S. edition, December 22, 2007.

"Fitch Takes Various Rating Actions on 29 Lehman NIM Notes." *Business Wire*, May 28, 2008.

Flaherty, Anne. "Congress OKs Bill Easing Foreclosures." *Denver Post*, May 20, 2009.

Flessner, Mark A. "The Subprime Crisis: Are Predatory Lenders to Blame?" In *First Focus: The Subprime Crisis—A Thomson West Report*, ed. Jodine Mayberry, 181. Andrews Publications, 2008.

"Flimsy Foundations: The Global Housing Market." *Economist*, U.S. edition, December 11, 2004.

Forte, Joseph Philip. "Disruption in the Capital Markets: What Happened?" *Probate and Property*, September–October 2008.

Frank, Ted. "Prime Target." *Wall Street Journal*, April 25, 2007.

Garber, Peter M. "Famous First Bubbles: The Fundamentals of Early Manias." MIT Press. p. 109. 2000.

"Getting It Right on the Money: Financial Literacy." *Economist*, U.S. edition, April 5, 2008.

Gibson, Bryan, and David M. Sanbonmatsu. "Optimism, Pessimism, and Gambling: The Downside of Optimism." *Chicago Tribune*, September 18, 2005.

Gorton, Gary B. "The Subprime Panic." Working Paper 14398. National Bureau of Economic Research, October 2008.

"Greenspan's History on Mortgages." *Washington Times*, F34, Feb. 10, 2006.

Hagerty, James. "Builders Fight Bush Plan on Low-Cost Housing." *Wall Street Journal*, June 17, 2004.

Hagerty, James. "Empowered Official Will Regulate Mortgage Giants." *Wall Street Journal*, July 25, 2008.

Hagerty, James. "FHA, Relic of Past, Is Rebounding—Agency Is Becoming Centerpiece of Bid to Prop Up Housing." *Wall Street Journal*, March 6, 2008.

Hagerty, James. "Treasury's Blueprint-Housing: New U.S. Panel Aims to Fill Gaps in Mortgage-Sector Oversight." *Wall Street Journal*, March 31, 2008.

Hagerty, James, and John D. McKinnon. "Regulators Hit Fannie, Freddie with New Assault—Officials to Boost Powers, Signal that Government Won't Back Mortgage Firms." *Wall Street Journal*, April 28, 2004.

Hagerty, James, Ruth Simon, and Damian Paletta. "U.S. Seizes Mortgage Giants—Government Ousts CEO's of Fannie, Freddie; Promises Up to $200 Billion in Capital." *Wall Street Journal*, September 8, 2008.

Hall, Kevin G. "Agencies Failed to Rein in Subprime Lending." *Knight Ridder Tribune Washington Bureau*, April 24, 2007.

Hardaway, Robert. "The Great American Housing Bubble: The Road to Collapse." (The Fallout From the Bailout: The Impact of the 2008 Bailout on Lending Regulation, Securities Regulation and Business Ethics, Dayton, OH), March 20, 2009.

Hardaway, Robert. "Price Index Sleight of Hand Haunts in Credit Crisis." *Rocky Mountain News*, September 22, 2007.

Harney, Kenneth. "Your Mortgage: Score One for Fannie Mae and Freddie Mac." *Los Angeles Times*, February 4, 1996.

Harney, Kenneth. "Zip Code 'Redlining': A Sweeping View of Risk." *Washington Post*, February 2, 2008.

Herz, Robert H., and Macdonald, Linda A. Understanding the Issues: Some Facts about Fair Value (fin. accounting standards bd. 2008), available at http://www.fasb.org/articles&reports/uti_fair_value _may_2008.pdf.

Hevesi, Dennis. "Giving Credit Where Credit Was Denied." *New York Times*, June 8, 1997.

Hilsenrath, Jon, Ianthe Jeanne, Carrick Mollencamp, and Mark Whitehouse. "Lehman's Demise Triggered Cash Crunch around Globe-Decision to Let Firm Fail Marked a Turning Point in Crisis." *Wall Street Journal*, September 29, 2008.

Hoak, Jon S. "Business Ethics and Corporate Responsibility after the 2008 Bailout." (The Fallout From the Bailout: The Impact of the 2008 Bailout on Lending Regulation, Securities Regulation and Business Ethics, Dayton, Ohio), March 20, 2009.

Hockett, Robert C. "Bringing It All Back Home: How to Save Main Street, Ignore K Street, and Thereby Save Wall Street." *Fordham Urban Law Journal* 36, no. 3 p. 427(April 2009): 427.

Holmes, Steven. "Fannie Mae Eases Credit to Aid Mortgage Lending." *New York Times*, September 30, 1999.

Horowitz, Robert A., and Laureen E. Galeoto. "The Subprime Meltdown —A Perfect Storm." In *First Focus: The Subprime Crisis—A Thomson West Report*, ed. Jodine Mayberry, 49. Andrews Publications, 2008.

Hudson, Michael. "Debt Bomb—Lending a Hand: How Wall Street Stoked the Mortgage Meltdown." *Wall Street Journal*, June 27, 2007.

Hudson, Mike, and Scott Reckard. "The Nation: Workers Say Lender Ran Boiler Rooms." *Los Angeles Times*, February 4, 2005.

"HUDwinked." *Wall Street Journal*, July 16, 2004.

Hunt, John Patrick. "One Cheer for Credit Rating Agencies: How the Mark-to-Market Accounting Debate Highlights the Case for Rating-Dependent Capital Regulation." *South Carolina Law Review* 60 no. 3 P. 749 (Spring 2009): 749.

Husock, Howard. "Credit Where It's Not Due." *Wall Street Journal*, February 10, 2004.

Immergluck, Daniel. "Private Risk, Public Risk: Public Policy, Market Development, and the Mortgage Crisis. *Fordham Urban Law Journal* 36, no. 3 p. 447 (April 2009): 447.

"In Come the Waves." June 16, 2005. http://www.economist.com/business/ displaystory. *In Come the Waves*, *The Economist*, June 16, 2005.

Inserra, Thomas. "Restoring Confidence: Learning From the S&L Crisis to Address the Subprime Mortgage Problem." *First Focus: The Subprime Crisis—A Thomson West Report*, p. 85, 2008.

Ito, Peter W. Esq. "Fallout and Survival in the Subprime Crisis." In *First Focus: The Subprime Crisis—A Thomson West Report*, ed. Jodine Mayberry, 35. Andrews Publications, 2008.

Jaworski, Robert M. "Jaworkski on Subprime: Final Guidance." *Emerging Issues 862*. August 27, 2008.

Kling, Arnold. "Fannie Mae and Freddie Mac." *Capitol Hill Hearing Testimony*. Congressional Quarterly, Inc. December 9, 2008.

Kopecki, Dawn. "Fannie Mae Used Regional Offices to Lobby Congress, HUD Says." *Wall Street Journal*, October 13, 2005.

"In Come the Waves—The Global Housing Boom." *Economist*, U.S. edition. June 18, 2005.

Ip, Greg, Kate Kelly, Michael Phillips, and Robin Sidel. "The Week that Shook Wall Street: Inside the Demise of Bear Stearns." *Wall Street Journal*, March 18, 2008.

Karnitschnig, Matthew, Monica Langley, and Deborah Solomon. "Bad Bets and Cash Crunch Pushed Ailing AIG to Brink." *Wall Street Journal*, September 18, 2008.

Kirk, Donald R. "How to Prepare for Subprime-Related Litigation." In *First Focus: The Subprime Crisis—A Thomson West Report*, ed. Jodine Mayberry, 67. Andrews Publications, 2008.

Kitzinger, Lindsay, and David B. H. Martin. "Disclosure Implications of Fair Value Accounting and the Subprime Mortgage Crisis." American Law Institute, July 24–25, 2008.

Kohn, Donald L. "The Changing Business of Banking: Implications for Financial Stability and Lessons from Recent Market Turmoil." *Federal Reserve*, April 17, 2008.

Korngold, Gerald. "Legal and Policy Choices in the Aftermath of the Subprime and Mortgage Financing Crisis." *South Carolina Law Review* 60, no. 3 P. 727 (Spring 2009): 727.

Kroszner, Randall S. "The Challenges Facing Subprime Mortgage Borrowers." November 5, 2007. Randall S. Kroszner, Governor, Federal Reserve System, Address at the Consumer Bankers Association 2007 Fair Lending Conference, Washington, D.C. (November 5, 2007). This is from a speech by Randall S. Kroszner found on Federal Reserve site, http://www.federalreserve.gov/newsevents/speech/kroszner 20071105a.htm

Kroszner, Randall S. "Prospects for Recovery and Repair of Mortgage Markets." *Federal Reserve*, May 22, 2008.

Lapine, Kenneth M. "Lapine on Cleveland v. Deutsche Bank." 2008 *Emerging Issues 1839*. August 27, 2008.

Levitin, Adam J. "Hydraulic Regulation: Regulating Credit Markets Upstream." *Yale Journal on Regulation* 26, no. 2 p. 143 (Summer 2009): 143.

Lipshaw, Jeffrey M. "Disclosure and Judgment: We Have Met Madoff and He Is Ours." (The Fallout From the Bailout: The Impact of the 2008 Bailout on Lending Regulation, Securities Regulation and Business Ethics, Dayton, OH), March 20, 2009.

Lowenstein, Roger. "Who needs the Mortgage-Interest Deduction?" *New York Times*, March 5, 2006.

Lucchetti, Aaron. "Credit Crunch: Ratings Raised a Red Flag—Moody's Analyst Aired Concerns on CDOs to No Avail." *Wall Street Journal*, June 7, 2008.

Martin, William R., and Kerry Brainard Verdi. "The Subprime Mortgage Crisis: Somebody Has to Pay." In *First Focus: The Subprime Crisis—A Thomson West Report*, ed. Jodine Mayberry, 107. Andrews Publications, 2008.

Mayer, Christopher J., and Karen Pence. "Subprime Mortgages: What, Where, and to Whom?" Working Paper 14083. National Bureau of Economic Research, June 2008.

McCall, Brain M. "Learning From Our History: Evaluating the Modern Housing Finance Market in Light of Ancient Principles of Justice." *South Carolina Law Review* 60, no. 3 (Spring 2009): 707.

McCarrick, John F. Esq. "Insurance Coverage and the Subprime Mess: Who Pays the Cleanup Costs?" In *First Focus: The Subprime Crisis—A Thomson West Report*, ed. Jodine Mayberry, 127. Andrews Publications, 2008.

Miller, Robert T. "A Conservative Case for the Paulson Plan." (The Fallout From the Bailout: The Impact of the 2008 Bailout on Lending Regulation, Securities Regulation and Business Ethics, Dayton, OH), March 20, 2009.

Mishkin, Frederic. "How Should We Respond to Asset Price Bubbles?" *Federal Reserve*, May 15, 2008.

Mitchell, Lawrence. "The Speculation Economy; How Finance Triumphed Over Industry." Berret-Koehler Publishers, Inc., 2007.

"Monetary Myopia." *Economist*, January 14, 2006.

"Mortgage Crisis." *CQ Researcher* 17, no. 39 (November 2, 2007): 913.

Mulligan, Howard. "As Lawmakers Tackle the Subprime Crisis, Professional Vigilance Is a Must: New Laws, Stricter Guidelines in the Works." In *First Focus: The Subprime Crisis—A Thomson West Report*, ed. Jodine Mayberry, 77. Andrews Publications, 2008.

Murray, Sara, and Jonathan Karp. "Will New Rules on Mortgages Help Borrowers? Bill Seen Likely to Encourage Lower Rates on Bigger Loans, but Benefits May Be Limited." *Wall Street Journal*, February 7, 2008.

Norris, Floyd. "Will Bubbles Spoil Fed's Reputation?" *New York Times*, September 30, 2005.

O'Hara, Matthew J. "Would a Prudent ERISA Fiduciary Invest in Subprime Mortgage Securities?" In *First Focus: The Subprime Crisis—A Thomson West Report*, ed. Jodine Mayberry, 117. Andrews Publications, 2008.

O'Neal, Joseph, Jr. "Bankruptcy Reform in the Wake of the Subprime Crisis: Is It Enough?" In *First Focus: The Subprime Crisis—A Thomson West Report*, ed. Jodine Mayberry, 99. Andrews Publications, 2008.

Opdyke, Jeff. "Green Thumb: Figuring Out Big-Mortgage Helper Plan." *Wall Street Journal*, March 22, 2008.

Peterson, Christopher L. "Predatory Structured Finance." *Cardozo Law Review* 28: 2185, 2007.

Pittman, Sally. "Arms, But No Legs to Stand on: Subprime Solutions Plague the Subprime Mortgage Crisis." *Texas Tech Law Review*, Summer 2008.

Phillips, Sandra. "Reducing Home Mortgages Foreclosures in a Predatory Lending Environment: A Case Study of a Mid-Sized City in Central New York." *Fordham Urban Law Journal* 36, no. 3 p. 489 (April 2009): 489.

Plank, Thomas E. "Regulation and Reform of the Mortgage Market and the Nature of Mortgage Loans: Lessons from Fannie Mae and Freddie Mac." *South Carolina Law Review* 60, no. 3 P. 779 (Spring 2009): 779.

Porras, Ileana. "The City and International Law: In Pursuit of Sustainable Development." *Fordham Urban Law Journal* 36, no. 3 p. 537 (April 2009): 537.

Ramirez, Steven. "Predatory Government." (The Fallout From the Bailout: The Impact of the 2008 Bailout on Lending Regulation, Securities Regulation and Business Ethics, Dayton, OH), March 20, 2009.

"Report Notes Jump in Subprime-Related Suits, News Brief—Subprime Litigation." In *First Focus: The Subprime Crisis—A Thomson West Report*, ed. Jodine Mayberry. Andrews Publications, 2008.

"Restructured Products; Credit-Rating Agencies." *Economist*, U.S. edition, February 9, 2008.

Robison, Brian E. "Litigation in the Wake of the Subprime Lending Collapse: What Has Happened and Where We Are." In *First Focus: The Subprime Crisis—A Thomson West Report*, ed. Jodine Mayberry, 59. Andrews Publications, 2008.

"The Role of Market Speculation in Rising Oil and Gas Prices: A Need to Put the Cop Back on the Beat Staff Report." Washington Post, December 25, 2005.

Romano, Carlin. "The Wall Street/Main Street Bug: Curing Symptoms of Synecdoche." *Chronicle Review*, October 17, 2008.

Romano, Roberta. "Does the Sarbanes-Oxley Act Have a Future?" *Yale Journal on Regulation* 26, no. 2 p. 229 (Summer 2009): 229.

Sanchez, Jesus. "Countrywide Braces for Drop-Off; Refinancings Send Profits Soaring 60%, but the Market has Topped Out, Mortgage Lender Says." *Los Angeles Times*, July 25, 2003.

Sanders, Edmund. "Banks Moving into Subprime Lending Arena; Finance: Regulators Increasingly Are Becoming Concerned as More Lenders Court Customers with Credit Problems." *Los Angeles Times*, May 13, 1999.

Schwarcz, Steven L. *"Markets, Systemic Risk, and the Subprime Mortgage Crisis."* Duke Law School Faculty Scholarship Series, Mar. 1, 2008, *available at* http://lsr.nellco.org/cgi/viewcontent.cgi?article=1136 &context=duke_fs.

Schwarcz, Steven L. "Understanding the Subprime Financial Crisis." *South Carolina Law Review* 60, no. 3 P. 549, Spring 2009.

Sewell, Dennis. "Clinton Democrats Are to Blame for the Credit Crunch." *Spectator*, October 4, 2008, 14.

Shaffer, Andrew. "Bankruptcy and Receivership: An Alternative to 'Bailout'?" (The Fallout From the Bailout: The Impact of the 2008 Bailout on Lending Regulation, Securities Regulation and Business Ethics, Dayton, OH), March 20, 2009.

Shea, Gary. "Financial Market Analysis Can Go Mad (In the Search for Irrational Behavior During the South Sea Bubble)." *Economic History Review* 60, no. 4 p. 742 (2007): 742.

Shea, Gary. *Financial market analysis can go mad (in the search for irrational behaviour during the South Sea Bubble).* 60 The Economic History Review 742 (2007), available at http://onlinelibrary.wiley.com/doi/ 10.1111/j.1468-0289.2007.00379.x/full.

Sherry, Peter J., Jr. "Ford." (The Fallout From the Bailout: The Impact of the 2008 Bailout on Lending Regulation, Securities Regulation and Business Ethics, Dayton, OH), March 20, 2009.

Shilling, A. Gary. "The Fed is to Blame." *Forbes* 174, no. 2 (July 26, 2004): 178.

Simon, Ruth. "Investors Press Lenders on Bad Loans—Buyers Seek to Force Repurchase by Banks; Potential Liability Could Reach Billions." *Wall Street Journal*, May 28, 2008.

Simon, Ruth. "Mortgage Lenders Loosen Standards—Despite Growing Concerns, Banks Keep Relaxing Credit Score, Income and Debt Load Rules." *Wall Street Journal*, July 26, 2005.

Simon, Ruth. "U.S. News: Mortgages Made in 2007 Go Bad at Rapid Clip—Delinquencies Worse Than 2006 Vintage; New Stress on Banks." *Wall Street Journal*, August 7, 2008.

"Splitting Headaches; Bond Insurers and the Markets." *Economist*, U.S. edition, February 23, 2008.

Stanton, Thomas. "Fannie Mae and Freddie Mac: Committee: House Oversight and Government Reform." CQ Congressional Testimony. Congressional Quarterly, Inc. December 9, 2008.

Stix, Gary. "The Science of Bubbles: The Worst Economic Crisis Since the Great Depression Has Prompted a Reassessment of How Financial Markets Work and How People Make Decisions about Money." *Scientific American*, July 2009, 78.

"Supervision and Regulation." Federal Reserve System: Purposes and Functions, 59. Bd. of Governors of the Fed. (9th ed. 2005).

"Tarp Oversight: Committee House Financial Services." *CQ Congressional Testimony*, December 10, 2008.

Texas Commercial Bank. "Public Disclosure, Community Reinvestment Act Performance Evaluation." Charter Number 10225. September 9, 1996.

Traiger & Hinckley LLP. "The Community Reinvestment Act: A Welcome Anomaly in the Foreclosure Crisis." January 7, 2008.

"Update on Subprime Lending." 2008 *Emerging Issues 81*, 2008.

"U.S. Savings Rate Sinks to Lowest Since Great Depression." *International Herald Tribune*, February 1, 2007.

Ventura, Michael. "The Psychology of Money." *Psychology Today* 28, no. 2 p. 50 (March–April 1995): 50.

"Weekend at Henry's." *Wall Street Journal*, September 8, 2008.

Wei, Lingling. "Stated Income Home Mortgages Raise Red Flags." *Wall Street Journal*, August 22, 2006.

Weisman, Steven R. "Fed Sets Rules to Stop Deceptive Lending Practices." *New York Times*, July 15, 2008.

Whalen, R. Christopher. "The Subprime Crisis—Cause, Effect, and Consequences." *Journal of Affordable Housing and Community Development Law*, Spring 2008.

"When Dragon's Stumble." *Economist* 318, no. 7695 (February 23, 1991): 32.

White, Alan. "Borrowing While Black: Applying Fair :Lending Laws to Risk-Based Mortgage Pricing." South Carolina Law Review, Vol. 60 Number 3, P. 677, Spring 2009.

White, Alan. "The Case for Banning Subprime Mortgages." (The Fallout From the Bailout: The Impact of the 2008 Bailout on Lending Regulation, Securities Regulation and Business Ethics, Dayton, OH), March 20, 2009.

White, Alan. "Rewriting Contracts, Wholesale: Data on Voluntary Mortgage Modifications from 2007 and 2008 Remittance Reports." *Fordham Urban Law Journal* 36, no. 3 (April 2009): 9.

"Whitewashing Fannie Mae." *Wall Street Journal*, December 11, 2008.

Wronski, Andrew J. "Will Legislative Reforms Hurt Borrowers in the Long Run?" In *First Focus: The Subprime Crisis—A Thomson West Report*, ed. Jodine Mayberry, 187. Andrews Publications, 2008.

Yingling, Edward. "Troubled Asset Purchase Program Oversight; Committee: House Financial Services." *CQ Congressional Testimony,* November 18, 2008.

Young, Michael R. "Fair Value Accounting and Subprime." *Practising Law Institute: Corporate Law and Practice Course Handbook Series*, September–October 2008.

"50 Years of Housing Milestones." The National Association of Home Builders. April 2003, available at http://www.ewcupdate.com/fckeditor/userfiles/baec_net/A%20Century%20of%20Progress(1).pdf.

Ziegler, Edward H. "The Case for Megapolitan Growth Management in the 21st Century: Regional Urban Planning and Sustainable Development in the United States." *Urban Lawyer* 41, no. 1 (Winter 2009).

Ziegler, Edward H. "Megapolitan Growth Management for Sustainable Development in the 21st Century: Finally Closing the Door on the Economic, Environmental, Infrastructure, and Other Human Costs and Calamities of Exclusionary and Auto-Dependant Local Urban Planning Schemes." *Zoning and Planning Law Report* 30, no. 4 (April 2009).

Ziegler, Edward H. "Urban Sprawl, Growth Management and Sustainable Development in the United States: Thoughts on the Sentimental Quest for a New Middle Landscape." *Virginia Journal of Social Policy and the Law* 11, no. 1 p. 26 (Fall 2003): 26.

MISCELLANEOUS

Adrian, Tobias, and Hyun Song Shin. "Financial Intermediaries, Financial Stability and Monetary Policy." August 5, 2008.

Comptroller of the Currency. "Community Reinvestment Act Performance Evaluation: Texas Commerce Bank." September 9, 1996.

General Accounting Office. "Financial Markets Regulation: Financial Crisis Highlights Need to Improve Oversight of Leverage at Financial Institutions and Across System." July 2009.

Hoshi, Takeo, and Anil K. Kashyap. "Will the U.S. Bank Recapitalization Succeed? Lessons From Japan." NBER Working Paper 14401. http://www.nber.org/papers/w14401.

"Role of Federal Housing Administration in Housing Crisis; Committee: Senate Appropriations; Subcommittee: Transportation, Housing and Urban Development, and Related Agencies." *CQ Congressional Testimony,* April 2, 2009.

"The Fallout from the Bailout: The Impact of the 2008 Bailout on Lending Regulation, Securities Regulation, and Business Ethics." A Symposium, University of Dayton School of Law. March 20, 2009.

Trager Hinckley LLP. "The Community Reinvestment Act: A Welcome Anomaly in the Foreclosure Crisis." January 7, 2008.

ELECTRONIC MEDIA

"A Long Road of Learning." http://www.alumni.hbs.edu/bulletin/2001/june/profile.html (last visited Oct. 1, 2010).

Angelo Mozilo. Feb. 12, 2009, http://www.time.com/time/specials/packages/article/0,28804,187351_1877350_1877339,00.html. *Angelo Mozilo - 25 People to Blame for the Financial Crisis*, TIME, Feb. 11, 2009, http://www.time.com/time/specials/packages/article/0,28804,1877351_1877350_1877339,00.html.

Bill Clinton. Feb. 12, 2009. http://www.time.com/time/specials/packages/printout/0,29239,1877351_1877350_187732. *Bill Clinton - 25 People to Blame for the Financial Crisis*, TIME, Feb. 11, 2009, http://www.time.com/time/specials/packages/article/0,28804,1877351_1877350_1877322,00.html.

Chaney, Tiffany, and Paul Emrath. "US vs. European Housing Markets," May 5, 2006. http://www.nahb.org/generic.aspx?genericContentID=57411&print=truehttp://www.nahb.org/generic.aspx?genericContentID=57411&print=truehttp://www.nahb.org/generic.aspx?genericContentID=57411&print=truehttp://www.nahb.org/generic.aspx?genericContentID=57411&print=truehttp://www.nahb.org/generic.aspx?genericContentID=57411&print=truehttp://www.nahb.org/generic.aspx?genericContentID=57411&print=true (last visited October 1, 2010).

Coleman, Major D., Michael Lacour-Little, and Kerry D. Vandell. "Subprime Lending and the Housing Bubble: Tail Wags Dog." September 3, 2008. http://papers.ssrn.com/so13/papers.cfm?abstract_id=1262365 (last visited October 1, 2010).

Dietz, Robert. Housing Tax Expenditure Analysis. May 27, 2008. www.housingeconomics.com. May 27, 2008, *available at* http://www.nahb.org/generic.aspx?sectionID=734&genericContentID=96447&channelID=311.

Economics for Your Life. www.camilleconomics.com" www.camilleconomics.com. *ECONOMICS for Your Life*, Camilli Economics (2006), *available at* http://www.camillieconomics.com/PDF/Economics%20for%20Your%20Life,%20Vol%201.2.pdf.

"H. R. 1852: Expanding American Homeownership Act of 2007." http://www.govtrack.uswww.govtrack.uswww.govtrack.uswww.govtrack.uswww.govtrack.uswww.govtrack.us/congress/bill.xpd?bill=h110-1852&tab=summary (last visited *October 1, 2010)*.

"H. R. 3915: Mortgage Reform and Anti-Predatory Lending Act of 2007." www.govtrack.us. http://www.govtrack.us/congress/bill.xpd ?bill=h110-3915&tab=summary

Hardaway, Robert. "Over Regulation Caused the Housing Crisis." October 1, 2008. http://www.buffalonews.com/149/story/451501 .html. Robert Hardaway, *Over-regulation Caused the Housing Crisis*, Sept. 30, 2008, http://www.buffalonews.com/incoming/ article119761.ece.

"History of the U.S. Tax System, Fact Sheet: Taxes." http://www.treasury .gov/Pages/default.aspx (last visited October 1, 2010).

"Housing's Contribution to Gross Domestic Product." www.nahb.org. http://www.nahb.org/generic.aspx?genericContentID=66226

"Who Regulates Fannie Mae." http://www.fanniemae.com/faq/ cs_faq3.jhtml?p=FAQ (last visited October 1, 2010).

Hunter, Kathleen. "Congress Meddles with State Lending." http:// www.stateline.org/live/ViewPage.action?siteNodeId=136&language Id=1&contentId. Kathleen Hunter, *Congress Meddles with State Lending*, STATELINE, June 1, 2005, *available at* http://www.stateline.org/live/ ViewPage.action?siteNodeId=136&languageId=1&contentId=34787

Market Crashes: The Tulip and Bulb Craze. Investopedia. http://www .investopedia.com/features/crashes/crashes2.asp

Paul, Ron. "Don't Blame the Market for the Housing Bubble." http:// www.lewrockwell.com/paul/paul376.htmlhttp://www.lewrockwell .com/paul/paul376.htmlhttp://www.lewrockwell.com/paul/paul376 .htmlhttp://www.lewrockwell.com/paul/paul376.htmlhttp://www .lewrockwell.com/paul/paul376.htmlhttp://www.lewrockwell.com/ paul/paul376.html (last visited October 1, 2010).

Press Release from: Fannie Mae. April 11, 2000. http://www.csrwire.com/ PressReleasePrint.php?id=35 http://www.csrwire.com/press_releases/ 25741-Fannie-Mae-Chairman-Announces-New-Loan-Guidelines-to -Combat-Predatory-Lending-Practices

Seymour, Julia. "Despite Media 'Mythmaking,' Capitalism Didn't Fail." http://www.businessandmedia.org/articles/2008/20081001141844 .aspx.

Single Black Female, in her own House. November 18, 2004. http:// www.economist.com/world/unitedstates/printout. *Single Black Female, in Her own House, The Economist*, Nov. 18, 2004.

Sowell, Thomas. "Bankrupt 'Exploiters.'" July 22, 2008. http:// townhall.com/columnists/ThomasSowell/2008/07/22/bankrupt _exploiters_part_i (last visited October 1, 2010).

Sowell, Thomas. "Bankrupt 'Exploiters': Part II." July 23, 2008. http:// townhall.com/columnists/ThomasSowell/2008/07/23/bankrupt _exploiters_part_ii (last visited October 1, 2010).

TABLES

"Average Size (Sq. Ft) of an American Home." http://www.nahb.org. http://www.nahb.org/fileUpload_details.aspx?contentID=80051

Eurostat, http://epp.eurostat.ec.europa.eu/cache/ity_offpub/KS-DZ-08 -001/EN/KS-DZ-01-001-En.PDF http://epp.eurostat.ec.europa.eu/ cache/ITY_OFFPUB/KS-DZ-08-001/EN/KS-DZ-08-001-EN.PDF

"Federal Funds Rate from 1990 to 2007." http://www.federalreserve.gov/ ecobredata/releases/statisticsdata.htm

"Home Ownership Rates." http://www.nahb.org. Tiffany Chaney & Paul Emrath, *US vs. European Housing Markets*, NAHB, May 5, 2006, *available at* http://www.nahb.org/generic.aspx?genericContentID =57411.

"Household Saving Rates for Selected Countries." Organization for Economic Cooperation and Development. (2007).

HousingEconomics.com. Various tables. http://www.housingeconomics .com (last visited October 1, 2010).

Housing vs. GDP (in trillions) 1945–2008. http://www.housing bubblebust.com/Fed/GDPvsHSG.htm. *Is The Housing Bubble Fuelling GDP Growth?*, Dec. 21, 2005, *available at* http://www.housing bubblebust.com/Fed/GDPvsHSG.html.

"Nominal Median Home Prices." Based on data available at http:// www.econ.yale.edu/~shiller/data.htm (last visited October 1, 2010).

"Percentage of Consumer Budget Spent on Housing by Country." Data from Bureau of Labor Statistics http://bls.gov/ro2/ce9805.htm

"Housing Statistics 2008," http://www.communities.gov.uk/documents/ statistics/pdf/1095351.pdf (last visited October 1, 2010).

http://www.stats.govt.nz/store/2007/11/household-economic-survey -year-ended0jun30-07-hotp.htm Geoff Bascand, Household Economic Survey: Year ended 30 June 2007 (2007), *available at* http://www .stats.govt.nz/browse_for_stats/people_and_communities/house- holds/householdeconomicsurvey_hotpyejun07.aspx

Properties with Foreclosure Activity. "RealtyTrac Press Releases of U.S. Foreclosure Market Report."

"Ratio of Home Prices to Household Income." http://www.business week.com/investor/content/oct2008/pi20081017_950382.htm?chan =top+news_top+news+index+-+temp_top+story. *The State of the Nation's Housing 2007*, Harvard Joint Center for Housing Studies (2007) (using data available from Additional table: Metropolitan Area House Price-Income Ratio, 1980-2006, *available at* http://www.jchs. harvard.edu/publications/markets/son2007/metro_affordability _index_2007.xls).

"Rooms Per House by Country." www.nahb.org

"Savings Rate Compared." *OECD Economic Outlook* 82, no.2 (December 2007).

"Tax Deductions for Home Ownership by Country." www.nahb.org. Tiffany Chaney & Paul Emrath, *US vs. European Housing Markets,* NAHB, May 5, 2006, *available at* http://www.nahb.org/generic .aspx?genericContentID=57411.

"Total of Top Three Housing Related Tax Expenditures." Data available at http://www.jct.gov/publications.html?func=startdown&id=1192. Joint Comm. on Taxation, *Estimates of Federal Tax Expenditures for Fiscal Years 2008-2012* (2008) (referring to data on p. 50 under Table 2. - Tax Expenditure Estimates by Budget Function, Fiscal Years 2008-2012).

www.housingeconomics.comwww.housingeconomics.comwww .housingeconomics.comwww.housingeconomics.comwww.housing economics.com

STATUTES

12 U.S.C.A. § 2901.
12 U.S.C.A. § 2902.
12 U.S.C.A. § 2903.
12 U.S.C.A. § 2904.
12 U.S.C.A. § 2905.
12 U.S.C.A. § 2906.
26 U.S.C.S. § 163.
12 U.S.C. § 2901, Title VII.
12 U.S.C.S. § 1723.
12 U.S.C.S. § 5201.
12 U.S.C.S. § 5202.
12 U.S.C.S. § 5211.
12 U.S.C.S. § 5213.
12 U.S.C.S. § 5219.
12 U.S.C.S. § 5220.
12 U.S.C.S. § 5223.
12 U.S.C.S. § 5225.
12 U.S.C.S. § 5227.
12 U.S.C.S. § 5232.
12 U.S.C.S. § 5237.

Appendix A

Securitization

STEP-BY-STEP BREAKDOWN OF THE SECURITIZATION PROCESS

The securitization process begins when a bank acquires a mortgage from a home buyer and then proceeds to sell that mortgage. Banks discovered that they could yield a larger profit by selling mortgages versus retaining them. As a result, mortgages were sold and subsequently assigned to various companies. The various companies would have attained numerous mortgages and then would put mortgages into various pots. As a result of forming these pots, bonds would then be issued that were backed by securities.

This process acts as a positive and fundamental operation, because securitization allows the funding lender to divest itself of the risk of the loan and create additional liquidity by selling it as part of a parcel of loans in the secondary market. The most common method of converting a loan portfolio into a tradable security as described above is the mortgage backed security (MBS), essentially a bond backed by residential mortgages. A collateralized debt obligation (CDO) may also contain a mortgage loan or numerous mortgage loans. A CDO falls in line with an MBS; however, almost anything can be contained into a CDO. These things can include: pools of mortgage loans, car loans, commercial mortgages, credit card debt, and unpaid parking tickets. A CDO may even be comprised primarily of a credit default swap (CDS). A CDS is a credit derivative that bears a resemblance to an insurance contract on a product in the event of bankruptcy or default.

Originally, Fannie Mae and Freddie Mac were the organizations who were buying and issuing these bonds. However, as the housing market boom began to take off, other companies embarked on the purchase and issuance of bonds. These modern companies would essentially borrow money overnight in order to enable the company to lend out at a higher rate. Securities were guaranteed as collateral with a counterparty in barter for short-term borrowing. The proceeds of the short-term loan were then used to purchase more securities. However, when the value of the securities decreased, the counterparty required the funds to post more collateral. This was often not practicable, so assets were seized that has been designated as collateral.

Since there was this new secondary market, companies were able to leverage positions with the additional capital. Thus, MBS comprised a high percentage of bank assets. In addition, such leverage was possible due to a lack of oversight by lenders, resulting in upwards of $30 in capital for each dollar of equity.

This method of securitization was productive while the prices of houses were on the rise. However, once house values began to level off and stop appreciating, this scheme was no longer advantageous. The reason for this is because once prices stopped going up, the banks that were going to soon be held liable began to require more collateral. However, this demand was not feasible because the drop in home prices prevented the ability to provide more collateral.

Appendix B

Itemized Deductions for Individuals and Corporations

(All text in **bold** is verbatim from the statute; all text not in bold is author's summary; emphasis in *italics* is added by author)

26 U.S.C.A. §163

(h) Disallowance of deduction for personal interest.—

(1) **In general.—In the case of a taxpayer other than a corporation,** *no deduction shall be allowed under this chapter for personal interest paid or accrued during the taxable year.*

(2) **Personal interest.—For purposes of this subsection, the term** *"personal interest" means any interest allowable as a deduction under this chapter other than—*

. . .

(D) *any qualified residence interest* **(within the meaning of paragraph (3)),**

(3) **Qualified residence interest.—For purposes of this subsection—**

(A) **In general.—The term "qualified residence interest" means any interest which is paid or accrued during the taxable year on—**

(i) **acquisition indebtedness with respect to any qualified residence of the taxpayer, or**

(ii) **home equity indebtedness with respect to any qualified residence of the taxpayer.**

For purposes of the preceding sentence, the determination of whether any property is a qualified residence of the taxpayer shall be made as of the time the interest is accrued.

(B) *Acquisition indebtedness.—*

(i) In general.—The term "acquisition indebtedness" means any indebtedness which—

    (I) is incurred in acquiring, constructing, or substantially improving any qualified residence of the taxpayer, and

    (II) is secured by such residence.

    Such term also includes any indebtedness secured by such residence resulting from the refinancing of indebtedness meeting the requirements of the preceding sentence (or this sentence); but only to the extent the amount of the indebtedness resulting from such refinancing does not exceed the amount of the refinanced indebtedness.

(ii) *$1,000,000 Limitation.—The aggregate amount treated as acquisition indebtedness for any period shall not exceed $1,000,000 ($500,000 in the case of a married individual filing a separate return).*

(C) *Home equity indebtedness.—*

(i) In general.—The term "home equity indebtedness" means any indebtedness (other than acquisition indebtedness) secured by a qualified residence to the extent the aggregate amount of such indebtedness does not exceed—

    (I) the fair market value of such qualified residence, reduced by

    (II) the amount of acquisition indebtedness with respect to such residence.

(ii) Limitation.—The aggregate amount treated as home equity indebtedness for any period shall not exceed $100,000 ($50,000 in the case of a separate return by a married individual).

(D) *Treatment of indebtedness incurred on or before October 13, 1987.—*

(i) In general.—In the case of any pre-October 13, 1987, indebtedness

    (I) such indebtedness shall be treated as acquisition indebtedness, and

    (II) the limitation of subparagraph (B)(ii) shall not apply.

(ii) Reduction in $1,000,000 limitation.—The limitation of subparagraph (B)(ii) shall be reduced (but not below zero) by the aggregate amount of outstanding pre-October 13, 1987, indebtedness.

       (iii) Pre-October 13, 1987, indebtedness.—The term "pre-October 13, 1987, indebtedness" means—

            (I) any indebtedness which was incurred on or before October 13, 1987, and which was secured by a qualified residence on October 13, 1987, and at all times thereafter before the interest is paid or accrued, or

            (II) any indebtedness which is secured by the qualified residence and was incurred after October 13, 1987, to refinance indebtedness described in subclause (I) (or refinanced indebtedness meeting the requirements of this subclause) to the extent (immediately after the refinancing) the principal amount of the indebtedness resulting from the refinancing does not exceed the principal amount of the refinanced indebtedness (immediately before the refinancing).

      (iv) Limitation on period of refinancing.—Subclause (II) of clause (iii) shall not apply to any indebtedness after—

            (I) the expiration of the term of the indebtedness described in clause (iii)(I), or

            (II) if the principal of the indebtedness described in clause (iii)(I) is not amortized over its term, the expiration of the term of the 1st refinancing of such indebtedness (or if earlier, the date which is 30 years after the date of such 1st refinancing).

    (E) Mortgage insurance premiums treated as interest.—

     (i) In general.—*Premiums paid or accrued for qualified mortgage insurance by a taxpayer during the taxable year in connection with acquisition indebtedness with respect to a qualified residence of the taxpayer shall be treated for purposes of this section as interest which is qualified residence interest.*

     (ii) Phaseout.—The amount otherwise treated as interest under clause (i) shall be reduced (but not below zero) by 10 percent of such amount for each $1,000 ($500 in the case of a married individual filing a separate return) (or fraction thereof) that the taxpayer's adjusted gross income for the taxable year exceeds $100,000 ($50,000 in the case of a married individual filing a separate return).

    (iii) Limitation.—Clause (i) shall not apply with respect to any mortgage insurance contracts issued before January 1, 2007.

    (iv) Termination.—Clause (i) shall not apply to amounts—

            (I) paid or accrued after December 31, 2010, or

            (II) properly allocable to any period after such date.

Appendix C

Home Mortgage Disclosure Act of 1975

(All text in **bold** is verbatim from the statute; all text not in bold is author's summary; emphasis in *italics* is added by author)

12 U.S.C.A. § 2801

(a) **Findings of Congress**
The Congress finds that *some depository institutions have sometimes contributed to the decline of certain geographic areas by their failure pursuant to their chartering responsibilities to provide adequate home financing to qualified applicants on reasonable terms and conditions.*

(b) **Purpose of chapter**
The purpose of this chapter is to provide the citizens and public officials of the United States with sufficient information to enable them to determine *whether depository institutions are filling their obligations to serve the housing needs of the communities and neighborhoods in which they are located and to assist public officials in their determination of the distribution of public sector investments in a manner designed to improve the private investment environment.*

12 U.S.C.A. § 2803

(a) **Duty of depository institutions; nature and content of information**
   (1) *Each depository institution* **which has a home office or branch office located within a primary metropolitan statistical area,**

metropolitan statistical area, or consolidated metropolitan statistical area that is not comprised of designated primary metropolitan statistical areas, *as defined by the Department of Commerce shall compile and make available, in accordance with regulations of the Board, to the public for inspection and copying at the home office,* and at least one branch office within each primary metropolitan statistical area, metropolitan statistical area, or consolidated metropolitan statistical area that is not comprised of designated primary metropolitan statistical areas in which the depository institution has an office the number and *total dollar amount of mortgage loans which were*

(A) *originated* (or for which the institution received completed applications), or

(B) *purchased by that institution during each fiscal year* (beginning with the last full fiscal year of that institution which immediately preceded the effective date of this chapter).

(2) The information required to be maintained and made available under paragraph (1) shall also be itemized in order to clearly and conspicuously disclose the following:

(A) The *number and dollar amount for each item referred to in paragraph (1), by census tracts for mortgage loans secured by property located within any county with a population of more than 30,000,* within that primary metropolitan statistical area, metropolitan statistical area, or consolidated metropolitan statistical area that is not comprised of designated primary metropolitan statistical areas, otherwise, by county, for mortgage loans secured by property located within any other county within that primary metropolitan statistical area, metropolitan statistical area, or consolidated metropolitan statistical area that is not comprised of designated primary metropolitan statistical areas.

(B) *The number and dollar amount for each item referred to in paragraph (1) for all such mortgage loans which are secured by property located outside* that primary metropolitan statistical area, metropolitan statistical area, or consolidated metropolitan statistical area that is not comprised of designated primary metropolitan statistical areas.

(b) *Itemization of loan data* - Any item of information relating to mortgage loans required to be maintained under subsection (a) of this section shall be further itemized in order to disclose for each such item—

(1) the *number and dollar amount of mortgage loans which are insured* under title II of the National Housing Act [12 U.S.C. 1707 et seq.]

or under title V of the Housing Act of 1949 [42 U.S.C. 1471 et seq.] or which *are guaranteed* under chapter 37 of title 38;

(2) the *number and dollar amount of mortgage loans made to mortgagors who did not,* at the time of execution of the mortgage, *intend to reside in the property securing the mortgage loan;*

(3) the *number and dollar amount of home improvement loans;* and

(4) the *number and dollar amount of mortgage loans and completed applications involving mortgagors or mortgage applicants grouped according to census tract, income level, racial characteristics, and gender.*

Appendix D

Community Reinvestment Act of 1977

(All text in **bold** is verbatim from the statute; all text not in bold is author's summary; emphasis in *italics* is added by author)

12 U.S.C.A. § 2901

(a) **The Congress finds that—**
   (1) *regulated financial institutions are required by law to demonstrate that their deposit facilities serve the convenience and needs of the communities in which they are chartered to do business;*
   (2) *the convenience and needs of communities include the need for credit services as well as deposit services; and*
   (3) **regulated financial institutions have** *continuing and affirmative obligation to help meet the credit needs of the local communities in which they are chartered.*
(b) **It is the purpose of this title [12 USCS §§ 2901 et seq.] to require each appropriate Federal financial supervisory agency to use its authority when examining financial institutions, to encourage such institutions to help meet the credit needs of the local communities in which they are chartered consistent with the safe and sound operation of such institutions.**

12 U.S.C.A. § 2903

(a) **In general. In connection with its examination of a financial institution, the appropriate Federal financial supervisory agency shall—**

(1) *assess the institution's record of meeting the credit needs of its entire community,* including low- and moderate-income neighborhoods, consistent with the safe and sound operation of such institution; and

(2) *take such record into account in its evaluation of an application for a deposit facility by such institution.*

(b) Majority Owned Institutions. —In assessing and taking into account, under subsection (a), the record of a nonminority-owned and nonwomen-owned financial institution, the appropriate Federal financial supervisory agency may consider as a factor capital investment, loan participation, and other ventures undertaken by the institution in cooperation with minority- and women-owned financial institutions and low-income credit unions provided that these activities help meet the credit needs of local communities in which such institutions and credit unions are chartered.

(c) Financial holding company requirement

(1) In general. An election by a bank holding company to become a financial holding company under section 1843 of this title shall not be effective if—

(A) the Board finds that, as of the date the declaration of such election and the certification is filed by such holding company under section 1843(l)(1)(C) of this title, not all of the subsidiary insured depository institutions of the bank holding company had achieved a rating of "satisfactory record of meeting community credit needs", or better, at the most recent examination of each such institution; and

12 U.S.C.A. § 2906

(a) Required

(1) In general. Upon the conclusion of each examination of an insured depository institution under section 2903 of this title, *the appropriate Federal financial supervisory agency shall prepare a written evaluation of the institution's record of meeting the credit needs of its entire community,* including low-and moderate-income neighborhoods.

(b) Public section of report

(1) Contents of written evaluation. The public section of the written evaluation shall—

(i) state the appropriate Federal financial supervisory agency's conclusions for each assessment factor identified in the regulations prescribed by the Federal financial supervisory agencies to implement this chapter;

(ii) discuss the facts and data supporting such conclusions; and

(iii) contain the institution's rating and a statement describing the basis for the rating.

(2) Assigned rating. The institution's rating referred to in paragraph (1)(C) [FN1] shall be 1 of the following:

(A) *"Outstanding record* of meeting community credit needs".

(B) *"Satisfactory record* of meeting community credit needs".

(C) *"Needs to improve record* of meeting community credit needs".

(D) *"Substantial noncompliance* in meeting community credit needs".

Appendix E

Housing and Community Development Act of 1992

(All text in **bold** is verbatim from the statute; all text not in bold is author's summary; emphasis in *italics* is added by author)

TITLE IX, SUBTITLE A, § 910 - REPORT ON COMMUNITY DEVELOPMENT LENDING

(a) In general. **Not later than 12 months after the date of enactment of this section, the Board of Governors of the Federal Reserve System, in consultation with the Comptroller of the Currency, the Chairman of the Federal Deposit Insurance Corporation, the Director of the Office of Thrift Supervision, and the Chairman of the National Credit Union Administration, shall submit a report to the Congress comparing residential, small business, and commercial lending by insured depository institutions in low-income, minority, and distressed neighborhoods to such lending in other neighborhoods.**

(b) Contents of report. **The report required by subsection (a) shall—**

    (1) *compare the risks and returns of lending in low-income, minority, and distressed neighborhoods with the risks and returns of lending in other neighborhoods;*

    (2) *analyze the reasons for any differences in risk and return between low-income, minority, and distressed neighborhoods and other neighborhoods;*

    (3) *if the risks of lending in low-income, minority, and distressed neighborhoods exceed the risks of lending in other neighborhoods, recommend ways of mitigating those risks.*

Appendix F

Home Ownership and Equity Protection Act of 1994

(All text in **bold** is verbatim from the statute; all text not in bold is author's summary; emphasis in *italics* is added by author)

15 U.S.C.A. § 1639

(a) Disclosures

  (1) **Specific disclosures - In addition to other disclosures required under this subchapter, for each mortgage referred to in section 1602(aa) of this title, the creditor shall provide the following disclosures in conspicuous type size:**

    (A) **"You are not required to complete this agreement merely because you have received these disclosures or have signed a loan application."**

    (B) **"If you obtain this loan, the lender will have a mortgage on your home. You could lose your home, and any money you have put into it, if you do not meet your obligations under the loan."**

  (2) **Annual percentage rate - In addition to the disclosures required under paragraph (1), the *creditor shall disclose—***

    (A) **in the case of a credit transaction with a *fixed rate of interest, the annual percentage rate and the amount of the regular monthly payment; or***

    (B) **in the case of *any other credit transaction, the annual percentage rate of the loan, the amount of the regular monthly payment, a statement that the interest rate and monthly payment may increase, and the amount of the maximum monthly payment,* based on the maximum interest rate allowed pursuant to section 3806 of Title 12.**

Appendix G

Regulations Assigning Regulatory Authority to the Secretary of Housing Regarding Fannie Mae and Freddie Mac

(All text in **bold** is verbatim from the statute; all text not in bold is author's summary; emphasis in *italics* is added by author)

24 C.F.R. § 81.1 (DECEMBER 1, 1995)

(a) Authority. The Secretary has general regulatory power respecting the Federal National Mortgage Association ("Fannie Mae") and the Federal Home Loan Mortgage Corporation ("Freddie Mac") (referred to collectively as Government-sponsored enterprises ("GSEs")) and is required to make such rules and regulations as are necessary and proper to ensure that the provisions of the Federal Housing Enterprises Financial Safety and Soundness Act of 1992 ("FHEFSSA"), codified generally at 12 U.S.C. 4501–4641; the Fannie Mae Charter Act, 12 U.S.C. 1716–1723h; and the Freddie Mac Act, 12 U.S.C. 1451–59, are accomplished.

Under the act, the Secretary is responsible for establishing housing goals to require GSEs to extend access to mortgage credit to very-low- and low-income families and families in central cities, rural areas, and other undeserved areas.

FHEFSSA directs the Secretary to *establish three separate housing goals for the GSE's mortgage purchases financing: housing for low-income families; for central cities, rural areas, and other underserved areas housing; and special affordable housing to meet the unaddressed needs of low-income families in low-income areas and very-low-income families.*

The purpose of these regulations is to promote access to mortgage credit throughout the Nation (including central cities, rural areas, and other underserved areas) by increasing the liquidity of mortgage investments and improving the distribution of investment capital available for residential mortgage financing. Specifically, the three goals are as follows:

24 C.F.R. § 81.11-§ 81.12 (DECEMBER 1, 1995) – LOW- AND MODERATE-INCOME HOUSING GOALS

(a) Purpose of the goal. This annual goal for the purchase by each GSE of mortgages on housing for low- and moderate-income families ("the Low- and Moderate-Income Housing Goal") is intended to achieve increased purchases by the GSEs of such mortgages.

The *annual goals for each GSE's purchases of mortgages on housing or low- and moderate-income families are:*

In 2005, 52 percent of the total number of dwelling units financed by that GSE's mortgage purchases unless otherwise adjusted by HUD in accordance with FHEFSSA. In addition, as a Low- and Moderate-Income Housing Home Purchase Subgoal, 45 percent of the total number of home purchase mortgages in metropolitan areas financed by that GSE's mortgage purchases shall be home purchase mortgages in metropolitan areas which count toward the Low- and Moderate-Income Housing Goal. These percentages increase over a period of four years so by 2009, the new annual goals for each GSE's purchases of mortgages are 56 percent of the total number of dwelling units financed and 47 percent of the total number of home purchase mortgages in metropolitan areas.

24 C.F.R. § 81.13 (DECEMBER 1, 1995) – CENTRAL CITIES, RURAL AREAS, AND OTHER UNDERSERVED AREAS HOUSING GOAL

(a) Purpose of the goal. This annual goal for the purchase by each GSE of mortgages on housing located in central cities, rural areas, and other underserved areas is intended to achieve increased purchases by the GSEs of mortgages financing housing in areas that are underserved in terms of mortgage credit.

The *annual goals for each GSE's purchases of mortgages on central cities, rural areas, and other underserved areas are:*

In 2005, 37 percent of the total number of dwelling units financed by that GSE's mortgage purchases unless otherwise adjusted by HUD in accordance with FHEFSSA. In addition, as a central cities, rural areas, and other underserved areas housing subgoal, *32 percent of the total number of home purchase mortgages in metropolitan areas financed by that GSE's mortgage purchases shall be home purchase mortgages in metropolitan areas which count toward the central cities, rural areas, and other underserved areas housing goal.* These percentages increase over a period of four years so by 2009, the new annual goals for each GSE's purchases of mortgages are 39 percent of the total number of dwelling units financed and 34 percent of the total number of home purchase mortgages in metropolitan areas.

24 C.F.R. § 81.14 (DECEMBER 1, 1995) – SPECIAL AFFORDABLE HOUSING GOAL

(a) Purpose of the goal. This goal is intended to achieve increased purchases by the GSEs of mortgages on rental and owner-occupied housing meeting the then-existing unaddressed needs of, and affordable to, low-income families in low-income areas and very-low-income families.

The annual goals for each GSE's purchases of mortgages on rental and owner-occupied housing are:

In 2005, 22 percent of the total number of dwelling units financed by each GSE's mortgage purchases unless otherwise adjusted by HUD in accordance with FHEFSSA. The goal for the year 2005 shall include mortgage purchases financing dwelling units in multifamily housing totaling not less than 1 percent of the average annual dollar volume of combined (single-family and multifamily) mortgages purchased by the respective GSE in 2000, 2001, and 2002, unless otherwise adjusted by HUD in accordance with FHEFSSA. In addition, as a Special Affordable Housing Home Purchase Subgoal, *17 percent of the total number of home purchase mortgages in metropolitan areas financed by each GSE's mortgage purchases shall be home purchase mortgages in metropolitan areas, which count toward the Special Affordable Housing Goal in the year 2005 unless otherwise adjusted by HUD in accordance with FHEFSSA;*

These percentages increase over a period of four years so by 2009, the new annual goals for each GSE's of mortgages on rental and owner-occupied housing are 27 percent of the total number of dwelling units financed and 18 percent of the total number of home purchase mortgages in metropolitan areas.

OTHER NOTES REGARDING 24 C.F.R. § 81

As required by the FHEFSSA, on October 13, 1993, the Secretary published notices of interim housing goals establishing requirements necessary to implement the transition housing.

The Interim Notice for Fannie Mae established that, of the dwelling units financed by Fannie Mae's mortgage purchases: (1) In 1993 and 1994, 30 percent should be affordable to low- and moderate-income families; 28 percent and, in 1994, 30 percent should be located in central cities; during the 1993 –1994 period, at least $16.4 billion in mortgages should meet the Special Affordable Housing Goal.

The GSEs commented that various parts of the proposed rule were not legally sustainable because the Secretary's actions were, for example, "unreasonable," "arbitrary," "capricious," "not supported by a cogent rationale," "in direct conflict with the plain meaning of the Act," or "an improper exercise of the Secretary's discretion" HUD has carefully reviewed these concerns and applicable case law, n13 and has concluded that its exercise of regulatory authority in promulgation this final rule is, in all respects, well within the discretion accorded to HUD by Congress under FHEFSSA and is well supported by ample evidence and considered reasoning.

Appendix H

Performance Tests, Standards, and Ratings, in General

(All text in **bold** is verbatim from the statute; all text not in bold is author's summary; emphasis in *italics* is added by author)

12 C.F.R. § 25.21 (SEPTEMBER 10, 1997)

(a) *Performance tests and standards.* **The OCC assesses the CRA performance of a bank in an examination as follows:**

    (1) *Lending, investment, and service tests.* **The OCC applies the lending, investment, and service tests, as provided in §§ 25.22 through 25.24, in evaluating the performance of a bank, except as provided in paragraphs (a)(2), (a)(3), and (a)(4) of this section.**

    (2) *Community development test for wholesale or limited purpose banks.* **The OCC applies the community development test for a wholesale or limited purpose bank, as provided in § 25.25, except as provided in paragraph (a)(4) of this section.**

    (3) *Small bank performance standards.* **The OCC applies the small bank performance standards as provided in § 25.26 in evaluating the performance of a small bank or a bank that was a small bank during the prior calendar year, unless the bank elects to be assessed as provided in paragraphs (a)(1), (a)(2), or (a)(4) of this section. The bank may elect to be assessed as provided in paragraph (a)(1) of this section only if it collects and reports the data required for other banks under § 25.42.**

    (4) *Strategic plan.* **The OCC evaluates the performance of a bank under a strategic plan if the bank submits, and the OCC approves, a strategic plan as provided in § 25.27.**

(b) Performance context. The OCC applies the tests and standards in paragraph (a) of this section and also considers whether to approve a proposed strategic plan in the context of:

   (1) Demographic data on median income levels, distribution of household income, nature of housing stock, housing costs, and other relevant data pertaining to a bank's assessment area(s);

   (2) Any information about lending, investment, and service opportunities in the bank's assessment area(s) maintained by the bank or obtained from community organizations, state, local, and tribal governments, economic development agencies, or other sources;

   (3) The bank's product offerings and business strategy as determined from data provided by the bank;

   (4) Institutional capacity and constraints, including the size and financial condition of the bank, the economic climate (national, regional, and local), safety and soundness limitations, and any other factors that significantly affect the bank's ability to provide lending, investments, or services in its assessment area(s);

   (5) The bank's past performance and the performance of similarly situated lenders;

   (6) The bank's public file, as described in § 25.43, and any written comments about the bank's CRA performance submitted to the bank or the OCC; and

   (7) Any other information deemed relevant by the OCC.

(c) Assigned ratings. *The OCC assigns to a bank one of the following four ratings pursuant to § 25.28 and Appendix A of this part: "outstanding"; "satisfactory"; "needs to improve"; or "substantial noncompliance" as provided in 12 U.S.C. 2906(b)(2).* The rating assigned by the OCC reflects the bank's record of helping to meet the credit needs of its entire community, including low- and moderate-income neighborhoods, consistent with the safe and sound operation of the bank.

(d) Safe and sound operations. *This part and the CRA do not require a bank to make loans or investments or to provide services that are inconsistent with safe and sound operations.* To the contrary, the OCC anticipates banks can meet the standards of this part with safe and sound loans, investments, and services on which the banks expect to make a profit. Banks are permitted and encouraged to develop and apply flexible underwriting standards for loans that benefit low- or moderate-income geographies or individuals, only if consistent with safe and sound operations.

12 C.F.R. § 25.29 (SEPTEMBER 10, 1997) – EFFECT OF CRA PERFORMANCE ON APPLICATIONS

(a) CRA performance. Among other factors, the OCC takes into account the record of performance under the CRA of each applicant bank in considering an application for:

(1) The establishment of a domestic branch;

(2) The relocation of the main office or a branch;

(3) Under the Bank Merger Act (12 U.S.C. 1828(c)), the merger or consolidation with or the acquisition of assets or assumption of liabilities of an insured depository institution; and

(4) The conversion of an insured depository institution to a national bank charter.

(b) Charter application. An applicant (other than an insured depository institution) for a national bank charter shall submit with its application a description of how it will meet its CRA objectives. The OCC takes the description into account in considering the application and may deny or condition approval on that basis.

(c) Interested parties. The OCC takes into account any views expressed by interested parties that are submitted in accordance with the OCC's procedures set forth in part 5 of this chapter in considering CRA performance in an application listed in paragraphs (a) and (b) of this section.

(d) Denial or conditional approval of application. A bank's record of performance may be the basis for denying or conditioning approval of an application listed in paragraph (a) of this section.

Appendix I

Taxpayer Relief Act of 1997

(All text in **bold** is verbatim from the statute; all text not in bold is author's summary; emphasis in *italics* is added by author)

PUB. L. NO. 105-312

Sec. 121. Exclusion of Gain from Sale of Principal Residence

(a) **Exclusion**—*Gross income shall not include gain from the sale or exchange of property if, during the 5-year period ending on the date of the sale or exchange, such property has been owned and used by the taxpayer as the taxpayer's principal residence for periods aggregating 2 years or more.*

(b) **Limitations**—

  (1) **In General**—*The amount of gain excluded from gross income under subsection (a) with respect to any sale or exchange shall not exceed $250,000.*

  (2) *$500,000 Limitation for Certain Joint Returns*- **Paragraph (1) shall be applied by substituting "$500,000" for "$250,000" if-**

    (A) a husband and wife make a joint return for the taxable year of the sale or exchange of the property,

    (B) either spouse meets the ownership requirements of subsection (a) with respect to such property,

    (C) both spouses meet the use requirements of subsection (a) with respect to such property, and

    (D) neither spouse is ineligible for the benefits of subsection (a) with respect to such property by reason of paragraph (3).

Appendix J

American Recovery and Reinvestment Act of 2009

(All text in **bold** is verbatim from the statute; all text not in bold is author's summary; emphasis in *italics* is added by author)

26 U.S.C.A. § 36

(a) **Allowance of credit.**—In the case of an *individual who is a first-time homebuyer of a principal residence in the United States during a taxable year, there shall be allowed as a credit against the tax imposed by this subtitle for such taxable year an amount equal to 10 percent of the purchase price of the residence.*

(b) **Limitations.—**

    (1) **Dollar limitation.—**

        (A) **In general.**—Except as otherwise provided in this paragraph, the *credit allowed under subsection (a) shall not exceed $8,000.*

        (B) **Married individuals filing separately.**—In the case of a *married individual filing a separate return, subparagraph (A) shall be applied by substituting "$4,000" for "$8,000."*

        (C) **Other individuals.**—If two or more individuals who are not married purchase a principal residence, the amount of the credit allowed under subsection (a) shall be allocated among such individuals in such manner as the Secretary may prescribe, except that the total amount of the credits allowed to all such individuals shall not exceed $8,000.

Notes

Introduction

1. Gillian Tett, Fool's Gold: How the Bold Dream of a Small Tribe at J. P. Morgan Was Corrupted by Wall Street Greed and Unleashed a Catastrophe 181 (Simon and Shuster 2009) (hereinafter Tett).

2. Stan Liebowitz, *The Real Scandal—How Feds Invited the Mortgage Mess*, N.Y. Post, http://www.nypost.com/seven/02052008/postopinion/opedcolumnists/the_real_scandal_243911.htm?page=0 (last visited Oct. 1, 2010).

3. *See generally* Tett, *supra* note 1, at 181; George Soros, A New Paradigm for Financial Markets: The Credit Crisis of 2008 and What It Means (Public Affairs 2008); Paul Krugman, The Return of Depression Economics and the Crisis of 2008 (W.W. Norton & Company Ltd. 2009); Richard Posner, A Failure of Capitalism (Harvard University Press 2009); Richard Bookstaber, A Demon of Our Own Design (John Wiley & Sons, Inc. 2007); Mark Zandi, Financial Shock: 360 Look at the Subprime Mortgage Implosion and How to Avoid the Next Financial Crisis (Pearson Education, Inc. 2009); Niall Ferguson, The Ascent of Money: A Financial History of the World (The Penguin Press 2008); William Cohan, House of Cards: A Tail of Hubris and Wretched Excess On Wall Street (Doubleday 2009).

4. Roger Lowenstein, *Who Needs the Mortgage-Interest Deduction*, N.Y. Times, Mar. 5, 2006. *See also* Ron Paul, *Don't Blame the Market for the Housing Bubble* (Mar. 20, 2007), http://www.LewRockwell.com (last visited Sept. 5, 2009) (hereinafter Paul, *Don't Blame the Market*) ("[F]ed intervention in the economy—through the manipulation of interest rates and the creation of money—caused the artificial boom in mortgage lending."); Hans Bader, *Affordable Housing, Diversity Mandates Caused Mortgage Crisis*, Open Market, Aug. 5, 2008, at 1, http://www.openmarket.org/2008/08/05/affordable-housing-diversity-mandates-caused-mortgage-crisis/ (last visited Sept. 5, 2009) ("As a *Washington Post* story shows, the high-risk loans that led to the mortgage crisis were the product of regulatory pressure, not a lack of

regulation. In 2004, even after banking officials warned that subprime lenders were saddling borrowers with mortgages they could not afford, the U.S. Department of Housing and Urban Development helped fuel more of that risky lending. Eager to put more low-income and minority families into their own homes, the agency required that two government-chartered mortgage finance firms purchase far more 'affordable' loans made to these borrowers. HUD stuck with an outdated policy that allowed Freddie Mac and Fannie Mae to count billions of dollars they invested in subprime loans as a public good that would foster affordable housing . . . Lenders also face the risk of being sued for discrimination if they fail to make loans to people with bad credit, which often has a racially-disparate impact (proving that such impact is unintentional is costly and difficult, and not always sufficient to avoid liability under antidiscrimination laws). They also risk possible sanctions under the Community Reinvestment Act."); Thomas Sowell, *Bankrupt "Exploiters,"* Townhall, July 22, 2008, http://townhall.com/columnists/ThomasSowell/2008/07/22/bankrupt_exploiters?page=2 (last visited Sept. 5, 2009) ("It was government intervention in the financial markets, which is now supposed to save the situation, that created the problem in the first place.").

5. Viral V. Acharya & Matthew Richardson, Restoring Financial Stability: How to Repair a Failed System 32 (John Wiley & Sons, Inc. 2009).

6. Dennis Sewell, *Clinton Democrats Are to Blame for the Credit Crunch*, Spectator, Oct. 4, 2008, at 14 (hereinafter Sewell) (citing David Streitfeld & Gretchen Morgenson, *Building Flawed American Dreams*, N.Y. Times, Oct. 19, 2008 ["By . . . allowing lenders to hire their own appraisers, which often resulted in inflated house valuations, . . . HUD fueled the mortgage engine."]).

7. First Focus: The Subprime Crisis—A Thomson West Report 61 (Jodine Mayberry ed., Andrews Publications 2008) (hereinafter First Focus) (article by Brian E. Robinson, *Litigation in the Wake of the Subprime Lending Collapse: What Has Happened and Where We Are* [hereinafter Robinson]).

8. *See* M. Ahmed Diomande, James Heintz & Robert Pollin, *Why U.S. Financial Markets Need a Public Credit Ratings Agency*, Wall St. Watch, Aug. 2009, at 4. *See generally Monetary Myopia—Alan Greenspan*, Economist, Jan. 14, 2006; David Enrich & Damian Paletta, *Failed Lender Played Regulatory Angels—Red Flags Flew but Lamb's Banks Kept Pouring Out Loans, Till They Collapsed*, Wall St. J., Oct. 3, 2008, at A1; Lou Beach, *Bank Shot*, New Republic, Feb. 13, 2008, at 1.

9. Eamonn K. Moran, *Wall Street Meets Main Street: Understanding the Financial Crisis*, 13 N.C. Banking Inst. 5, 32–44 ("The factor that levered a serious housing market bubble and collapse into a threat to the United States financial markets and, indeed, the world financial system, was the financial innovations that developed on Wall Street as a result of securitization").

10. *Id., supra* note 5.

11. Rick Jelliffe, *Success Has a Thousand Fathers. . .*, O'ReillyXML, May 22, 2008, http://www.oreillynet.com/xml/blog/2008/05/success_has_a_thousand_fathers.html (last visited Oct. 1, 2010) (A popular version of a quote taken from President John F. Kennedy after the Bay of Pigs disaster).

12. Joseph O'Neill, *"Bankruptcy Reform in the Wake of the Subprime Crisis: Is it Enough?"* in First Focus, *supra* at 99.

13. Peter Ito, *Fallout and Survival in the Subprime Crisis*, in First Focus, *supra* at 35.

14. Realty Trac, *U.S. Foreclosure Activity Increases 75% in 2007 According to RealtyTrac U.S. Foreclosure Market Report*, in First Focus at 195.

15. Howard Mulligan, *As Lawmakers tackle the Subprime Crisis, Professional Vigilance is Must: New Laws, Stricter guidelines in the Works*, in First Focus, *supra* at 77.

16. Robinson, in First Focus.

17. Ronel Elul, *The Economics of Asset Securitization*, Q3 Fed. Res. Bank of Philadelphia Bus. Rev. 16, 16-25 (2005) (An in-depth discussion of the economics of asset securitization).

18. See Robert Ridge and Lauren Rushak, *Identifying the Categories of Disputes emerging from the Subprime Meltdown*, compiled in First Focus at 11; see also Scott Bertschi, "Courts Will Dilute Liability among Participants in Subprime Mortgages" , Id. At 73.

19. *See* John Whitlock and Matthew Martel, *A Sampling of Subprime-related Litigation Faced by Mortgage Lenders in Bankruptcy*, compiled in First Focus at 93.

20. *See generally* Brian Robinson, *Litigation in the Wake of the Subprime Lending Collapse: What Has Happened and Where We Are*, in First Focus at 59 (hereinafter Robinson).

21. *Id.* at 59.

22. John P. Doherty & Richard Hans, *The Pebble and the Pool: the Global Expansion of Subprime Litigation*, compiled in First Focus at 25.

23. Donald Kirk, *How to Prepare for Subprime-Related Litigation*, compiled in First Focus, *supra* at 67.

24. *Id.* at 69.

25. *Id.*

26. See Robinson, in First Focus, *supra* at 59.

27. William Martin and Kerry Verdi, *The Subprime Mortgage Crisis: Somebody Has to Pay*, in First Focus, *supra* at 107.

28. H. W. Brands, Traitor to His Class 329 (Doubleday 2008) (2008).

29. *See* CARS: Car Allowance Rebate System, http://www.cars.gov (last visited Sept. 5, 2009).

30. Ilyce Glick, *$15,000 Home Buyer Tax Credit Gets Another Boost*, CBSMoneyWatch.com, Aug. 24, 2009, http://moneywatch.bnet.com/saving -money/blog/home-equity/15000-home-buyer-tax-credit-gets-another -boost/931/?tag=col1;blog-river.

31. Roger Lowenstein, *Who Needs the Mortgage-Interest Deduction*, N.Y. Times, Mar. 5, 2006. *See also* Paul, *Don't Blame the Market*.

32. The Community Reinvestment Act, 12 U.S.C. § 2901 (2009); *see also* Raymond H. Brescia, *Part of the Disease or Part of the Cure: The Financial Crisis and the Community Reinvestment Act*, 60 S.C. L. 617, 619 (2009).

33. Forbes, June 22, 2009, at 15.

34. Sewell.

35. *Id.*

36. *Id.* at 2.

37. *Id.*

38. *Id.*

Chapter 1: Overview: An Allegory

1. Daniel McGinn, House Lust: America's Obsession with Our Homes 19 (2008) at 3 (cited in note 139 of Kristen David Adams, *Subprime Mortgage and Discriminatory Lending: Homeownership: American Dream or Illusion of Empowerment?*, 60 S.C. L. Rev. 573, 598).

2. See for comparison Kristen David Adams, Homeownership: American Dream or Illusion of Empowerment?, 60 S. C. L. Rev. 573, 611–613 (Citing W. Reg'l Advocacy Project, Without Housing: Decades of Federal Housing Cutbacks, Massive Homelessness, and Policy Failures i [2006] at 25 [citing Executive Office of the President, President's Advisory Panel on Fed. Tax Reform, Simple, Fair, and Pro-Growth: Proposals to Fix America's Tax System 27, 72–74 (2005), http://www.taxpolicycenter.org/taxtopics/upload/tax-panel-2.pdf].) (The mortgage interest deduction for homeowners is the second-largest single break in the entire tax code, and the wealthy receive the bulk of this benefit. A recent bipartisan presidential advisory panel on taxation found that over 70 percent of tax filers received no benefit from mortgage interest deductions, and only 54 percent of taxpayers who pay interest on their mortgages received this tax benefit. More than 55 percent of the federal expenditures under this program went to 12 percent of taxpayers with incomes greater than $ 100,000—often to finance luxury or second homes. The presidential panel found that these mortgage interest breaks, which allow for deductions on mortgages up to $1 million for first or second homes, exceed what is necessary to encourage increased homeownership in society or to help people buy a first home.)See also Winton Pitcoff, *Has Homeownership Been Oversold?*, Shelterforce, Jan.–Feb. 2003, at 1–2 ("Since the Mortgage Interest Deduction and related benefits are available only to those with incomes high enough to itemize deductions, 63 percent of these deductions goes to those in the top one-fifth of the income distribution, and only 18 percent goes to those in the bottom fifth.").

3. See for comparison The Community Reinvestment Act, 12 U.S.C. § 2901 (2009); *See also* Raymond H. Brescia, *Part of the Disease or Part of the Cure: The Financial Crisis and the Community Reinvestment Act*, 60 S.C. L. Rev. 617, 619 (2009).

4. See for comparison, Dennis Sewell, *Clinton Democrats Are to Blame for the Credit Crunch*, The Spectator, Oct. 4, 2008.

5. Compare to rise in California house prices in 2005.

6. See for comparison, William D. Cohan, House of Cards: A Tale of Hubris and Wretched Excess on Wall Street (Doubleday, 2009).

7. See for comparison, Gillian Tett, Fool's Gold: How the Bold Dream of a Small Tribe at J. P. Morgan Was Corrupted by Wall Street Greed and Unleashed a Catastrophe 181 (Simon and Shuster 2009).

8. See for comparison, *Id.* at 52–56.

Chapter 2: Blind Faith

1. Gillian Tett, Fool's Gold: How the Bold Dream of A Small Tribe at J. P. Morgan was Corrupted by Wall Street Greed and Unleashed a Catastrophe (Free Press, 2009) [hereinafter Tett], at 211.

2. Case Schiller Index, *available at* http://www.econ.yale.edu/-schiller/data.htm.

3. Compare S&P/Case Schiller Home Prices Indices, *available at* http://www.metroarea.standardandpoors.com (last visited June 21, 2009) (showing a progressively steeper increase in percentage of home prices), and Consumer Price Indexes, *available at* http://www.bls.gov/cpi/ (last visited June 21, 2009).

4. H. W. Brands, Traitor to His Class (Doubleday, New York, 2008) [hereinafter Brands], at 238.

5. David Goldman, There goes another $30 billion, CNNMoney.com, June 1, 2009, http://money.cnn.com/2009/06/01/news/economy/gm_auto_bailout/?postversion=2009060112 (last visited Oct.11,2010).

6. Brands, at 320.

7. *Id.* at 329.

8. G. Soros, The Credit Crisis and What It Means (Perseus Books, 2008) [hereinafter Soros], at 146.

9. Need source.

10. See Charles P. Kindleberger and Robert Aliber, Manias, Panics, and Crashes: A History of Financial Crises (John Wiley and Sons, 2005), at 115–16.

11. Robert Hardaway, Price Index Sleight of Hand Haunts in Credit Crisis, Rocky Mountain News, Sept. 22, 2007, at B-2.

12. Tett, at 121.

13. Community Reinvestment Act http://www.ffiec.gov/CRA/history.htm and Comptroller of the Currency Administrator of National Banks, Community Reinvestment Act Information, http://www.occ.treas.gov/crainfo.htm.

14. Tett, at 122.

15. *Id.*

16. Soros (citing J. Mason and J Rosner, *How Resilient Are Mortgage Backed Securities to Collateralized Debt Obligation Market Disruption?* paper delivered at the Hudson Institute, Washington, D.C., February 15, 2007, 11).

17. M. Zandi, Financial Shock (FT Press, 2008), at 61, chart 3.5.

18. Soros.

19. Wall Street Journal, Jan. 16, 2008, at A1.

20. O. Blanchard, *The Crisis: Basic Mechanism, and Appropriate Policies*, International Monetary Fund Working Paper (2009), at 3.

21. *Getting It Right on the Money—Financial Literacy*, The Economist, Apr. 5, 2008.

22. *Id.* at 3.

23. *Id.*

24. Tett.

25. Tett, *supra* at 66.

26. Cited in B. Malkiel, *The Efficient Market Hypothesis and Its Critics*, 59 Journal of Economic Perspectives 77–78 (Winter, 2003).

27. *Id.* at 78.

28. *Id.*

29. Cited at *Id.*

Chapter 3: Greed

1. Kristen David Adams, HomeOwnership: American Dream or Illusion of Empowerment, 60 S. Car. L. Rev. 574, 610(Spring, 2009) (citing Western Regional Advocacy Project, Without Housing: Decades of Federal Housing Cutbacks, Massive Homelessness, and Power Failures).

2. *Id.* at 612.

Chapter 4: Regulation

1. A. Friedlaender, The Dilemma of Freight Transport Regulation vii (1969). In particular, the following inefficiencies and inequities [of regulation] were singled out [by President Kennedy]: the dulling of managerial initiative; the inability of carriers to divest themselves of traffic that fails to cover costs; . . . the substitution of cost-increasing service competition for cost-reducing rate competition; . . . and, finally, the decline of the common carrier relative to private and exempt carriage.

2. Cited in Forbes, June 22, 2009, at 15.

3. By 301 AD, economic regulation was well established as an instrument of state power. In that year the emperor Diolectian issued his famous edict threatening death for violations of laws setting a "just price." H. Spiegel, The Growth of Economic Thought 63 (1983). By 1359, private companies had obtained monopoly powers by charter from their respective governments. In that year, the society of Merchant Adventurers obtained a charter, and benefits of regulation; in 1600, the East India Company received its charter. Both attempted to suppress the competition, whom they called "free-traders" and "interlopers."

4. See Robert M. Hardaway, *Transportation Regulation: Turning the Tide*, Transp. L. J. (1985) at 102113.

5. P. Samuelson, Economics 51–52 (8th ed. 1972) at 372.

6. S. Breyer, Regulation and its Reform 60–63 (1982) (hereinafter Breyer).

7. George Stigler, *The Theory of Economic Regulation*, 2 Bell. J. Econ. & Mgmt. Sci. 3, 10–12 (1971) at 6.

8. Ch. 601, 52 Stat. 973 (1938); *See generally* Paul S. Dempsey, *Rise and Fall of the Civil Aeronautics Board—Opening Wide the Floodgates of Entry,* 11 Transp. L. J. 91, 182 (1979) at 91.

9. Breyer, *supra* note 6, at 206.

10. *See generally* Michael E. Levine, *Revisionism Revised? Airline Deregulation and the Public Interest,* 44 Law & Contemp. Probs. (Winter, 1981), at 180.

11. G. Kolko, Railroads and Regulation 7 (1970) at 35 (citing *Hearings before the House Comm. on Commerce,* 48th Cong., 1st Sess. 1–2 (1884) (testimony by John P. Green)).

12. William A. Jordan, *Producer Protection, Prior Market Structure and the Effects of Government Regulation,* 15 J. L. & Econ. 151 (1972) at 168.

13. *Id., supra* note 11.

14. *Id., supra* note 1.

15. *See Oversight of the CAB Practices and Procedures: Hearings before the Subcomm. on Administrative Practice and Procedure of the Senate Comm. on the Judiciary,* 94th Cong., 1st Sess. 454 (1975) (statement of William A. Jordan).

16. Staff of senate subcomm. On administrative practice and procedure of the senate comm. On the judiciary, 94th cong., 1st sess., report on cab practices and procedures 41 (comm. Print 1975).

17. 1984 CAB Draft Report, *supra* note 234, at 20.

18. The Community Reinvestment Act, 12 U.S.C. § 2901 (2009). *See also* Raymond H. Brescia, *Part of the Disease or Part of the Cure: The Financial Crisis and the Community Reinvestment Act,* 60 S.C. L. 617, 619 (2009).

Chapter 5: Local Exclusionary Practices

1. Village of Euclid v. Amber Realty Co., 272 U.S. 365 (1926).

2. Ziegler, Edward H., The Case for Megapolitan Growth Management in the 21st Century: Regional Urban Planning and Sustainable Development in the United States, Urban Lawyer, Vol. 41, Issue 1 (Winter 2009), pp. 147–182.

3. Peter Whoriskey, *Density Limits Only Add to Sprawl,* Wash. Post, Mar. 9, 2003, at A01.

4. Daniel P. Selmi, James A. Kushner, & Edward H. Ziegler, Land Use Regulation: Cases and Materials 551 (Wolters Kluwer, 2008) (hereinafter Selmi et al.).

5. *Id.* at 551, citing Michael Bush, *Insiders are Bailing on Home-builders Stocks,* MSN Money Management Focus, Sep. 3, 2003.

6. 522 F. 2nd 897 (9th Cir. 1974).

7. James Clingermayer, *Quasi-judicial Decision-Making and Exclusionary Zoning,* 31 Urb. Affairs Rev. 544 (1966), cited in Selmi et al., *supra,* at 549.

8. Mark Baldassare, Trouble in Paradise: The Suburban Transformation in America (Columbia University Press, 1986).

9. 205 F. 2nd 118, (3d Cir. 2000) at 125.

10. Michael Berger, *Building Blues,* L.A. Daily Jour., May 3, 2001, at 7.

11. San Silver, *New Greens Focus Growth, Not Fight It* (Mar. 2003), at 3; cited in Selmi et al., supra, at 560.

12. Edward Ziegler, *Megapolitan Growth Management for sustainable Development in the 21st Century: Finally Closing the Door on The Economic, Environmental, Infrastructure, and Other Human Costs and Calamities of Exclusionary and Auto-Dependent Local Urban Planning Schemes,* Zoning and planning law report, Vol. 32, No. 4 (Apr. 2009).

Chapter 6: Bubbles of the Past

1. Anne Goldgar, Tulipmania: Money, Honor, and Knowledge in the Dutch Golden Age 3 (University of Chicago, 2007) (hereinafter Goldgar).

2. Mike Dash, *When the Tulip Bubble Burst,* Bus. Wk., Apr. 24, 2000, http://www.businessweek.com/2000/00_17/b3678084.htm.

3. *Id.* at 241. *See also* Frontline, *Famous Bubbles: From Tulipmania to Japan's Bubble Economy,* http://www.pbs.org, at 1.

4. *Id.* at 40.

5. *Id.*

6. *Id.* at 142.

7. Charles Mackay, Memoirs of Extraordinary Popular Delusions and the Madness of Crowds 87 (Robinson, Levey, and Franklyn 1852) (hereinafter Mackay).

8. Earl A. Thompson, *The Tulipmania: Fact or Artifact,* 130 Public Choice 99, 103–04 (2006).

9. Mackay, *supra* note 7, at 65.

10. *What Does the Future Hold for Real Estate?,* Knowledge @ Emory, http://knowledge.emory.edu/article.cfm?articleid=618 (last visited Sept. 28, 2010).

11. See Peter M. Garber, Famous First Bubbles: The Fundamentals of Early Manias (MIT Press, 2000) (hereinafter Garber).

12. Didier Sornette, Why Stock Markets Crash: Critical Events in Complex Financial Systems 9 (Princeton Univ. Press 2003).

13. *Id.*

14. Goldgar, supra note 1, at 232.

15. Dr. Samuel Johnson, The Works of the English Poets from Chaucer to Cowper 414 (Harvard Univ. Library 1810) (referring to the poem, "The South Sea Project").

16. *See* Richard S. Dale, Johnnie E. V. Johnson, & Leilei Tang, *Financial Markets Can Go Mad: Evidence of Irrational Behavior during the South Sea Bubble,* 58 Econ. Hist. R. 233 (2005) (hereinafter Dale, Johnson & Tang).

17. Dale, Johnson & Tang, *supra* note 16, at 234.

18. *Id.* at 234.

19. *Margin: Borrowing Money To Pay for Stocks,* SEC.gov, *available at* http://www.sec.gov/investor/pubs/margin.htm.

20. Garber, *supra* note 11, at 115.

21. Garber, *supra* note 11, at 115, 117.

22. Garber, *supra* note 11, at 115 (referring to this "help" as "bribes").

23. Dale, Johnson & Tang, *supra* note 16, at 235.

24. *Id.*

25. Garber, *supra* note 11, at 115.

26. *Id.*

27. Dale, Johnson & Tang, *supra* note 16, at 236.

28. *Id.*

29. *Id.*

30. Garber, *supra* note 11, at 119.

31. *Id.*

32. *Id.*

33. *Id.*

34. Dale, Johnson & Tang, *supra* note 16, at 240.

35. Richard S. Dale, Johnnie E. V. Johnson, & Leilei Tang Financial Markets Can Go Mad @260.

36. Martha L. Olney, Buy Now, Pay Later: Advertising, Credit, and Consumer Durables in the 1920s 7 (The University of North Carolina Press 1991) (hereinafter Olney, Buy Now, Pay Later).

37. *Id.*

38. *Id.* at 9.

39. *Id.*

40. Louis D. Johnston & Samuel H. Williamson, *What Was the U.S. GDP Then?*, MeasuringWorth.com, available at http://www.measuringworth.org/usgdp (last visited Nov. 5, 2010).

41. Olney, Buy Now, Pay Later, *supra* note 36, at 27.

42. *Id.*

43. *Id.* at 34.

44. *Id.*

45. *Id.* at 49.

46. Bureau of Economic Analysis, *Personal Saving Rate*, BEA.gov, *available at* http://www.bea.gov/briefrm/saving.htm (last visited Nov. 5, 2010).

47. Milan V. Ayres, *Installment Selling and Finance Companies*, 196 Annals Am. Acad. Pol. & Soc. Sci. 121, 121 (1938) (hereinafter Ayres).

48. Olney, Buy Now, Pay Later, supra note 36, at 119.

49. Ayres, supra note 47, at 124.

50. Olney, Buy Now, Pay Later, supra note 36, at 106.

51. *Id.*

52. *Id.* at 109.

53. Martha L. Olney, *Avoiding Default: The Role of Credit in the Consumption Collapse of 1930*, 114 Q. J. of Econ. 319, 321 (1999) (hereinafter Olney, *Avoiding Default*).

54. Randall E. Parker, The Economics of the Great Depression 5 (Edward Elgar Publishing, 2007).

55. *Id.*

56. *Id.* at 4–5.

57. *Id.* at 13–14.

58. *Id.*

Chapter 7: Economic Education

1. See, e.g., Robert Hardaway, America Goes To School: Law, Reform, and Crisis in Public Education. Praeger (1995).

2. Robert Hardaway, America Goes To School: Law, Reform, and Crisis in Public Education. Praeger (1995) 4(citing Arthur Fisher, Science + Math + F: Crisis in Education, Popular Science (August 1992), 58).

3. National Center for Education Statistics, http://nces.ed.gov/nations reportcard/civics/interpreting.asp.

4. N. Mead & B. Sandene, *The Nation's Report Card: Economics 2006*, (NCES 2007-475) (National Center for Education Statistics, Institute of Education

Sciences, U.S. Department of Education. Washington, DC, 2007) (hereinafter Mead & Sandene).

5. *Id.* at 1.

6. Community Reinvestment Act, Federal Reserve Board (FRB), http://www.federalreserve.gov/dcca/cra/.

Chapter 8: Speculation

1. 60 Fed. Reg. 61846, 61848 (Dec. 1, 1995).

2. *Id.*

3. Pub. L. No. 111-6, § 1006 (codified as amended at 26 U.S.C. § 36).

4. A&E's *Flip This House*: About the Show, http://www.aetv.com/flipthishouse/flip2_aboutshow.jsp (last visited Oct. 19, 2008).

5. Mary Umberger, *Study: It's Hip to Flip in the Hottest Markets*, Chi. Trib., Sept. 18, 2005, at C1.

6. Christopher Cagan, *Real Estate Flipping: Gold Mine, Mistake or Fraud?* (2005), http://www.facorelogic.com/uploadedFiles/Newsroom/Studies _and_Briefs/Studies/FlippingStudy_r3(1).pdf (last visited Sept. 29, 2010).

7. Merriam Webster's Collegiate Dictionary (10th ed. 1998) at 478.

8. Reuven Brenner, Gambling and Speculation: A Theory, a History, and a Future of Some Human Decisions 90 (Cambridge University Press, 1990).

9. *Id.* at 91.

10. MTV Cribs: Main, http://www.mtv.com/ontv/dyn/cribs/series.jhtml (last visited Oct. 20, 2008).

11. National Association of Realtors, *Median Sales Price of Existing Single-Family Homes for Metropolitan Areas* (2008), http://www.realtor.org/Research.nsf/files/MSAPRICESF.pdf/$FILE/MSAPRICESF.pdf (last visited Sept. 29, 2010).

12. Les Christie, *Second-Home Sales at All-Time High: Vacation Homes and Investment Properties Show Double-Digit Growth in 2005* (2006), http://money.cnn.com/2006/04/05/real_estate/second_homes/index.htm (last visited Oct. 28, 2008).

13. Michael Ventura, *The Psychology of Money*, Psychol. Today, Mar.–Apr. 1995, at 86.

14. Brenner, *supra*, at 63.

15. *Id.* at 83.

16. *Id.* at 84–86.

17. Bryan Gibson & David M. Sanbonmatsu, *Optimism, Pessimism, and Gambling: The Downside of Optimism*, 30 No. 2 Personality & Soc. Psychol. Bull. 149, 149 (2004) (hereinafter Gibson & Sanbonmatsu).

18. *Id.* at 158.

19. *Id.*

20. *Id.*

21. Peter J. Adams, Gambling, Freedom, and Democracy 84 (Routledge 2008) (hereinafter Adams).

22. *Id.*

23. *Id.*

24. Gibson & Sanbonmatsu, *supra*, at 153.

25. *Id.*

26. Dan Gainor, with Julia A. Seymour & Genevieve Ebel, *The Great Media Depression: News Reports View Economy Far Worse Now Than during the 1929 Stock Market Crash* (2005) http://www.businessandmedia.org/specialreports/2008/GreatDepression/GD%20Report%20Final.pdf (last visited Sept. 29, 2010).

27. *Id.*

28. Adams, *supra*.

29. *Id.* at 85–88.

Chapter 9: Psychology

1. *Wall Street Lays another Egg*, Vanity Fair (Dec. 2008).

2. David G. Myers, Psychology (7th ed., Worth, 2004) (hereinafter Myers) at 336–37.

3. *Id.*

4. *Id.*

5. Albert Bandura, Dorothea Ross, & Sheila A. Ross, *Transmission of Aggression Through Imitation of Aggressive Models*, 63 No. 3 J. Abnormal & Soc. Psychol. 575, 575 (1961).

6. Myers, supra.

7. Bandura, *supra*, at 577.

8. Myers, *supra*.

9. *Id.*

10. *Id.*

11. Myers, *supra*, at 312–13.

12. *Id.*, at 313.

13. *Id.*

14. Ivan P. Pavlov, Conditioned Reflexes: An Investigation of the Physiological Activity of the Cerebral Cortex (1927).

15. Myers, *supra*.

16. *Id.*

17. Umberger, *supra*. Mary Umberger, *Study: It's Hip to Flip in the Hottest Markets*, Sept. 18, 2005, at C1.

18. Myers, *supra*, at 737–38.

19. *Id.*

20. Muzafer Sherif et al., Intergroup Conflict and Cooperation: The Robbers Cave Experiment (University Book Exchange, 1961).

21. Myers, *supra*.

22. *Id.*

23. MTV, *supra*. MTVCribs, *available at* http://www.mtv.com/shows/cribs/series.jhtml (last visited Oct. 23, 2010).

24. Adams, supra, at 89. Peter J. Adams, Gambling, Freedom, and Democracy 89 (Routledge 2008).

25. Joel Best, Flavor of the Month: Why Smart People Fall for Fads 21 (Univ. of Cal. Press 2006) (hereinafter Best).

26. *Id.*, p. 71.

27. *Id.*, p. 72.

28. *Id.*, p. 82.

29. Gibson & Sanbonmatsu, *supra* at 159.

30. Best, *supra*, at 121.

31. *Id.*

32. *Id.* at 155.

33. Irwin Kellner, *What Goes Up Must Come Down*, http://www
.marketwatch.com/news/story/goes-up-must-come-down/story.aspx
?guid=%7B2AB533B3-6489-4552-B450-EFEE0C09527E%7D (last visited
Mar. 1, 2009).

34. Best, *supra*, at 156.

35. *Id.*

36. A&E's *Flip This House, supra.*

37. Best, *supra*, at 159.

38. Gary Stix, *The Science of Bubbles and Busts*, Sci. Am., July 2009, at 78.

39. *Id.*

40. *Id.*

41. *Id.* (quoting Robert J. Shiller, Professor of Economics, Yale University).

42. *Id.* (citing Bernd Weber, Antonio Rengel, Matthias Wilbral, & Armin
Falk, *The Medial Prefrontal Cortex Exhibits Money Illusion*, Proc. Nat'l Acad.
Sci. USA, March 31, 2009).

43. *Id.* at 80–81.

44. *Id.* at 80.

45. *Id.* at 80–81.

46. *See id.*

47. *Id.* at 81.

48. *Id.* at 84.

49. *Id.* at 84–85.

Chapter 10: Bankruptcy Laws

1. For a historical analysis of the rise of consumer credit in the United
States, *see generally* Lendol Calder, Financing the American Dream: A Cultural
History of Consumer Credit (Princeton University Press, 1999) (hereinafter
Calder).

2. Calder at 39.

3. Martin Feldstein, *How to Save an "Underwater" Mortgage*, Wall St. J.,
August 8–9, 2009, at A13.

4. Christopher L. Peterson, *Subprime Meltdown: The Law and Finance of the
American Home Mortgage Foreclosure Crisis*, 2008 Utah L. Rev. 1107, 1108
(2008) (citation omitted).

5. Elizabeth Warren, *A Principled Approach to Consumer Bankruptcy*, 71 Am.
Bankr. L.J. 483, 492 (1997).

6. Charles Jordan Tabb, The Law of Bankruptcy § 1.1 (2d ed. 2009) (hereinafter Tabb).

7. The social utility of providing individual debtors with a fresh start is
deeply rooted in American bankruptcy law. In perhaps the most cited

recitation of the fresh start principle, the Supreme Court of the United States stated as follows in *Local Loan Co. v. Hunt*: "One of the primary purposes of the Bankruptcy Act is to 'relieve the honest debtor from the weight of oppressive indebtedness, and permit him to start afresh free from the obligations and responsibilities consequent upon business misfortunes.' This purpose of the act has been again and again emphasized by the courts as being of public as well as private interest, in that it gives to the honest but unfortunate debtor who surrenders for distribution the property which he owns at the time of bankruptcy, a new opportunity in life and a clear field for future effort, unhampered by the pressure and discouragement of pre-existing debt." Local Loan Co. v. Hunt, 292 U.S. 234, 244 (1934) (internal citations omitted).

8. Tabb at § 1.25.

9. Katherine Porter, *Misbehavior and Mistake in Bankruptcy Mortgage Claims*, 87 Tex. L. Rev. 121, 129 (2009) ("Most consumers who file Chapter 13 bankruptcy cases are homeowners.") (citation omitted).

10. Alan M. White, 36 Fordham Urb. L. J. 509, 512 (2009) (citation omitted). "Cram-down is a feature of bankruptcy law that allows a debtor to pay a creditor the value of the collateral instead of the full value of the loan." Nina Liao, *Cramming Down the Housing Crisis: Amending 11 U.S.C. § 1322(b) to Protect Homeowners and Create a Sustainable Bankruptcy System*, 93 Minn. L. Rev. 2240, 2242 (2009) (internal citations omitted).

11. *See generally* 11 U.S.C. § 362 (2009).

12. *See generally* 11 U.S.C. § 1322(b) (2009).

13. John Eggum, Katherine Porter, & Tara Twomey, *Saving Homes in Bankruptcy: Housing Affordability and Loan Modification*, 2008 Utah L. Rev. 1123, 1126 (2009) (hereinafter Eggum et al.) (citation omitted).

14. *Id.* (citation omitted).

15. *Id.* (citation omitted).

16. 11 U.S.C. § 1322(b)(2) (2009). Both academics as well as the Democrats in the current Congress have advocated for the revision to the Bankruptcy Code so as to enable debtors to modify the terms of a principal residential mortgage. *See, e.g.*, Eggum et al. To date, these efforts have proved unavailing. Indeed, in May 2009, the U.S. Senate rejected a bill that would have amended the Bankruptcy Code to enable bankruptcy judges to lower interest rates and reduce loan obligations to the current market appraisal of the property. Jane Birnbaum, *Law Makes Debt Relief Harder for Homeowners*, N.Y. Times, May 14, 2009, at B1.

17. Eggum et al. at 1130 (citation omitted).

Chapter 11: Banking Practices and Redlining

1. The Public Papers and Addresses of Franklin D. Roosevelt 40–42 (Samuel Rosenman, ed., vol. 13, Harper 1950).

2. Samuel L. Clements (Mark Twain) & Charles Dudley Warner, The Gilded Age: A Tale of Today 263 (Harper & Brothers 1873; reprint ed., author's national ed., 10 vols., 1915, vol. 1).

3. Burt Ely, Editorial, *We Need Fundamental Mortgage Reform*, Wall St. J., Sept. 8, 2008, at A19.

4. Patrick Barta, *Measuring New Risks in Mortgage Markets*, Wall St. J., June 5, 2000, at A1.

5. Greg Ip, James R. Hagerty, & Jonathan Karp, *Housing Bust Fuels Blame Game—Democrats Seize On Opponents' Role; Bipartisan Failures*, Wall. St. J., Mar. 19, 2008, at A1.

6. Jeff Bailey, *In One City, Home Sellers Find It Pays to Cut Out Middleman*, N.Y. Times, June 8, 2007, at A1.

7. Marc Lifsher, *Gov. Vetoes Loan Oversight Bill*, L.A. Times, Sept. 26, 2008, at C3.

8. *States to Track Mortgage Brokers*, L.A. Times, Jan. 3, 2008, at C3.

9. Rick Brooks & Ruth Simon, *Subprime Debacle Traps Even Very Credit-Worthy*, Wall St. J., Dec. 3, 2007, at A1.

10. *Id.*

11. The Mortgage Lender Implode-o-Meter, http://www.ml-implode.com (last visited Sept. 30, 2010).

12. Robert Shiller, The Subprime Solution 51 (2008). Princeton University Press

13. Gretchen Morgenson, *Crisis Looms in Mortgages*, N.Y. Times, Mar. 11, 2007, at A1.

14. Rick Brooks & Constance Mitchell Ford, *The United States of Subprime – Data Show Bad Loans Permeate the Nation*, Wall St. J., Oct. 11, 2007, at A1 (hereafter Brooks & Ford).

15. As defined by the Home Ownership Equity Protection Act (HOEPA), a high-rate mortgage, often subprime, is any mortgage where the Annual Percentage Rate (APR) exceeds 8 percent over the comparable treasury rate for a first-lien mortgage, 10 percent over the comparable treasury for a second-lien mortgage, or any mortgage loan in which the total points and fees exceed 8 percent of the loan amount. The comparable treasury is the treasury security with similar duration. For example, a 30-year fixed-rate mortgage takes its yield from the 30-year treasury bill, whereas a five-year adjustable-rate mortgage looks at a five-year treasury.

16. *Id.* at A1.

17. *Id.* at A1.

18. Donald Kohn, Vice Chairman Federal Reserve, Speech at the Federal Reserve Bank of Richmond's Credit Market Symposium: The Changing Business of Banking, Apr. 17, 2008 (hereinafter Kohn Speech).

19. Brooks & Ford at A1.

20. *Id.*

21. *Insecurities; American Banks*, The Economist, Nov. 13, 2004,

22. Michael Hudson, *Debt Bomb—Lending a Hand: How Wall Street Stoked the Mortgage Meltdown*, Wall St. J., June 27, 2007, at B1.

23. *Id.*

24. *Id.*

25. Gretchen Morgenson, *Crisis Looms in Mortgages*, N.Y. Times, Mar. 11, 2007, at 1.

26. Mitchell Pacelle & Jathon Sapsford, *Banking—Size, Smiles, and Scandals*, Wall St. J., Feb. 9, 2004 at R8.

27. *Id.*

28. Jathon Sapsford, *Critics Cry Found on Bank Review*, Wall St. J., Jan. 8, 2004, at B1.

29. Ben Bernanke, Chairman Federal Reserve, Speech at the Federal Reserve Bank of Chicago Annual Conference on Bank Structure and Competition: Risk Management in Financial Institutions, May 15, 2008.

30. Jesus Sanchez, *Countrywide Braces for Drop-Off*, L.A. Times, Jan. 25, 2003, § 3 at 3.

31. *Id.*

32. Kenneth Harney, *Your Mortgage: FHA Eases Qualifications for First Timers*, L.A. Times, Feb. 5, 1995, § K at 3.

33. Kohn Speech.

34. Michael D. Calhoun, President and Chief Operating Officer, Center for Responsible Lending, Testimony to the Committee on House Financial Services, Sept 30 2009.

35. *See generally* Robert S. England, *Inside the Market Correction*, Mortgage Banking, May 1, 2007, at 44.

36. Jay Romano, *Mortgage ABC's in a Borrower's Market*, N.Y. Times, Mar. 15, 1998, § 11 at 1.

37. Alina Tugend, *What You Need to Know to Get a Mortgage*, N.Y. Times, June 1, 2008, § RE at 1.

38. Ruth Simon, *Mortgage Lenders Loosen Standards*, Wall St. J., July 25, 2005, at D1 (hereinafter Simon, *Mortgage Lenders*).

39. London Interbank Offer Rate, which measures the average interest rate banks charge each other at various intervals.

40. Lenders typically set the margin rate at the maximum possible before the loan qualifies for additional Section 32 disclosures under the Homeowner Equity Protection Act (HOEPA).

41. Ruth Simon, *Rising Rates to Worsen Subprime Mess*, Wall St. J., Nov. 24, 2007, at A1.

42. Since HOEPA disallows negative-equity mortgages for high-cost loans, lenders cleverly set the margin of this product low enough that the APR did not push it into Section 32 violation.

43. Simon, *Mortgage Lenders*, at D1.

44. Kenneth Harney, *Your Mortgage: Score One for Fannie Mae*, L.A. Times, Feb. 4, 1996, § K at 4.

45. Peralte Paul, *Banker's Hour*, Atlanta Journal-Constitution, Aug. 30, 2007, at 1C.

46. Michael Hudson, *Debt Bomb—Lending a Hand: How Wall Street Stoked the Mortgage Meltdown*, Wall St. J., June 27, 2007, at B1.

47. *Id.*

48. Mike Hudson and E. Scott Reckard, *Workers Say Lender Ran "Boiler Room,"* L.A. Times, Feb. 4, 2005, at A1.

49. Ruth Simon, *Mortgages Made in 2007 Go Bad at Rapid Clip*, Wall St. J., Aug. 7, 2008, at A3.

50. *Id.*

51. Randall Kroszner, Governor Federal Reserve, Speech at State Bank Supervisors Annual Conference, May 22, 2008.

52. Carrick Mollenkamp and Serena Ng, *Wall Street Wizardry Amplified Crisis*, Wall St. J., Dec. 27, 2007 at A1.

53. *The Great Untangling; Credit Derivatives*, The Economist, Nov. 8, 2008.

54. *When It Goes Wrong—Securitization*, The Economist, Sept. 22, 2007.

55. *Year End Review in Markets and Finance 2008*, Wall St. J., Jan. 2, 2008 at R9.

56. Donald Kohn, Vice Chairman Federal Reserve, Speech at the Federal Reserve Bank of Richmond's Credit Market Symposium, April 17, 2008.

57. *Id.*

58. *Confessions of a Risk Manager*, The Economist, Aug. 7, 2008.

59. *Bearish Turns*, The Economist, June 21, 2008.

60. Kate Kelly, Serena Ng, & Michael Hudson, *Subprime Uncertainty Fans Out*, Wall St. J., July 18, 2007, at C1.

61. Robin Sidel, Greg Ip, Michael M. Phillips, & Kate Kelly, *The Week That Shook Wall Street: Inside the Demise of Bear Stearns*, Wall St. J., Mar. 18, 2008, at A1.

62. Ben Bernanke, Chairman Federal Reserve, at the Federal Deposit Insurance Corporation's Forum on Mortgage Lending for Low and Moderate Income Households, July 8, 2008.

63. *The $2 Bailout*, Economist, Mar. 19, 2008.

64. Franklin D. Raines, Former CEO of Fannie Mae, Testimony to the House Committee on Oversight and Government Reform, Dec. 9, 2008 (hereinafter Raines Testimony).

65. Id.

66. Id.

67. Arnold Kling, Adjunct Scholar of the Cato Institute, Testimony to the House Committee on Oversight and Government Reform, Dec. 9, 2008.

68. Raines Testimony.

69. *Id.*

70. *Id.*

71. *Id.*

72. *Suffering a Seizure*, The Economist, Sep. 8, 2008.

73. James Lockhart III, Director of the Federal Housing Finance Authority, Testimony to the House Financial Services Committee, Sep. 25, 2008.

74. *Id.*

75. *Id.*

76. Matthew Karnitschnig, Carrick Mollenkamp, Susanne Craig, & Annelena Lobb, *Lehman Races to Find a Buyer*, Wall St. J., Sep. 12, 2008, at A1.

77. Susanne Craig, *Lehman Struggles to Shore Up Confidence*, Wall St. J., Sep. 11, 2008, at A1.

78. *Id.*

79. *Id.*

80. Susanne Craig, *Lehman Faces Mounting Pressures*, Wall St. J., Sep. 10, 2008, at A1.

81. Diya Gullapalli, *For Neuberger Deal, Fateful Few Months*, Wall St. J., Dec. 5, 2008, at C11.

82. Carrick Mollencamp, Mark Whitehouse, Joe Hilsenrath, & Ianthe Jeanne Dugan, *Lehman's Demise Triggered Cash Crunch Around Globe*, Wall St. J., Sept. 29, 2008, at A1).

83. *Id.*

84. *Size Matters*, The Economist, Sep. 18, 2008.

85. *Id.*

86. *When Fortune Frowned*, The Economist, Oct. 9, 2008.

87. Serena Ng, Liz Rappaport & Carrick Mollenkamp, *Credit Shows Signs of Easing on Bank Rescue*, Wall St. J., Oct. 15, 2008, at A1.

88. Liz Peek, *Credit Spreads Widen Despite Signs of Recovery*, N.Y. Sun, Sep. 4, 2008.

89. *Blocked Pipes*, The Economist, Oct. 2, 2008, (hereinafter *Blocked Pipes*).

90. *Id.*

91. Jon Hilsenrath, Diya Gullapalli, & Randall Smith, *U.S., Britain Up Ante in Fight to Stop Crisis*, Wall St. J., Oct. 8, 2008, at A1.

92. *Blocked Pipes.*

93. Ben Bernanke, Federal Reserve Chairman, Speech at the Economic Club of New York, Oct. 15, 2008.

94. *Id.*

95. Carl Hulse & David Herszenhorn, *Defiant House Rejects Huge Bailout*, N.Y. Times, Sep. 30, 2008, at A1.

96. E. S. Browning & Tom Lauricella, *Dow Falls 777.68 Points on Bailout's Delay*, Wall St. J., Sept. 30, 2008, at C1.

97. Richard Simon & Nicole Gaouette, *A Hard Vote and Complex Task*, L. A. Times, Oct. 4, 2008, at A1.

98. *Id.*

99. Deborah Solomon & Damian Paletta, *Paulson Wants Rest of TARP Funds from Congress*, Wall St. J., Dec. 20, 2008, at A6.

100. *Id.*

101. Aline van Duyn, Michael Mackenzie, & Nicole Bullock, *Corporate Bonds Find Hope from New Issue*, Fin. Times, Jan. 7, 2009.

102. Michael Mackenzie, *US Set for Further Mortgage Rates Fall*, Fin. Times, Jan. 7, 2009.

103. *Id.*

104. Jessica Holzer, *Foreclosure Mitigation Makes Little Headway*, Wall St. J., Dec. 23, 2008, at A4.

105. *Id.*

106. *Fear of Financials Takes Stocks Down*, L.A. Times, July 15, 2008, at C6.

107. Sheila Bair, Chairman Federal Deposit Insurance Corporation, Speech to the House Financial Services Committee, Sept. 17, 2008.

108. *Id.*

109. *Id.*

110. *Id.*

111. *Id.*

112. William Apgar & Mark Duda, *The Twenty-Fifth Anniversary of the Community Reinvestment Act*, Federal Reserve Bank of New York Economic Policy Review, June 1, 2003 (hereafter Apgar & Duda).

113. *Id.*

114. *Id.*

115. *Id.*

116. *Id.*

117. *Id.*

118. *Id.*

119. *Id.*

120. Traiger & Hinckley, LLP, The Community Reinvestment Act: A Welcome Anomaly in the Foreclosure Crisis, http://www.traigerlaw.com/publications/traiger_hinckley_llp_cra_foreclosure_study_1-7-08.pdf (last visited Sept. 30, 2010) (hereafter Traiger & Hinckley).

121. *Id.*

122. Apgar & Duda.

123. Traiger & Hinckley.

Chapter 12: The Federal Reserve

1. David M. Jones, The Buck Starts Here: How the Federal Reserve Can Make or Break Your Financial Future 50 (Prentice Hall 1995) (hereinafter Jones, Buck Starts Here).

2. *Id.*

3. David M. Jones, The Politics of Money: The Fed under Alan Greenspan 13 (New York Institute of Finance 1991) (hereinafter Jones, Politics of Money).

4. David M. Jones, Unlocking the Secrets of the Fed 98 (2002) (hereinafter Jones, Unlocking the Secrets).

5. Carl H. Moore, The Federal Reserve System—A History of the First 75 Years 1–9 (McFarland 1990) (a quick summary of the political struggle and a quick summary of the Federal Reserve Act).

6. Bernard Shull, The fourth branch: the Federal Reserve's unlikely rise to power and influence 29–36 (Praeger 2005) (hereinafter Shull) (timeline of the Panic of 1907).

7. Edwin Kemmerer & Donald Kemmerer, The ABC of the Federal Reserve System 32 (12th ed., Harper and Brothers Publishers 1950) (hereinafter Kemmerer & Kemmerer).

8. *Id.* at 33.

9. Shull at 42–48 (events leading up to the federal reserve act).

10. Donald Kettl, Leadership at the Fed 4 (Yale University Press 1986) (hereinafter Kettl).

11. Martin Mayer, The Fed 68 (The Free Press 2001) (hereinafter Mayer) (quoting Carter Glass as cited in Robert Choate, *Bank on Transparency*, Fin. Times (London), Mar. 2, 1998, at 18).

12. *Id.* (quoting H. Parker Willis, Chief of Staff to Glass, as cited in Report of the Committee on the Working of the Monetary System, para 768 at 273 (Augus 1959).

13. Kemmerer & Kemmerer at 31.

14. *Id.* at 124.

15. *Id.* at 138.

16. Mayer at 81–92 (laying out what would lead to "The Accord").

17. *Id.* at 83.

18. *Id.* at 92.

19. Kettl at 2.

20. From Richard E. Mooney & Edwin L Dale Jr., eds. Inflation and Recession 23 (Doubleday and Co. 1958) Quoted in David M. Jones, Fed Watching and Interest Rate Projections: a Practical Guide (New York Institute of Finance 1986) (hereinafter Jones, Fed Watching).

21. *Id.* at 11.

22. Jones, Fed Watching, at 13.

23. Jones, Politics of Money, at 29.

24. Jones, Buck Starts Here, at 56.

25. Jones, Politics of Money, at 25.

26. Jones, Buck Starts Here, at 51.

27. Jones, Unlocking the Secrets, at 98.

28. Jones, Buck Starts Here, at 52.

29. Remarks by Governor Ben S. Bernanke at the Redefining Investment Strategy Education Symposium, Dayton, OH, Mar. 30, 2005, http://www.federalreserve.gov/BOARDDOCS/SPEECHES/2005/20050330/default.htm (last viewed Sep. 30, 2010).

30. *Id.*

31. *Id.*

32. *Id.*

33. Bob Tedeschi, *What Really Moves Interest Rates*, N.Y. Times, Aug. 20, 2006.

34. Federal Reserve System, The Federal Reserve System: Purposes and Functions 23 (online Fed publication), http://www.federalreserve.gov/pf/pf.htm (last viewed Sep. 30, 2010) (hereinafter Federal Reserve System: Purposes and Functions).

35. John B. Taylor, *Housing and Monetary Policy*, Policy Panel at the Symposium on Housing, Housing Finance, and Monetary Policy sponsored by the Federal Reserve Bank of Kansas City, Jackson Hole, WY, Sept 2007. (Taylor also states that this sharp deviation in policy also explains why interest rates stayed low when rates went up. Taylor explains that the large deviation led investors to believe that a shift in policy was in the future and thus long term interest rates would stay low.)

36. Testimony of Chairman Alan Greenspan, *Federal Reserve Board's Semi-annual Monetary Policy Report to the Congress before the Committee on Banking, Housing, and Urban Affairs*, U.S. Senate, Feb. 16, 2005.

37. Daniel L. Thornton, *The Unusual Behavior of the Federal Funds and 10-Year Treasury Rates: A Conundrum or Goodhart's Law?*, September 2007, Federal Reserve Bank of St. Louis Working Paper Series, http://research.stlouisfed.org/wp/2007/2007-039.pdf (last visited Sep. 30, 2010) (this hypothesis is supported by an array of documentary and statistical evidence).

38. Laurence H. Meyer, *Before the Spring 1998 Banking and Finance Lecture*, Widener University, Chester, Pennsylvania April 16, 1998, http://www.federalreserve.gov/Boarddocs/Speeches/1998/199804162.htm (last viewed Sep. 30, 2010).

39. Remarks by Governor Ben S. Bernanke before the New York Chapter of the National Association for Business Economics, New York City, Oct. 15, 2002, *Asset-Price "Bubbles" and Monetary Policy.*

40. Federal Reserve System: Purposes and Functions at 60.

41. *See id.* at 59–60.

42. *See* David Cho & Nell Henderson, *Senators Blame Mortgage Crisis on "Neglect" by Fed, Greenspan,* Wash. Post, Mar. 23, 2007 (hereinafter Cho & Henderson) (referring to the Feds passing of the Home Ownership and Equity Protection Act [HOEPA] where the Fed set guidelines regarding unfair and deceptive lending practices but could only enforce the rules against those banks whom they had power to supervise).

43. Mayer at 60.

44. *Id.* at 62.

45. *Supra* Cho & Henderson.

46. Federal Reserve Press Release, July 14, 2008, http://www.federalreserve .gov/newsevents/press/bcreg/20080714a.htm (last viewed Sept. 30, 2010).

47. *Id.*

48. Predatory Lending and the Federal Reserve, Peter Skillern, Financial Markets Center, October 2000, *Peter Skillern is Executive Director of the Community Reinvestment Association of North Carolina.* http://www.fmcenter.org.

49. Id. Laurence H Meyer, April 16, 1998.

50. Remarks by Chairman Alan Greenspan, *Economic Challenges in the New Century,* Before the Annual Conference of the National Community Reinvestment Coalition, Washington, D.C., March 22, 2000, http://www.federalreserve .gov/boarddocs/speeches/2000/20000322.htm (last viewed Sept. 30, 2010).

Chapter 13: TAX POLICY

1. *See* Roger Lowenstein, *Who Needs the Mortgage-Interest Deduction,* N.Y. Times, March 5, 2006.

2. Roger Lowenstein, *Who Needs the Mortgage-Interest Deduction,* N.Y. Times, March 5, 2006; I.R.S., Publication 936, Home Mortgage Interest Deduction 8 (2008).

3. U.S. Department of Treasury, History of the U.S. Tax System, http:// www.ustreas.gov/education/fact-sheets/taxes/ustax.shtml.

4. U.S. Department of Treasury, History of the U.S. Tax System, http:// www.ustreas.gov/education/fact-sheets/taxes/ustax.shtml.

5. U.S. Department of Treasury, History of the U.S. Tax System, http:// www.ustreas.gov/education/fact-sheets/taxes/ustax.shtml.

6. U.S. Department of Treasury, History of the U.S. Tax System, http:// www.ustreas.gov/education/fact-sheets/taxes/ustax.shtml.

7. Daniel Immergluck, Private Risk, Public Risk: Public Policy, Market Development, and the Mortgage Crisis, 36 FORDHAM URB. L.J. 447, 452 (2009).

8. Michael J. Lea, Innovation and the Cost of Mortgage Credit: A Historical Perspective, 7 Housing Pol'y Debate 147, 162 (1996), available at http:// www.mi.vt.edu/data/files/hpd%207(1)/hpd%207(l)%201ea.pdf.

9. *See* Ernest Fisher, *Changing Institutional Patterns of Mortgage lending*, 5 Journal of Finance 307, 307-310 (1950) (cited in Immergluck, *supra* note 7, at 453 – Immergluck cited the actual figure for home ownership at just under 48%, stating that is unlikely that home ownership "hit rates substantially above 50% . . . "); cited verbatim in Robert Hardaway, Great American Housing Bubble: Re-examining Cause and Effect 35 U. Dayton L. Rev. 33 (Fall 2009) p. 46.

10. www.NAHB.org (National Association of Home Builders).

11. U.S. Census Bureau, CB09-104, Census Bureau Reports On Residential Vacancies And Homeownership 1 (2009), available at http://www.census.gov/hhes/www/housinglhvs/qtr2009/files/q209press.pdf.; Tiffany Chaney & Paul Emrath, US vs. European Housing Markets (May 5, 2006), Housing Economics.com, http://www.nahbregistration.com/generic.aspx?sectionD=734&genericContentID=57411&channelID=311.

12. U.S. Census Bureau, CB10-103, Census Bureau Reports on Residential Vacancies and Homeownership in the Second Quarter (2010), available at http://www.census.gov/hhes/www/housing/hvs/qtr210/files/q210 press.pdf.

13. HousingEconomics.com

14. National Association of Home Builders, www.NAHB.org.

15. U.S. Census Bureau, Census of Housing: Historical Census of Housing Tables Home Values (2004), http://www.census.gov/hhes/www/housing/census/historic/values.html; U.S. Census Bureau ; U.S. Census Bureau, Median and Average Sales Prices of New Homes Sold in United States http://www.census.gov/const/uspriceann.pdf.

16. Dan Immergluck, Credit To The Community 36 (Richard D. Bingham & Lany C. Ledebureds., 2004); cited verbatim in Robert Hardaway, Great American Housing Bubble: Re-examining Cause and Effect 35 U. Dayton L. Rev. 33 (Fall 2009) p. 46.

17. Press Release, Danilo Pelletiere, Research Dir., Nat'l Low Income Hous. Coal., Mortgage Interest Deduction (May 6, 2009) (available at "http://www.nhtf'org/detail/article'cfin?articleid=6061 &id=46) ("I want you to know that we will preserve the part of the American dream which the home-mortgage-interest deduction symbolizes.") cited verbatim in Robert Hardaway, Great American Housing Bubble: Re-examining Cause and Effect 35 U. Dayton L. Rev. 33 (Fall 2009) p. 46.

18. U.S. Department of Treasury, History of the U.S. Tax System, http://www.ustreas.gov/education/fact-sheets/taxes/ustax.shtml.

19. T axpayer Relief Act of 1997, Pub. L. No. 105-34, 111 Stat. 788 (codified as amended in scattered sections of 5 U.S.C., 19 U.S.C., 26 U.S.C., 29 U.S.C., 31 U.S.C., 42 U.S.C., and 46 app.).

20. George W. Bush, President of the U.S., President Bush's 2002 Speech at the Conference on Minority Home Ownership, George Washington University (Oct. 15, 2002), http://www.freerepublic.com/focus/f-news/2094023/posts (emphasis added); see also George W. Bush, President of the U.S., Remarks by the President on Homeownership at the Department of Housing and Urban Development, Washington, D.C. (June 18, 2002), http://www.hud.gov/news/speeches/ presremarks.cfm cited verbatim in Robert

Hardaway, Great American Housing Bubble: Re-examining Cause and Effect 35 U. Dayton L. Rev. 33 (Fall 2009) p. 52.

21. The Community Reinvestment Act, 12 U.S.C. § 2901 (2006); see also Raymond H. Brescia, Part of the Disease or Part of the Cure: The Financial Crisis and the Community Reinvestment Act, 60 S.C. L. REv. 617, 619 (2009).

22. See, e.g. Richard E. Mendales, Collateralized Explosive Devices: Why Securities Regulation Failed to Prevent the CDO Meltdown, and How to Fix It, 2009 U. ILL. L. REv. 1359 (2009). cited verbatim in Robert Hardaway, Great American Housing Bubble: Re-examining Cause and Effect 35 U. Dayton L. Rev. 33 (Fall 2009) p. 37.

23. American Recovery and Reinvestment Act of 2009, Pub. L. No. 111-5, 123 Stat. 225 (2009) (to be codified at 42 U.S.C. § 17384); First-Time Home Buyer Tax Credit, http://www.federalhousingtaxcredit.com/2009/faq.php.

Chapter 14: Real Estate Practices

1. Fred Wright, *The Effect of the New Deal Real Estate Residential Finance and Foreclosure Policies Made in Response to the Real Estate Conditions of the Great Depression*, 57 Ala L. Rev. 231, 233 (2005) (hereinafter Wright).

2. Alabama, *Song of the South*, on Southern Star (RCA Records 1989).

3. *Fed. Home Bank BD.*, 1 Fed. Home Loan Bank Rev. 3 (1934) (hereinafter *Fed. Home Bank BD.*).

4. David M. Kennedy, Freedom from Fear: The American People in Depression and War, 1929–1945 370 (1999).

5. *Fed. Home Loan Bank BD.*, *supra*, note 3.

6. *Id.*

7. Wright, *supra* note 1 at 238.

8. Nathaniel S. Keith, Politics and the Housing Crisis since 1930 21 (1973).

9. Gail Radford, Modern Housing for America: Policy Struggles in the New Deal Era 119, at 239 n. 24 (1996).

10. Guy S. Claire, Adminstocracy: The Recovery Laws and Their Enforcement 34, 35 (1934).

11. Kenneth T. Jackson, *Race, Ethnicity, and the Real Estate Appraisal: The Home Owners Loan Corporation and the Federal Housing Administration*, 6 J. Urb. Hist. 419, 24 (1980).

12. Wright, *supra* note 1 at 233.

13. Julia Patterson Forrester, *Mortgaging the American Dream: A Critical Evaluation of the Federal Government's Promotion of Home Equity Financing*, 69 Tul. L. Rev. 373, 378 (1994) (hereinafter Forrester, *Mortgaging*).

14. U.S. General Accounting Office, Tax Policy: Many Factors Contributed to the Growth in Home Equity Financing in the 1980s 3 (1993) (hereinafter GAO Report).

15. Gary Klein, *Preventing Foreclosures: Spotting Loan Scams Involving Low-Income Homeowners*, 27 Clearinghouse Rev. 116, 117 (1993).

16. *Id.; also see* Jack Meyers et al., *Firm Wrote Loans at 39% Interest*, Boston Herald, June 17, 1991, at 1, 20.

17. David Reiss, *Subprime Standardization: How Rating Agencies Allow Predatory Lending to Flourish in the Secondary Mortgage Market*, 33 Fla. St. U.L. Rev. 985, 997 (2006).

18. U.S. General Accounting Office, Consumer Protection: Federal and State Agencies Face Challenges in Combating Predatory Lending 21, 18 (2004).

19. *Democratic Candidates on Mortgage Reform*, Amer. Bankruptcy Inst. J. 27-1 ABIJ 10, (2008) (hereinafter *Democratic Candidates*).

20. *Id.*

21. *Predatory Mortgage Lending: Hearing before the S. Comm. on Banking, Housing, and Urban Affairs*, 107th Cong. 398, at 347 (2001).

22. *See Democratic Candidates.*

23. Julia Patterson Forrester, *Still Mortgaging the American Dream: Predatory Lending, Preemption, and Federally Supported Lenders*, 74 U. Cin. L. Rev. 1303 at 1314 (2006) (hereinafter Forrester, *Still Mortgaging*).

24. U.S. Dep't. of Housing & Urban Dev. & U.S. Dep't. of Treasury, Curbing Predatory Home Mortgage Lending: A Joint Report 13 at 24 (2000).

25. *Id.* See also 1993 Hearings on Problems in Lending, See Problems in Community Development Banking, Mortgage Lending Discrimination, Reverse Redlining, and Home Equity Lending: Hearings Before the Senate Comm. on Banking Housing and Urban Affairs, 103d Cong., 1st Sess. 447 at 253 (Feb. 17, 1993). [hereinafter 1993 Hearings on Problems in Lending].

26. *Mortgage Reform Bill Advances in House*, Amer. Bankruptcy Inst. J., 26-10 ABIJ 10, at 9 (2007).

27. *Id.*

28. *Id.*

29. Forrester, *Mortgaging, supra* note 13 at 392.

30. David Schmudde, *Lessons from the Subprime Mortgage Debacle*, 24-3 Practical Real Estate Lawyer (May 2008) (hereinafter Schmudde).

31. *See* GAO Report supra note 14 at 12–14.

32. Schmudde *supra* note 30.

33. John C. Weicher, The Home Equity Lending Industry: Refinancing Mortgages for Borrowers with Impaired Credit 13, 31 (Hudson Institute 1997).

34. Forrester, *Still Mortgaging, supra* note 23 at 1312 (2006).

35. Daniel P. Smith, *Real Estate and Home Life, Putting the Internet in its Place*, Chi. Sun-Times, Oct. 17, 2008.

36. *Id.*

37. Frank Nelson, Book Review; An Investment Pro's Guide to the Internet Frontier, L.A. Times, Feb. 17, 2008.

Chapter 15: Credit Rating Agencies

1. Chris Meyer, Email to Belinda Ghetti and Nicole Billick (Dec. 15, 2006), http://oversight.house.gov/images/stories/Hearings/Committee_on_Over sight/E-mail_from_Belinda_Ghetti_to_Nicole_Billick_et_al._December_16 _2006.pdf.

2. Richard M. Levich, Giovanni Majnoni & Carmen Reinhart, Ratings, Rating Agencies and the Global Financial System 20 (Richard M. Levich, Giovanni Majnoni & Carmen Reinhart eds., Kluwer Academic Publishers 2002) (hereinafter Levich et al.).

3. *Id.* at 21.

4. *Id.* at 22.

5. *Id.* at 22.

6. *Id.* at 22.

7. *Id.* at 22.

8. *Id.* at 22.

9. *Id.* at 22.

10. *Id.* at 24.

11. *Id.* at 24.

12. *Id.* at 24.

13. *Id.* at 24.

14. *Id.* at 26.

15. Lawrence J. White, *Agency Problems—and Their Solution*, The American, Jan. 24, 2009, http://www.american.com/archive/2009/agency-problems2014and-their-solution (last visited Sept. 30, 2010) (hereinafter White).

16. Levich et al., *supra* note i, at 34.

17. *Id.* at 35.

18. *Id.* at 35.

19. *Id.* at 35.

20. White, *supra* note xiv.

21. *Id.*

22. *Id.*

23. *Id.*

24. Levich et al., supra note i, at 47.

25. White, *supra* note xiv.

26. *Id.*

27. Levich et al., *supra* note i, at 21.

28. *Id.*

29. *Id.*

30. Eric Dinallo, *Buyers Should Pay for Bond Ratings*, Wall St. J., Mar. 3, 2009, http://online.wsj.com/article/SB123604378798715285.html (last visited Sept. 30, 2010).

31. Paulette Miniter, *Don't Rely on Credit Ratings Alone*, SmartMoney, Oct. 29, 2008, http://www.smartmoney.com/investing/bonds/Do-Not-Rely-on-Credit-Ratings-Alone (last visited Sept. 30, 2010).

32. *Id.*

33. Rachelle Younglai, Treasury Wants to Stay Out of Credit Ratings, Reuters India, Aug. 5, 2009, http://in.reuters.com/article/governmentFilingsNews/idINN0545168020090805.

34. *Id.*

35. *Id.*

36. *Id.*

Chapter 16: Appraisers

1. Briefing Morning Call (Allentown, PA), Aug. 29, 2007.

2. Thomson Financial News, US Econ: US April S&P/Case-Shiller 20-City Home Price Index Down 15.4% YOY. Date: 8/25/2009 available at http://www.forbes.com/feeds/afx/2009/08/25/afx6812423.html (Forbes).

3. Wegener, *A Lawyer's Guide to Rural Property Appraisals*, 3 Property & Probate 19 (Sept.–Oct. 1989).

4. Real Estate Financing (Matthew Bender & Company, Inc., a member of the LexisNexis Group, 2009) (hereinafter Real Estate Financing).

5. Gay v. Broder, 109 Cal. App. 3d 66 (Cal. App. 4th Dist. 1980).

6. *Id.*

7. *Regional Report/MI Bank Suing Appraiser over Twin Cities Home Loans*, St. Paul Pioneer Press, Aug. 5, 2009.

8. *Id.*

9. Sadtler v. Jackson-Cross Co., 402 Pa. Super. 492 (Pa. Super. Ct. 1991).

10. *Id.*

11. Barry v. Roskov, 232 Cal. App. 3d 447.

12. *Id.*

13. *Id.*

14. *Id. See also* Real Estate Financing.

15. Carolyn Said, *N.Y.' s Cuomo Alleges Appraiser, Lender Collusion Upped Home Values*, S.F. Chronicle, Nov. 2, 2007, http://www.sfgate.com/cgi-bin/article.cgi?file=/c/a/2007/11/02/MNO8T4NNM.DTL#ixzz0Ph15fKLr (last visited Oct. 1, 2010).

16. Thomas J. Inserra, MAI, SRA CEO, Zaio Group, *Restoring Confidence: Learning From the S&L Crisis To Address the Subprime Mortgage Problem* (hereinafter Inserra). http://www.zaio.com/PDF/PressRelease/Restoring_Confidence _by_Thomas_Inserra.pdf, last accessed date October 19, 2010.

17. *DLA Piper 2008 "State of the Market" Real Estate Survey Unveils Grim Outlook; Developments at Lehman Brothers, AIG and Merrill Lynch Push Credit Crisis Past Savings and Loan Crisis; Real Estate Markets Not Expected to Stabilize until 2010*, Bus. Wire, Sept. 23, 2008.

18. Inserra.

19. Federal Deposit Insurance Corporation, *FDIC Law, Regulations, Related Acts*, http://www.fdic.gov/regulations/laws/rules/8000-3100.html (last visited Oct. 1, 2010).

20. David Streitfeld, *Appraisal Shift Gives Lenders More Power, and Draws Critics* (series), N.Y. Times, Aug. 19, 2009, A1 (hereinafter Streitfeld).

21. James R. Hagerty, *Appraisers under Fire Again*, Wall St. J., Aug. 18, 2009, D1.

22. Id. *See also* Streitfeld at A1.

23. *Id.*

24. Id. *See also* Briefing Morning Call.

25. Id. *See also* Streitfeld at A1.

26. Id. *See also* Streitfeld at A1.

27. Anne Kates Smith, *Appraising the Home Appraisers*, 62 Kiplinger's Personal Finance (15289729, issue 11).

28. Id. *See also* Streitfeld at A1.

29. Id. *See also* Streitfeld at A1.

30. Id. *See also* Streitfeld at A1.

31. Mara Der Hovanesian, *Report: 1 in 5 Mortgages Are Underwater, In Nevada, More Than Half of All Mortgage Borrowers Are Upside Down.* http://www .zaio.com/PDF/PressRelease/Restoring_Confidence_by_Thomas_Inserra.pdf, last accessed date October 19, 2010.

32. U.S. Department of the Treasury, *Financial Regulatory Reform: A New Foundation: Rebuilding Financial Supervision and Regulation,* June 30, 2009.

33. Id. *See also* Streitfeld at A1.

34. Id. *See also* Hagerty at D1.

35. James R. Hagerty & Ruth Simon, *U.S. News: Appraisals Roil Real Estate Deals—Conservative Approach to Home Pricing Makes It Harder to Refinance or Sell,* Wall St. J., June 9, 2009, A3.

36. Id. *See also* Hagerty at D1.

Chapter 17: Accounting

1. Donald R. Kirk, *How to Prepare for Subprime-Related Litigation.* First Focus: The Subprime Crisis—A Thomson West Report (2008).

2. Jack M. Cathey, Myrtle W. Clark & Richard G. Schroeder, Financial Accounting Theory and Analysis (8th ed., 2005) (hereinafter Cathey, Clark & Schroeder).

3. Jesse Westbrook, *SEC, FASB Resist Calls to Suspend Fair-Value Rules, Bloomberg,* http://www.bloomberg.com/apps/news?pid=20601087&sid =agj5r6nhOtpM& (last visited Oct. 15, 2008) (hereinafter Westbrook).

4. Financial Accounting Standards Board, *Statements of Financial Accounting Standards No. 115: Accounting for Certain Investments in Debt and Equity Securities* 5 (1993) (hereinafter FASB 115).

5. Cathey, Clark & Schroeder, *supra* note 2.

6. FASB 115, *supra* note 4, at 6–9.

7. *Id.*

8. Financial Accounting Standards Board, *Statement of Financial Accounting Standards No. 157: Fair Value Measurements* 6 (2006).

9. Financial Accounting Standards Board, *Statement of Financial Accounting Standards No. 159: The Fair Value Option for Financial Assets and Financial Liabilities* (2007).

10. *Id.*

11. *All's Fair,* Economist, Sept. 18, 2008, (hereinafter *All's Fair*).

12. Westbrook, *supra* note 3.

13. Financial Accounting Standards Board, *supra* note 4, at 5.

14. Financial Accounting Standards Board, *supra* note 9, at 1.

15. *Id.* at 3.

16. *All's Fair, supra* note 11.

17. Financial Accounting Standards Board, *supra* note 8, at 9–10.

18. *All's Fair, supra* note 11.

19. Financial Accounting Standards Board, *Statement of Financial Accounting Standards No. 107: Disclosures about Fair Value of Financial Instruments* 5 (1991).

20. Halsey G. Bullen et al., *The Fundamental Financial Instrument Approach: Identifying the Building Blocks*, 168 J. Accountancy 71, 71–77 (Nov. 1989) (hereinafter Bullen)_.

21. *Id.*

22. *Id.*

23. Cathey, Clark & Schroeder, *supra* note 2.

24. *Id.*

25. Bullen, *supra* note 20.

26. Financial Accounting Standards Board, Bullen, *supra* note 20.

27. Alan Blankley & Richard Schroeder, *Accounting for Derivatives under SFAS No. 133*, Mid-Atlantic J. Bus. (2000).

28. Bullen, *supra* note 20.

29. Financial Accounting Standards Board,Cathey, Clark & Schroeder, *supra* note 2.

Chapter 18: Fallout: The Litigation Mess

1. Carrick Mollenkamp & Serena Ng, *UBS Forced to Set Aside Millions in CDO Case*, Wall St. J., Sept. 10, 2009, at C1 (hereinafter Mollenkamp & Ng).

2. Cited in Matthew L. Jacobs & Lorelie S. Masters, *Insurance Coverage and the Subprime Crisis: A Broad Overview*, http://www.lexisnexis.com/documents/pdf/20080407010256_large.pdf (last visited Oct. 1, 2010) (hereinafter Jacobs & Masters).

3. Cited in Faten Sabry, Anmol Sinha & Sungi Lee, *The Snowball Effect: A Brief Review of Subprime Securities Litigation*, Marsh & McLennan Companies, http://www.mmc.com/knowledgecenter/viewpoint/A_Brief_Review_of_Subprime_Securities_Litigation.php (last visited Oct. 1, 2010) (hereinafter Sabry, Sinha & Lee).

4. Mollenkamp & Ng at C1.

5. U.S. Securities and Exchange Commission, *Summary Report of Issues Identified in the Commission Staff's Examinations of Select Credit Rating Agencies.* July 2008 http://www.sec.gov/news/studies/2008/craexamination 070808.pdf (last visited Oct. 1, 2010).

6. *See* Donald R. Kirk, *How to Prepare for Subprime-Related Litigation*, First Focus: The Subprime Crisis—A Thomson West Report at 69 (Jodine Mayberry ed., Andrews Publications 2008) (hereinafter Kirk) (stating, "Shareholders claim agencies assigned bonds high ratings without disclosing they were backed by subprime mortgages"). *See also* Nathan Koppel, Andrew Edwards & Chad Bray, *Judge Limits Credit Firms' 1st-Amendment Defense*, Wall St. J., Sep. 7, 2009, http://online.wsj.com/article/SB125201681110884761.html (last visited Oct. 1, 2010) (stating "[the rating agencies have] also been criticized as being too close to issuers who foot the bill for their ratings"); Martha Graybow, *Credit Rating Agencies Fending Off Lawsuits from Subprime Meltdown*, Insurance J., http://www.insurancejournal.com/news/national/2008/07/

14/91841.htm (last visited Oct. 1, 2010) (noting that the agencies have been criticized for "being too close to issuers who foot the bill for their ratings"); Larry P. Ellsworth & Keith W. Porapaiboon, *Credit Rating Agencies in the Spotlight*, ABA Business Law Section, http://www.abanet.org/buslaw/blt/2009 -03-04/ellsworth.shtml (last visited Oct. 1, 2010) (describing a suit by the New Jersey Carpenters Vacation Fund against, among other defendants, Fitch, Moody's, and S&P).

   7. Credit Rating Agency Reform Act of 2006, 120 Stat. 1327.

   8. William R. Martin & Kerry Brainard Verdi, *The Subprime Mortgage Crisis: Somebody Has to Pay*, First Focus: The Subprime Crisis—A Thomson West Report (hereinafter Martin & Verdi).

   9. *Id.* at 110.

   10. *See* John Doherty & Richard Mans, *The Changing Landscape of Subprime Litigation*, Andrews Bankr. Litig., Jan. 14, 2008, at 3; cited in Kirk.

   11. Martin & Verdi.

   12. 15 U.S.C. § 78j(b).

   13. Kirk at 70.

   14. In re Citigroup Inc. Derivative Litigation, No. 3338-CC, consolidation order issued (Del. CH. Feb. 6, 2008).

   15. John P. Doherty & Richard F. Hans, *The Pebble and the Pool: The (Global) Expansion Of Subprime Litigation*, First Focus: The Subprime Crisis—A Thomson West Report.

   16. City of Cleveland v. Deutsche Bank Trust Co. et al., No. 08-CV-139 (N.D. Ohio); Mayor of Baltimore v. Wells Fargo Bank et al., No. 08-62 (D. Md.).

   17. Brian E. Robison, *Litigation in the Wake of the Subprime Lending Collapse: What Has Happened and Where We Are*, First Focus: The Subprime Crisis—A Thomson West Report.

   18. Kirk at 70.

   19. *Jacobs* & Masters.

   20. *Report Notes Jump in Subprime-Related Suits, News Brief—Subprime Litigation*, First Focus: The Subprime Crisis—A Thomson West Report, at 199.

   21. Kirk at 70.

   22. Sabry, Sinha & Lee.

   23. *Jacobs* & Masters.

   24. See Samuel et al. v. Countrywide KB Home Loans et al., No. 08-CV-350, complaint filed (D.S.C. Jan. 31, 2008).

   25. Sabry, Sinha & Lee.

   26. Martin & Verdi.

Glossary

   1. Morgan Stanley Smith Barney, *Individual Investors—Dictionary of Financial Terms*, http://www.morganstanleyindividual.com/customerservice/dictionary/ default.asp (last visited Oct. 1, 2010).

   2. Investopedia: A Forbes Related Company, *Financial Dictionary*, http:// www.investopedia.com/dictionary/default.asp (last visited Oct. 1, 2010).

   3. *Id.*

4. *Id.*
5. *Id.*
6. Morgan Stanley Smith Barney, *supra* note 1.
7. *Id.*
8. *Id.*
9. Investopedia, *supra* note 2.
10. *Id.*
11. *Id.*
12. *Id.*
13. *Id.*
14. *Id.*
15. Morgan Stanley Smith Barney, *supra* note 1.
16. Investopedia, *supra* note 2.
17. *Id.*
18. *Id.*
19. *Id.*
20. *Id.*
21. *Id.*

Index

About the Author

ROBERT M. HARDAWAY is professor of law at the University of Denver Sturm College of Law, Denver, Colorado, cum laude graduate of Amherst College, and Order of the Coif graduate of New York University Law School. He teaches civil procedure, evidence, and transportation law, and has taught constitutional law and criminal procedure. A former Deputy District Attorney for Arapahoe County, Colorado, Colorado Public Defender, and U.S. Navy JAG attorney, he has also taught at George Washington University Law School and Hastings Law School in San Francisco. He is the author of dozens of law review articles and 17 books and casebooks on law and public policy, as well as five published novels.